CHILDSCAPE, MEDIASCAPE

CHILDSCAPE, MEDIASCAPE
CHILDREN AND MEDIA IN INDIA

Edited by

Usha Raman
Sumana Kasturi

Orient BlackSwan

CHILDSCAPE, MEDIASCAPE: CHILDREN AND MEDIA IN INDIA

ORIENT BLACKSWAN PRIVATE LIMITED

Registered Office
3-6-752 Himayatnagar, Hyderabad 500 029, Telangana, India
e-mail: centraloffice@orientblackswan.com

Other Offices
Bengaluru, Chennai, Guwahati, Hyderabad, Kolkata,
Mumbai, New Delhi, Noida, Patna

First published by Orient Blackswan Private Limited 2023

ISBN 978-93-5442-730-5

Typeset in
Adobe Garamond Pro 11/13.5
by Le Studio Graphique, Gurgaon 122 007

039623

Printed in India at
Thomson Press, New Delhi 110 020

Published by
Orient Blackswan Private Limited
3-6-752 Himayatnagar, Hyderabad 500 029, Telangana, India
e-mail: info@orientblackswan.com

CONTENTS

TABLES AND FIGURES

Tables

Figures

ACKNOWLEDGMENTS

Four-and-a-half years. Two hundred and thirty five weeks. One thousand six hundred and forty five days. And uncountable hours.

When a book travels that long through time, it picks up a whole lot of pleases, sorrys and thank yous. This book started its journey as a proposal in June 2018, shepherded by Roopa Sharma through the publishing process at Orient BlackSwan. But even before that came the tentative emails to authors and collaborators, and the drawing in of a small but steady support system of just one person—the tenacious, dependable, ever-cheerful Devina Sarwatay, at the time just starting out on her doctoral project. Whether it was writing and following up on emails with authors, or helping with reference and style checks, her help was invaluable. She had no idea that this book would be just as big a challenge as her dissertation. We owe her much, but a simple thank you will have to suffice for now.

The twelve authors who so generously contributed their work are, of course, the core of the project, and we would like to thank each one of them for working with us to bring together their expertise and our vision for the book, and then so patiently rewriting, answering queries and refining their chapters over a much longer time period than any of us expected.

And a big thank you to our families, of course, who perhaps often wondered why we could not stop talking about children and media, even after we had submitted the final manuscript. After all, who can function without countless cups of lovingly brewed tea, often accompanied by indulgent eye-rolls and just the slightest hint of impatience with a fascination that veered from children fiddling with parents' mobile phones to young adults falling asleep over an endless scroll to school children taking their cues to life from cinema and comic books.

From Usha: Special thanks to Achala and Ananya, whose childhood years sparked many of my initial curiosities around how children learn from and with media.

From Sumana: Thank you to my family, but especially to Ani and Kai on whom I tried out many of my media literacy ideas, and who graciously allowed me to mine their thoughts and feelings about their engagement with media more often than they would have probably liked.

We'd like to express our gratitude to our copy-editor Anjali Aggarwal Gupta, whose painstaking combing through the text ensured that everything was in its place. We also thank Suchetana Ghosh Dostidar and the entire editorial team at OBS for their work on the manuscript and for bringing this book to its final iteration.

And finally, our continuing gratitude to all the young people who, as they experiment, experience and engage with various kinds of media, offer us insights into so many aspects of what it means to be humans living in this mediated world.

Usha Raman
Sumana Kasturi

CHILDREN AND MEDIA
A Two-way Street

Sumana Kasturi and *Usha Raman*

> A couple of decades ago, when my children were still children, I was telling them a story about animals fleeing the poisoned forest, their habitats ruined by humans, when my six-year-old remarked, 'But we don't do that anymore, do we?' To which I replied, 'Well, yes, we do—we're still chopping trees and poisoning the air in so many ways.' The response was quick and emphatic. 'No, but we don't do that! Humans do!' I was intrigued, but pressed her, 'But we are humans too.' This time, her answer was unequivocal. 'No, we're not humans, we are savages. We take care of forests.'
>
> We are 'savages' because we are brown. In most of the television and cinema she had watched in her six years of life, those who lived in forests, with nature, were people of colour, and those who came—either to plunder or rescue—were white. 'Savage' in her mind was simply a descriptor, without value, and was representative of non-Western, non-white peoples, while 'human' referred to the rest, in this case, those who engaged in extractive practices. (Usha Raman)

Children build their notions of the world and their place in it in multiple ways, some of which are better understood than others (Buckingham 2007; Singer and Singer 1990; Lester-Roushanzamir and Raman 1999). They develop a sense of who they are, how and where they relate to the rest of the world—other people, things, the natural and human-built environment—and, as they grow, acquire a sense of how to live in and with society. Institutions like family, community, school, religion—and media—all play a role in how children think; indeed, even what they think (Jordan 2004).

The anecdote above comes from the early 1990s, when these children were consuming mostly Western popular culture. One of the reasons for this was the general paucity of a wide range of locally produced children's media in India and from the global South generally. Between then and now, children's media has become more inclusive and there is much more diversity in production, not to speak of modes of dissemination. But the point of the story is that media content plays a role in feeding and shaping the child's imagination of the self and the world. The exchange is a telling example of how children create their understanding of the world, with all its hierarchies and differences, through what appears to be an incremental process of piecing together bits of information, fictional and real, combining these with experience as they grow older, constantly negotiating between the seen, the unseen and the hidden layers of meaning that reside in the corners of the everyday. But then they are also part of this world, writing into it their own meanings, participating in life even as they draw from it. To complicate this further, they are also located within the same media worlds that they consume—represented in different ways, writing meanings into the world's perceptions of childhood and those who inhabit it.

Within media and communication studies globally, children have always been subjects of intense attention, mostly due to concerns about 'media effects' resulting from sustained exposure to content and now use of devices. While a considerable body of work in the area has accumulated, drawing from Western contexts beginning from the post–World War II years, Indian media scholarship has shown little sustained interest or engagement in the area. The little that exists does so in isolated pockets, often in disciplines as varied as home science, education and psychology. This book is an attempt to bring together some of the scholarship in the country that looks at children's engagement with and representation in media, and outline some of the key questions that bear further exploration.

Childhoods and children's worlds are extremely complex phenomena to study. Even more so when we attempt to understand childhood (itself a shifting, growing, transforming experience) with/in media, which in recent years, has undergone tremendous change, largely attributable to the exponential growth of the Internet and associated media. Digital technology and networked media are together seen as having catalysed political, cultural and social change globally, intensifying the movement of ideas and practices across geographies, destabilising old modes of producing, consuming and circulating content (Deuze 2006).

To say these are turbulent times is perhaps a cliché that bears repeating in every age. But then, every age has its upheavals and troughs, and we can only speak to the one we live in. Our anxieties are many, but then so are our hopes. The place where both come to roost is the child of the present. Children seem to awaken our deepest fears (for them), our loftiest hopes (from them) and our unspoken discomforts (about their inner and invisible lives). Every one of us has been a child, yet it is a stage of being that we retain memory but very little understanding of. Further, this is not an understanding that is transferable in its entirety across generations, given the continuing changes in the world and the societies in which we live, and the consequent changes in children's contexts. Taken together with the unprecedented level of mediation we are experiencing (Couldry and Hepp 2017; Deuze 2011), from the ways in which we learn about the world to the modes in which we present ourselves to it, to the channels and forms through which we connect, to how we engage in commerce, work and entertainment, there is little that we can draw upon in terms of insights from our own experience—as children or with children of an earlier time. Some scholars have commented on the difficulty of taking a 'generational' position in terms of looking at children's experiences, and the dangers of thinking in terms of a 'born digital' frame particularly for today's children (Buckingham and Willett 2013; Palfrey and Gasser 2008). Of course, one must be careful to avoid either exceptionalism or nostalgia as we attempt to understand the lives of children with and within media.

It is difficult to ignore the level to which today's child is surrounded by media, broadly conceived. An average middle-class household in most countries of the world would have multiple devices that carry content and enable communication (phones, tablets, televisions, computers), and many more artefacts that carry stored information (books, newspapers, comics, games). Children also increasingly find themselves within media, beginning these days as early as ultrasound images to baby photographs to home videos and social media posts, and while some of these are self-generated by older children, others are created by adults and can become frames through which children see themselves (Weber and Dixon 2007; Montgomery 2015). This has also led to new concerns and complex debates around the circulation of child pornography on the Internet, in addition to issues of grooming and solicitation of minors online (Paasonen 2011).

Children—individuals below the age of 15 years—constitute a little over one-fourth of the world's population (Statista 2022). They represent an important consuming public—of information, entertainment, services and products—and even though they may not have the direct power to make financial decisions, they influence how spending decisions are made (Buckingham 2007, 2013; Cook 2009). This makes them the target of representational and persuasive media genres but, strangely enough, less visible in informational/news media as active and agentic participants in society or polity. However, ever since media studies carved out a space for itself as a discipline, children have been subjects of interest, with research about them often negotiating the boundaries of development studies, education, psychology, sociology, cognitive science and public health, among others. It is difficult, if not impossible, to box work in this area into one disciplinary framework. In fact, the field gains from the cross-linking and movement of ideas from one area to another, drawing on theoretical and methodological frameworks from multiple intellectual traditions. This has meant that scholars who engage with what we might call 'children's worlds' are located in many different disciplinary homes, as does the work they do. This is particularly true of Indian scholarship that relates to children and media; it is certainly not exclusive to departments of media and communication studies, as is evident from the work sampled in this volume.

In a somewhat similar manner, the study of media too has travelled across disciplinary walls, perhaps because media are no longer separate from life, but have become part of life. Communication scholars speak of the notion of mediatisation (Hepp and Krotz 2014), a state where all social life is mediated in some way (Livingstone 2009; Couldry and Hepp 2017), or where institutions reconfigure themselves in response to what has been referred to as a 'media logic' (Altheide and Snow 1992). Considering the current moment, as the world moves beyond the social, cultural and economic changes engendered by COVID-19, we can observe the dramatic ways in which digital technologies and social media took centre-stage during the peak of the pandemic, and continue to do so in a post-pandemic world. With so much of our lives taking place behind and in front of screens, and most social interaction mediated by devices, children's worlds were even more defined by what they saw, heard and engaged with, through media. Sheltered in place, many children were doing their lessons online, consuming entertainment online more than ever before and connecting with friends through digital platforms.

Those who do not have access to contemporary modes of connection and information dissemination of course continue to live and learn in ways we always have, yet we have seen a framing of education that is increasingly privileging the former and side-lining the latter. So mediation becomes the default condition for much of the way children experience the world. In fact, the pandemic has made clear just how much we have come to depend on media for so many aspects of life, with those without access to digital devices and connectivity simply dropping out of the reach of whatever education there is in these times.

In a world where media suffuses multiple facets of life, to draw a map of work relating to children and media, therefore, it is necessary that we look across disciplines and pull together the diverse ideas and ways of exploring children's worlds. We need to draw in educators who are increasingly resorting to media and mediation in teaching practice (media for examples beyond the textbook, mediation for blended learning and flipped classroom modes). We need to co-opt the work of those who teach media skills as well as media literacy—and those who might consciously and insistently eschew such practices from a position of active resistance to mediation and mediatisation.

In this introduction, we trace the contours of the research on children and media globally and see how it relates to the field in India. We organise this work under four main heads: issues of representation; media, children and globalisation; the political economy of children's media; and the shift from media effects to agency. This is by no means an exhaustive or a systematic review of the literature; our aim is to simply offer a broad overview within which the book chapters may be read. We then go on to describe the organisation of this book and the logic of the five sections into which the chapters have been placed.

Childhood Representations in the Media

Nearly every book that tackles the subject of childhood and media begins by noting that given advances in media technologies and changes in the media environment, the experience of childhood has changed in the current times. And this book is no different. While this is true across the world and across generations, our intention is to examine the terrain of research and thinking in this broad area of children and media in the Indian context.

The experience of childhood, often understood or assumed as natural and universal, is in fact very much a factor of geographic location and social or economic class. In the case of India (and perhaps some other locations as well), other markers such as gender, caste and religion also factor into the equation, significantly moderating the experience of childhood and the ways in which the child is imagined in public policy and constructed by the market.

As Western Europe and North America developed into so-called advanced societies—moving from industrialisation to urbanisation, to middle-class suburbia in the first half of the twentieth century, with post-war economies growing and thriving, the notion of the ideal childhood also transformed over this time. Research in the fields of psychology and child development—from Freud to Erikson, to Piaget (Steinberg and Kincheloe 1997; also Krcmar 2013)—developed alongside, constructing a distinct notion of what an ideal childhood should look like. These ideals and observations that were in fact rooted in socio-cultural attitudes of the time became conflated with biological stages of development, a conflation that has had far-reaching implications, for instance, on social and educational policy. Measurable indices that we now take for granted, such as standardised testing, IQ charts, and mental and behavioural parameters, may be seen as having resulted from this approach. Scholars of critical pedagogy consider that racial and economic privilege are significant contributing factors to achieving high scores on these scales, rather than merely biological superiority. This is an example of how socio-cultural representations of children and childhood can shape public policy, and educational models in particular, and why it is important for us as researchers to both be aware of the historical constructions of childhood and the ongoing effect of contemporary representations and consequent constructions of it. Thus, we base our exploration on the historical and socio-cultural construction of childhood rather than normative, developmental models (for example, Steinberg and Kincheloe 1997; Buckingham 2008).

Children are, willy-nilly, implicated in matters of politics, society, culture and economics. As Giroux (1994: 23) argues, 'Children's culture is a sphere where entertainment, advocacy, and pleasure meet to construct conceptions of what it means to be a child occupying a combination of gender, racial, and class positions in society through which one defines oneself in relation to a myriad of others.'

In India, the disparity in terms of class and caste (rather than race) is striking. Life experiences, access to education, technology and media, among other privileges, vary widely among different demographic groups. The experience of a child belonging to the dominant caste and middle class is vastly different from that of a child of a marginalised caste or different socio-economic background. With regard to media accessibility in particular, Indian children from middle- and upper-class families may have media practices and social contexts that are similar to their counterparts in countries of the global North, while there may be a world of difference between these children's consumption of media and related practices and those of children from marginalised or less privileged backgrounds.

Banaji (2017), in her in-depth ethnographic study about children and media in India, refers to these two very separate populations as 'media-rich' and 'media-poor'. She shows how middle-class and upper-caste children have relatively easy access to a wide variety of media technologies and social media platforms, and consume a range of media content; children from lower socio-economic strata and those who are lower on the caste hierarchy have a very different experience. While a few may have access to mobile phones and some forms of new media, many do not have any access at all, and even those who do have some form of shared access may not be able to use these in the same ways as a media-rich child would. Buckingham (2008) points out that a critical theory/cultural studies approach to studying children and media needs to recognise the diversity of childhoods as a function of class, gender and ethnicity. In the Indian context, the researcher would need to acknowledge the multiplicity of experiences of childhood in India, and take into account the complex intersectional identity of a child based on the various specific markers of difference.

Scholars from media studies and other disciplines have examined the representations of children and childhood in popular culture and media. On the one hand, they have explored what these representations may say about childhood in a particular era, and on the other, how these representations inform our perceptions of childhood. For instance, Postman (1994) has suggested that the advent of mass literacy and its recognition as an important aspect of adult life created the notion that young children should be taught to read and this training phase became both a rite of passage and a key component of experiencing childhood. Giroux (1994, 2020) and Jenkins (1998) both note the 'myth' of childhood innocence and the importance of recognising that narratives about children contribute to how we as a society construct, perceive and understand childhood. Similarly, scholars of visual and popular culture (Cvetkovic and Olson 2012) have noted the circulation of images of children as sweet, wide-eyed and innocent in popular nineteenth-century media such as postcards, magazines and calendars. These images which were perhaps aspirational and idealised became a touchstone of sorts for adults to latch on to (Krcmar 2013; Olson and Rampaul 2013) even as the reality for a vast number of children from working-class backgrounds may have been very different (Gillis 1996, as cited in Drotner 2013: 16).

This notion of childhood as a phase of carefree innocence endures and continues to populate both the popular imagination and media representations of it. Drotner (2013) notes that most television shows and 'family movies' are predicated on this idea of 'domesticated innocence'. Plotlines are often centred around how 'aberrations' to this norm are managed, handled and eventually fixed (Drotner 2013: 17). Drawing on Cunningham (1995) and Holland (2004) among others, she also makes the key point that these popular representations of childhood work to normalise a perceived 'typical' middle-class, heteronormative childhood that frames those outside of the norm as 'other', against which both adult fears and fantasies are projected. Moreover, women and girls are sexualised, and the 'other' (foreign, non-white, of a different religion, ethnicity or sexuality) is often portrayed as exotic, dangerous or ridiculous (Drotner 2013; Tsaliki 2015). Similar narratives continue to play out with regard to children and childhood as news and entertainment content is replete with such representations, images that are forced into the flat categories demanded by most mass media.

Media representations as well as academic constructions tend to be created 'for' and 'about' children by adults, often leaving little room for young people's own agency in shaping the knowledge that is produced about them. These constructions of childhood are circulated on multiple platforms and across time and geography, and thereby tend to be normalised as both natural and necessary.

When analysing representations of children in the media, two broad areas of concern emerge.

First, what are general representations of children in news, feature stories or entertainment? How are children portrayed in these contexts? Are they central to the narrative or marginal? Are they incidental appendages, deployed as symbols of a larger issue—as images of children in natural disasters or war zones often are—or are they treated as a more integral part of the narrative? Second, how does the child-centric media content portray/represent children? Are they shown as having agency and participation? What type of news and entertainment stories are being targeted at them?

Representations of children in global media have often been charged with being exploitative or unnecessarily emotive (Kędra and Sommier 2018). The viral photograph of Aylan Kurdi's small body washed up on the shores of the Turkish Mediterranean in December 2015 epitomised the Syrian refugee crisis and brought home the horror of the war in a way that no amount of reporting or statistical data could have done (Cole 2017). Researchers have noted that 'children's images are frequently used to symbolise the brutality of war, famine and genocide to arouse adult sympathy and humanise events' (Carter 2013: 257). At the other end of the spectrum, reporting of the courageous activism of Greta Thunberg, Malala Yousafzai and Emma Gonzalez (one of the young gun-regulation activists who collectivised after the Parkland school shooting in the US on 14 February 2018) demonstrates that young people today indeed have a voice and are willing to use it.

In India, Licypriya Kangujam, an eight-year-old climate change activist, Payal Jangid, winner of the Global Goals Changemaker Award, and more recently, Jyoti Kumari who transported her injured father across hundreds of miles on a bicycle during the 2020 COVID-19 lockdown are some of the children who have been in the news for their political stances and/or acts of bravery (Basak 2020; BBC 2020; The Week 2019; *The Indian Express* 2020). In contrast to the immense global press coverage of the former often in the context of their political stances, these heroic Indian children get far less exposure, and even that only in a few 'feel good', niche channels. Similar stories about young innovators in science and technology can be found, but only after some digging. It becomes clear then that while children can be heroes, they are more often portrayed in popular media as helpless bystanders in more complicated contexts with regard to location, gender or social class. We see that in India too, the news tends to fall along the lines mentioned previously—children as vulnerable and in need of protection and guidance (see Chapter 5 by Mehak Siddiqui, this volume), and very occasionally, stories of individual children performing acts of courage or innovation.

Overall, we are confronted by two ends of a spectrum with regard to representations of childhood, both in news and entertainment: Innocent children, sometimes precocious, as relatively passive consumers who are swept away by events beyond their control and needing protection vis-à-vis adventurous children, taking on villains and corporations and evil governments with aplomb. And while the news does indeed offer examples of both of these kinds of young people, the reality might be that many more young people fall along different points in that continuum: being active audiences in the way they read or adapt popular media narratives to their social contexts and showing agency in important situations and conversations.

With regard to entertainment, even a cursory survey suggests that children continue to be on the periphery in most narratives, acting as convenient fillers for comedy, cuteness or for fixing a plot hole. While early television and radio programming in India attempted to create educational and child-centric entertainment content (see Chapter 1 by Manisha Pathak-Shelat, this volume), popular children's entertainment in India has largely been borrowed from either the US, UK or Japan and dubbed into local Indian languages. Even locally produced content tends to follow along the lines of established and repetitive storylines that often echo caste, class and gender stereotypes or outright ignore any dimensions of diversity (Meenakshi 2017). Some of the more recent animated programming such as the popular show *Chhota Bheem* has attempted to draw from local histories and cultures but by and large follows the formulae set by Western shows.

What we continue to observe is that mainstream depictions of childhood and narratives for and about children tend to portray and speak to the default demographic of urban, educated, middle- and upper-class children. Children from less privileged backgrounds are less visible either as protagonists or implied audience. Following research in the US context about media content in that country, we may observe a similar handling of mainstream representation in India which depicts middle-class childhood as the norm and working class children as invisible, pitiful or deviant (for example, Sengupta 2009). Where race and class are the determining factors of visibility in Western media, caste and class are the markers in Indian media content. Recent efforts by boutique publishing houses such as Tulika and Tara Books, along with content for early readers created by Pratham Books, attempt to break this mould and introduce a greater diversity of child actors in the stories they tell (Sreenivas 2011; also Chapter 3 by Deepa Sreenivas in this volume). Similarly, some recent films (for example, the 2015 film *Kaka Muttai* that portrays the everyday desires of slum children) tell stories that centre the experiences of marginalised children without representing them as victims.

Media, Children and Globalisation

With social media and the variety of digital platforms available to the privileged Indian child, consuming media content from around the world requires nothing more than a single click on a phone, laptop or tablet (and access to a broadband network). YouTube videos with content from individual content creators as well as copyrighted content, Apple Music and Spotify, Instagram photo streams, Snapchat images and (until recently) TikTok videos are all part of the deluge of content that is easily and instantly accessible to the Indian child. An Indian teenager may listen to Billie Eilish, K-pop and the latest Indian film songs or the increasing range of indie music that is available online. She may follow YouTube sensation PewDiePie, join a streaming game on Twitch, or participate in meme pranks that sweep across the globe in a digital wave.

> As teenagers, my children watched Hasan Minhaj's stand-up clips, followed *Stranger Things* and obsessed over the latest Marvel Universe movie, while simultaneously enjoying an old Hindi or Telugu film. They rolled their eyes at Bollywood celebrity antics on social media, and repeated verbatim the dialogues from their favourite 5 Star or Center Fresh television advertisement, while

> dancing to songs from *Bahubali*, *Kalank* and the Arabic version of *Dhoom*. (Sumana Kasturi)

These transnational consumers may seamlessly bridge the gap between local and global, regional and national, as they devour media content from across the globe, but are in fact performing a more complex set of media practices that transcends simple understandings of local and global, heterogenisation and homogenisation. Parameswaran (2013: 75), drawing on Appadurai's explication of globalisation, emphasises that 'globalizing and localizing processes or various forms of global homogenization and local heterogenization, feed into and reinforce each other rather than act in a mutually exclusive fashion'.

Media convergence (Jenkins 2006) further amplifies the scale of consumption, projecting multiple streams of content via movies and television, music and fashion which allow young audiences to absorb, engage with and consume global media content at different yet simultaneous entry points. These young people's media-embedded lives show us they are often active and enthusiastic participants in global media culture, taking from it as well as writing into it. And herein lies the paradox that all those who think about childhood need to contend with.

Children in contemporary society are constructed as both vulnerable and with agency. We simultaneously depend on them to be responsible global citizens of the future (Parameswaran 2013), yet treat them as passive and peripheral while formulating policy.

As researchers and observers—as well as participants—in this global media culture, the questions we need to pose to ourselves, as well as to young people, involve issues of understanding, perception, engagement and perhaps even subversion. What understanding does an Indian teenager bring to a viewing of a global franchise such as Star Wars or a region-specific blockbuster such as *Bahubali* which has very distinct cultural and religious markers? Or how does a younger child consumer absorb and engage with the very British *Peppa Pig*, the Hispanic-American *Dora the Explorer* and the Indian cartoon phenomenon *Chhota Bheem*?

> I recently watched as my five-year-old niece, who speaks both Telugu and Hindi at home, in addition to an Indian-accented English learned at school, suddenly switched from her 'Indian' English to an American-accented one and thence to a British version. As I looked on bewildered, my son helpfully explained that she was channelling *Dora* and *Peppa*, going so far as to call her grandfather, who she normally calls 'Taatha', Grandpa Pig! (Sumana Kasturi)

Parameswaran (2013: 78) asks the question: How is global media consumed and read 'through the lenses of regional and local experiences and cultures' or is 'cultural located-ness irrelevant to their enjoyment and understanding of popular culture'? We need more closely observed work on how children consume and integrate such global media content into their understanding of the world and how such content also goes to build social and cultural norms that may differ from those in the adult worlds they intersect with (and live within).

The Political Economy Frame

Political economy and critical theory approaches in media studies focus on questions of power and inequality, and on how social and institutional structures may be designed to legitimise and maintain existing caste, class, race and gender hierarchies. This means we look at how the socio-economic structures and processes of the media industry influence how communication is shaped and distributed to audiences. How do the media portray culture and society? How do the power dynamics at play in society reflect in popular media? Thus, when it comes to children's media worlds, we have to ask: How do children 'read' and absorb these narratives and how does it affect their worldview? What are the motivations, expectations and responsibilities of media companies when they make content for children?

Drawing from the field of education which has a primary interest in children and how they learn, we can borrow the term 'cultural pedagogy' which is the understanding that while some learning takes place in formal educational contexts, both adults and children learn and gain perspective and understanding from many other social sites. And media are important socio-cultural sites of learning. They are an important site of knowledge production and identity formation for everyone, but especially for children (Steinberg and Kincheloe 1997; Giroux 2020).

A critical theory approach recognises that popular media/mass media/social media have the unique ability to engage our imagination, captivate our interest and, indeed, construct our worldview. As researchers we need to investigate these potent pedagogical sites to not only understand how appeal and desire work together to gain our affective engagement, but also to interrogate the larger institutional frameworks that enable and support the creation of media content. Political economy of communication has long held that media companies create consumers rather than audiences, and that their primary commodity is not content for audiences, but rather audiences for advertisers (Mosco 1996). Research on children as consumers, especially in the spheres of cultural studies and critical pedagogy, has drawn attention to how children are constructed as consumers, and how media corporations may work towards socialising their young audiences through savvy advertising, marketing and commercialised content (for example, Kasturi 2002). Buckingham (2013), however, warns against a simplistic understanding of how this may work, arguing that while the market may have considerable power in the stories it tells and the pleasures and meanings it generates, children themselves may have a role in how they understand and appropriate those meanings. We can see then, that there are no easy answers, and as researchers we need to continue to work towards a nuanced understanding of every aspect of children's media culture and practice.

Overall, a critically nuanced approach looks at both micro (content) and macro (institutional frameworks) aspects and asks the tough questions about power, inequality and economic concerns. In addition to questioning whose voices are privileged and whose are silenced, we also must ask: who owns these stories, what implications do they have for creating an equitable society and do monetary imperatives override education and entertainment? Who gains and who loses in this process, and what exactly is gained or lost?

As media conglomerates turn into global media monopolies, these concerns are tangible and, indeed, evident. Even a cursory survey of mass media and social media content will show that while the options for consuming content are ostensibly varied and wide, true diversity in stories and voices is limited. Similarly, one can see how cost effectiveness, ease of access and market imperatives result in children consuming repetitive, unimaginative, stereotypical or inappropriate content. The issues of homogenised content, depictions of aspirational or culturally foreign experiences, and a lack of recognition of difference in social, cultural and economic contexts may cause disconnect between content producers and audiences. The proliferation of web-only content has made space for many different kinds of stories to be told, but the business model for many of these endeavours has yet to be found. As large global streaming services gain dominance, it is not clear how and whether such efforts will be sustained. Here lies the possibility of drawing on and catering to marginal children's voices, but if the market logic of audiences takes hold of these spaces, it is not clear how diversity will survive and thrive. The one hope is that where there is a felt need and the capability has been built to exercise voice, communities of media consumers will not only claim but also create their own culturally relevant content.

The global media market also throws up more vexing questions of children as commodities in the digital age, with an intensification of criminal networks of child pornography and trafficking (Sarikakis and Shaukat 2007). There has been little scholarly attention on the toxic cultures of consumption and production in India from media scholars, although there is a growing body of work from legal and human rights perspectives. The same ease with which a child finds entertainment and education content also, potentially, makes the child reachable and groomable, both as voyeur and participant, an intersection that those interested in children's media worlds could productively—and responsibly—explore. The viral potential of social media messages further makes possible multiple sub-cultures of consumption that play an important role in attitude formation and norms making and breaking, as we have seen in such instances as the 'Bois Locker Room' case involving social media chats of a sexually explicit and violent nature among a group of high-school boys (Sebastian 2020).

For the critical media researcher, these are important questions. As popular media itself has contradictory narratives about how children should and do engage with media—teetering between celebratory accounts and moral panics (Chapter 2 by Devina Sarwatay, this volume)—thoughtful conversations on the subject by those who work in the fields of media, education and childhood, along with inputs from young people themselves can contribute to a more nuanced public discourse which in turn can influence policy initiatives in education, media and related areas.

From Effects to Agency

Early research on children and media focused almost entirely on effects. During the twentieth century, the emergence of mass communication technologies such as radio and television captured the public imagination; research and policy were focused on the innovative ways in which these new technologies could be used to efficiently convey messages to large groups of people. In addition to entertainment, their applicability in areas such as advertising, public information and political propaganda was apparent.

Additionally, it was at that time that mass communication as a field of study was in its infancy and effects research—focusing on the influence and effect of mass media on audiences—was the 'mainstream' approach to studying media and communication within the field. This approach was understandable given the larger debates of the day and the popularity of the 'dominant paradigm' for theory and research (McQuail 2010). Among the early topics of interest was the issue of children and how modes of mass communication would impact them. Krcmar (2013) also credits the emergence of the concept of adolescence as a separate and distinct stage of childhood influenced by developmental models of childhood, and the prevailing social, economic and political mores of the time, for the intense (and enduring) focus of communication research on the effects of mass media on children. This approach continues to maintain its central position in child-focused research as new media technologies have emerged over the decades. The following paragraph could have been written yesterday, but actually is from a time when videocassettes, video games and interactive cable were 'new technologies':

> Our focus is the nature of recurring research questions and accumulated wisdom regarding media effects. This research recognizes that each of these media was once a new technology. We are clearly most concerned with the ways in which the commercial media have viewed the child audience, their attempts to program for that audience, and the role of research in articulating public policy directions for regulating programming. Our basic assumption in this research project is that the current and growing debates about the introduction of the new video technologies and expected effects on children should be examined against the backdrop of earlier media innovations. (Wartella and Reeves 1983: 5).

As we can see, consequent to the emergence of each new technology, the ensuing strain of research on children and media continues to focus on effects. Wartella and Reeves (1983) go on to point out that popular discourse tends to focus on concerns of how new media (not New Media, as referring to digital media) technologies can be used for purposes of education, and how they are also being used for pleasure and leisure by children. As researchers, educators and parents, we can see that nearly three decades later, those concerns endure. While popular media may create moral panics around Internet dangers, and parents may wring their hands and respond with fear or despair, researchers have worked towards gaining a critical understanding of the ways in which young people use the Internet (Davies et al. 2014; McDool et al. 2016) and developing ways to counteract the potential risks. For example, the 5 Rights Foundation addresses issues of data and privacy, child rights, and child-centred design in order to build digital environments that are appropriate for children. Their 'Risky by Design' project identifies digital design features that are geared towards profit-making and pose significant risks to children's lives. The Global Kids Online project spearheaded by researcher Sonia Livingstone focuses on developing tools for research on children's use of the Internet and building a global database of research on the rights, opportunities and risks of children's online experiences. These are just a few of the initiatives that actively seek to make a difference in children's online lives.

In India, state-owned radio and television in the initial years had the overarching goal of development, literacy and education, and early research followed this mandate by attempting to study the effects and results of these initiatives. While other approaches have entered the sphere, as Manisha Pathak-Shelat points out in Chapter 1 in this volume, the main thrust of the (very small) children and media field in India continues to focus mainly on 'consumption and to a much lower extent to the contribution, creation and participation'. As we have already noted, much of the early research, both in India and elsewhere, tended to see the child audience as passive, vulnerable and innocent. Despite moving away from the technologically deterministic 'hypodermic needle' approach, it took a while for research to take an active audience approach with regard to children and media.

Early path-breaking work by the Birmingham School that focused on how audiences actively engaged with technology included looking at young people's practices around media (Du Gay et al. 2013); more recently, Nick Couldry's (2012) 'media as practice' approach has prompted such inquiry in the digital media landscape. Recent research on children and media has started to focus on children's media practices, socialisation patterns around media use, as well as bringing more children from more diverse backgrounds into the ambit of academic inquiry with a hope of breaking stereotypical frameworks. The recent expansion of the UNICEF-supported Global Kids Online project into India also holds promise by exploring contexts beyond the urban middle-class.

It is imperative that we step away from locating a potential for social change in the technologies and focus on the potential for change on the agency of young people. Several children's rights organisations in India and abroad are working on facilitative processes that can bring children into conversation with policy and planning initiatives that impinge on their lives. For example, Divya Disha, a Hyderabad-based civil society organisation, works with children to build their capacities to express themselves and to understand processes of governance so that they can speak directly to planners and programme implementers. Other initiatives by multilateral agencies such as UNICEF and UNESCO (for example, Voices of Youth) are also looking at building capacity among children and young people so that they add their voices to issues of governance and development. Whether on matters of urban planning, school infrastructures, or law and order, the effort here is to introduce children's perspectives to adult actors—while also creating a discursive space where children are seen as active participants in civic life. Such a rights-based approach serves to shift the perception of the child from a beneficiary of services to an informed and thinking participant. Sanjay Asthana, in his work among Palestinian youth, also finds that new modes of communication allow young people 'to author their own digital stories from a position of authority, to dissolve the boundaries between objective and subjective, thereby enabling the daily, personal, emotional registers through which they give an account of themselves' (Asthana 2017: 688). Media literacy efforts accordingly need to move away from seeing children as subjects that need to be educated, to participants who can intervene in media-making in unanticipated (by adults) and productive ways to fashion their own life-worlds. Media literacy and civic education then could go hand in hand, not as top–down delivery exercises but participatory engagement programmes.

As we have seen in the discussion so far, while many aspects of children's engagement with media have changed, the discourse around the topic often follows familiar patterns of response. Young people today are interacting with media in some familiar ways, but also in other ways that could not have been possible or imaginable in decades past. The greater ease of access that new media technologies have enabled allow children to seek, find and share content—appropriate and inappropriate—across media platforms. Mobile phones, handheld tablets and lightweight laptops as well as the apps that reside on every device facilitate an engagement with media that is dynamic, evolving and highly personalised. Further, these technologies have enabled another dimension to engagement allowing young people a greater role in actively engaging with content and, most importantly, in creating it as well. There are two steps to consider with regard to children as active 'produsers' (Bruns 2008) of media: one, children's general consumption and participation in media ecologies; two, children with agency, actively creating media content, utilising media platforms and understanding the way the media industry works in order to amplify their voices and become influencers. As Fisherkeller (2013) points out, the imperatives behind children producing media are diverse, including issues of intention, ability, resources and social support. Such agency does not necessarily need new technology and sophisticated equipment to be influential. As we will see in Vasuki Belavadi's chapter on Sangwari Khabariya, the rural community media outlet run by children, even 'older technologies' can allow young people a voice and empower them in unexpected ways. Still, digital media technologies have taken that capability to the next level, bringing on a wave of young social media users and creating media celebrities of a different kind. An Internet search for young Indian YouTubers produces a list of young comedians, chefs, dancers and teachers. These savvy produsers and their adult collaborators have learnt how to utilise media technologies, read audience interest and engage effectively online.

While popular media recognises and celebrates these children, as media researchers we need to simultaneously acknowledge the capabilities of these young people, while also seeking to better understand the cultural and socio-economic circuits of symbolism and power involved in the media-making, meaning-making and money-making of these young influencers. Nolas (2020) describes the concept of 'childhood publics' whereby we can begin to acknowledge the absence of children in political discourse, and the need for their inclusion in such conversations. She explains how normative understandings of citizenship with regard to gender have traditionally excluded women from participating in the larger public sphere in areas such as politics, economics or policy—exactly the kind of gaps that some non-governmental organisations like Divya Disha are attempting to fill. Similarly, the age restrictions on citizenship have served to exclude children from conversations pertinent to them. By focusing our attention on children's everyday cultural and communication practices, we can bring to the fore the value that childhood publics can bring to society as a whole.

Such research requires not only longitudinal ethnographic studies of young people's media experiences, but also a political economic probing of 'the complexities of the Big Data apparatus that operates under the hood of children's media culture' (Montgomery 2015: 270). Finally, as teachers, parents, researchers—the adults who are supposed to 'know better'—we need to go beyond limited, simplistic and technologically deterministic understandings of media literacy for young people. We need to be thinking about the nature of citizenship in a new digital age where—whether a child has access or not—issues of data privacy and surveillance, fake news and the undermining of democracy, digital capitalism and the push against net neutrality have influenced all our lives and will continue to do so for the foreseeable future. Thus, we should devote at least some of our energies to explore the connections between agency and citizenship, and see how we can empower young people with not only the tools to understand how media works, but also with the tools to use media technologies, systems and platforms to take an active role in public life, increase their civic engagement and engage with matters that move us towards a more just and equitable world (Lemish 2007; Herrera 2012; Carter 2013).

Why This Book?

Dafna Lemish, reminiscing about the beginnings of the *Journal of Children and Media*, recalls a conversation with her partner in which she was expressing her frustration at not finding an appropriate home for her work on the 'qualitative, gender-focused, emotion- and identity-driven studies of children and media' (Lemish 2019: 116), and recounts the suggestion from him that she create such a home. 'Why not?' she answered.

When looking for work on children and media in India, one has a similar sense of absence. The odd paper surfaces in a small conference, a scholar presents enthusiastically at an international symposium, a spirited conversation takes place between colleagues at a workshop, but searches across databases produce only a handful of articles and even fewer books. Notable among these have been Shakuntala Banaji's (2017) *Children and Media in India*, and more recently, Kiran Bhatia's and Manisha Pathak-Shelat's (2019) volume, *Challenging Discriminatory Practices of Religious Socialization among Adolescents.* Both these draw on deep engagements with young people in marginalised communities to offer insights on the ways in which children negotiate with and make meaning of their mediated environments, often taking on the role of agentic actors who intervene in processes of media-making and meaning-making. And while both, without doubt, represent high-quality scholarship in this area, they occupy a lonely space. We felt there was a need to populate this space with more work from a wider range of writers as well as a broader range of topics. We knew there were many people engaged in media literacy work; we also knew there were several scholars interrogating children's literature and games; and that there were some people conducting traditional media uses and gratifications work in relation to children and media. Yet strangely enough they had never been brought together within the shared covers of a book. In addition, there were other important voices working with children, in schools and other pedagogical sites, who had a keen interest in mediations of different kinds—through literature, film and of course digital tools. This deep engagement with children's concerns and the common interest in children's worlds drove the selection of contributions for this book.

How We Have Organised the Book

We recognise that any sort of organisation is arbitrary; all forms of categorisation reflect an attempt to impose an order for ease of understanding—and this is no different. As we have observed in the previous sections, the scholarship in this large and diverse field is spread across many disciplines and has different points of entry and departure. The 12 essays in the book have been organised into five sections, reflecting some of these different points of entry: Discourses, Representations, Interactions, Constructions and Negotiations. As with any categorisation or grouping scheme, the essays do have elements that might relate to a category other than the one they have been placed in.

The two essays in the first section, Discourses, offer a macro view of the field of study. In her opening essay, Manisha Pathak-Shelat describes the terrain of work on children and media in India, beginning by acknowledging that scholars in the field, coming as most do from the global North, 'seldom appreciate how social identities such as caste, class, gender and religion in vastly different geopolitical locations shape relations between children's media engagements, place, culture and lived realities' (Pathak-Shelat, this volume). She reviews how far we have come in our understanding of children and their media cultures and draws 'our attention to accomplishments and gaps, concerns and challenges, and areas for future research'. Her essay brings together the not insubstantial contributions of Indian scholars who have consistently worked on issues relating to children and media in a manner that we can now begin to recognise as a body of work. Attempting to trace the history of this field of inquiry in India from the 1980s to the early 2020s, she takes us from the early years of 'prosocial' television content for children on the national broadcaster Doordarshan and the initial studies around effects and consumption to more recent work that considers the transformations wrought by digital media. As has been the case in other areas of media studies, the more visible and more frequently cited scholarship tends to be from South Asian scholars located in the West, despite some successful collaborative work under the aegis of multilateral agencies such as UNICEF and UNESCO. Pathak-Shelat echoes Banaji (2017) in pointing out the urban, middle-class focus of much of the work on children and media, thus revealing a major gap that needs to be filled by scholars looking at the Indian context. She rounds off her essay by delineating some directions for future research while also exhorting young scholars to pay greater attention to more nuanced and critical methodological approaches. She tempers this with an acknowledgment that the politics and economics of academic research in India pose particular challenges to young scholars, but suggests that this could be overcome by building and nurturing productive collaborations within the region and globally.

If Pathak-Shelat draws the big picture, Devina Sarwatay zooms in on one specific dimension in Chapter 2 by peering at one layer—the digital—that arguably has been transformative. She excavates the popular discourse on children and media, identifying multiple threads that characterise the popular conversation around and in response to children and media—how they use it, what effect it has on them, and how this use and its impact should be managed in policy and practice. Even as the larger media studies discourse has moved away from looking at 'effects', we find that in general conversation and even in policymaking the idea of direct effects still has currency. As she attempts to understand and lay out the major themes that emerge from a careful scrutiny of mainstream media stories relating to digital media and children, Sarwatay hopes that this will 'offer a starting point from which to develop a more pointed inquiry and imagine future research' and encourage media literacy initiatives (Sarwatay, this volume).

The second section, Representations, has three essays that radically reframe the notion of how children are portrayed in media, taking this inquiry into newer media forms—and some older ones with a newer lens. Representation is a staple of media studies, with a long tradition that emphasises the need for inclusion and diversity in portrayals of all people, but more particularly those groups that have for long remained invisible. In children's media production, efforts like *Sesame Street* have been on the vanguard of making inclusive representation mainstream, yet even a cursory survey of Indian media products aimed at children would find several absences, but even more importantly perhaps, we find that there are limited and narrow ways of seeing children—and making space for them to be seen. The essays in this section interrogate this rather vexing issue and offer ways in which we might begin to address it. In Chapter 3, Deepa Sreenivas examines the problematic nature of representation in even the more recent inclusive books such as those published by progressive publishers like Tara Books and Tulika. Noting that most children's stories are written from a decidedly middle-class point of view, with children from other backgrounds seen from this location, Sreenivas asks what if such stories 'called for a disruption of the middle-class gaze itself?' What kind of mediations would be necessary at both visual and verbal levels for such a disruption to be accomplished? Speaking about a specific collection of stories that aims to do just this, she argues, 'narrative worlds are routinely deployed around the everyday lives…of children from privileged backgrounds'. It is important for adult interlocutors to ask these questions and seek answers that will guide the production of creative media products for children that facilitate 'returning the gaze' from a subaltern point of view. This would go a long way in making space for marginalised children to stake a claim to a public voice. Going back to the anecdote at the beginning of this piece, clearly, all children need to find themselves (and seek their possible futures) in literature, in the multiple ways they exist in the world.

Media representations do more than nudge a child to look at herself and the world in certain ways. They also reflect how adults see children, setting in motion an often vicious cycle of *see–think–believe–act* that has repercussions on policies, programming and infrastructures for children. In an analysis that spans video games, films and news media, Aditya Deshbandhu (Chapter 4) examines how both fictional and factual media accounts construct children. News narratives and, to some extent, cinema paint children as subjects that are vulnerable, fragile and without agency. Childhood, by extension, is a phase that requires regulation and protection. He contrasts this construction with examples of child characters in popular video games, who exhibit agency and the ability to influence their circumstances. This forces us to re-think how we understand risk and whether there are ways in which children's agency can be tapped in a manner that mitigates risk in specific contexts. This has implications not only for how we might nurture children's (and adults') imaginations of themselves but also for how policy relating to children—in contexts of 'vulnerability' and otherwise—might draw on their innate capacities.

In the third chapter in this section, Chapter 5, Mehak Siddiqui attempts to go beyond describing how children are portrayed in the news media to understanding whether and how they might be 'co-opted or framed within certain narratives or ideologies'. Using the COVID-19 crisis of 2020 as an entry point, she examines the coverage of children from disadvantaged backgrounds within the context of this and other contemporary moments of crisis. Suggesting that the coverage reflects 'our larger systemic biases about children', leading us to accord attention and sympathy to some while ignoring others, she moves on to position the child within politics, where the child as actor is only grudgingly acknowledged but more often than not is portrayed as victim. From here it is a short step to the appropriation of children as passive symbols in conflict, as we have seen in the case of refugee crises, where they become, quite literally, poster children for relief fundraising, in the process symbolically annihilating their role as 'central actors' (Block and Buckingham 2007). Siddiqui's analysis is particularly important in the context of the Indian subcontinent, where conflict and internal displacement have affected the lives of children in deeply troubling ways, yet the resilience and fortitude of these same children have often been disregarded by both media and policymakers.

We then move on to a set of essays that have as their site schools, possibly the place where the majority of studies on children are conducted. Given that many children spend a third to one-half of their waking hours in an educational institution, this is no surprise. The three chapters in this section, grouped under the theme 'Interactions', explore children's engagement with media, both old and new. Kamala Mukunda in Chapter 6 offers a practitioner's perspective to the conversations around young people and technology. As a senior teacher at a semi-residential school that restricts use of cell phones during the five-day school week, her essay introduces us to the debates and policy decisions surrounding smartphone use in schools around the world, and juxtaposes this with the responses of students and teachers at the school, considering in some detail the philosophy that drives their approach to personal technology. The chapter provides a nuanced understanding of the pros and cons of technology in the classroom context and emphasises the need to go beyond mere 'banning' to teaching young people how to relate to digital devices in healthy ways.

The two chapters that follow investigate device use and Internet harms from the viewpoint of the adolescent child. In Chapter 7, Anita Sareen Parihar explores the role of digital devices—the mobile phone, primarily—in the lives of teenage girls and their perceptions of harms from online interactions. She uses an action research approach where a media stimulus was used to generate discussion around the issues of interest—cyber bullying and risky behaviours online. Like the other essays in this section emphasise, children are far more aware of the possible dangers of Internet use than adults probably give them credit for. Thus, it is important to include their ideas and experiences when developing policies or framing regulations for child-facing media, or introducing safeguards for all media in relation to child users. Parihar, like Archana Kumari in Chapter 8, emphasises that creating opportunities to engage with young people around their use of social and digital media would allow for a more nuanced understanding of how to best position such media within their lives. Kumari looks at how children between the ages of 13 and 17 years from urban and peri-urban backgrounds understand social media and the Internet within the framework of their lives. While her observations derive from an admittedly small number of participants, the in-depth interviews allow for some important insights to emerge, particularly relating to the different expectations that urban and rural youth bring to the Internet and their mobile phones. Issues of access and control notwithstanding, young people appear to be much more savvy about how to handle this brave new world. These chapters use the term 'media literacy' to describe their intervention as well as what is needed to ultimately moderate one's responses to and engagement with media. As Devina Sarwatay emphasises in her essay, we need to have an evidence-based approach to developing media literacy programmes; these small experiments offer the beginnings of such an evidence-based inquiry, although much more work is needed.

Clearly we need to go beyond the small numbers and limited range of contexts and populations that these chapters focus on before we can have some sense of the range of experiences children in India are having with technology, even on the margins of access. The experiments with online education during the pandemic have only made this need even more urgent. The ways in which a savvy teenager in an elite private school in New Delhi or Mumbai interacts with and deploys technology might be no different from her contemporary in New York or London, but one may imagine differences in both imaginations of technology and the limits to access imposed by circumstances for children in less privileged situations. Much more work is needed in this space, and what we have here is but a glimpse of the many questions that could and must be explored if we are to make sense of how children everywhere interact with the contemporary mediascape in all its variety. This becomes particularly crucial in these times, when so much policy, particularly in the education sector, is driven by a technological imaginary that assumes that we will very soon reach universal digital coverage—something that is very far from the truth, with rural Internet penetration in 2019 estimated at 25 per cent (Kantar IMRB 2018). Clearly, this is an evolving story that needs to be followed by researchers with an interest in children's media lives, in school and out of it.

But what we are finding is that children who have access, even of the most rudimentary kind, do magical things with technology. The contributors in the last two sections point to this in perhaps surprising and hopeful ways. The two essays in the section Constructions describe and derive insights from children's intimate engagement with media-making. When children become participants in storytelling and have the opportunity to frame themselves and their worlds in ways they can control, all kinds of exciting possibilities emerge. In this context, Samina Mishra in Chapter 9 raises some pertinent points with regard to the role of the creative arts in childhood and learning. Using her skills as a filmmaker and writer, she works with young people in formal and non-formal settings and from different socio-economic backgrounds. Here, she makes a poignant case for teaching children to use creative arts—including filmmaking and writing—which she believes equips them with the creativity, empathy and resilience required to negotiate the challenges of contemporary life and the global workplace. In Chapter 10, Vasuki Belavadi brings his experience in community media to give us a glimpse into the challenges and rewards of teaching children from underprivileged backgrounds to become media practitioners. He recounts the instance of Sangwari Khabariya, a community media collective run by children in a rural area of Chhattisgarh and how the project has allowed young people who participate in the project to find their voice, develop agency and even make critical political observations. This work ties to other scholarship abroad which has pointed to positive evidence of agency and active participation in multiple studies involving children, both in 'normal' circumstances and those in conflict situations (Block and Buckingham 2007; Asthana 2017). These two essays, drawing from two very different micro-contexts, suggest that more such ethnographic and participatory work can fill out the patchwork of children's experiences in the country.

This segues into the final section, which we have labelled 'Negotiations', with two chapters that try to look at the complex mediascapes occupied by young people who are located at the margins. Media in these instances offer the promise of escape as well as survival, as young people learn how to write themselves into media and remake it in ways that are different from what was described in the previous section by Mishra and Belavadi. Chapter 11 by Nimmi Rangaswamy shifts the gaze from middle-class childhood and youth, observing how young teens in the urban slums of Chennai and Hyderabad construct the digital self through practices like friending, *coutouring* and encountering—practices that they are reinventing in contextually empowering ways. In effect, they are pioneers for their communities, in the forefront of figuring out digital etiquette through trial and error while exploring online social relationships in ways that traditional Indian society may not allow for.

In the final chapter in the volume, Kiran Bhatia offers a window into the lived realities of children living in a media-saturated world. Her research in a rural community near Ahmedabad explores the role of the media in socialising children to identify with their religious communities and enact patterns of behaviour that are concurrent with that identification. She lays a theoretical framework to show how mediated realities contribute to religious socialisation, arguing that understanding how such socialisation works will help implement better education and media literacy programmes. In the second half of her chapter, Bhatia makes some suggestions for critical media education initiatives that promote inter-faith dialogue and understanding in the context of the classroom. Both Bhatia and Rangaswamy—as do others in this volume—show how media can and do articulate notions of selfhood and identity among children. This echoes our argument that media of all kinds offer representations of life and identity that go towards creating frameworks of reference for social and cultural identities to religious and political ones.

There Is a Lot of Ground Yet to Be Covered

The 12 chapters in this volume represent a very thin slice of what we imagine will become a large and growing body of work on children and media in India. The rapid proliferation of media and the growing complexity of life—and children's lives—raise many questions that require sustained attention. As we have noted earlier, the expanding reach of digital media has created opportunities for participation in media in unprecedented ways, with children not only occupying positions of influence on social media (YouTube, TikTok[1] and Instagram) and in the gaming world (Twitch), but also becoming vulnerable to exploitation by corporate interests as a result of this influence. How children experience the social world is moderated by their engagement with the media, to different degrees. Even those children who are physically outside the 'network' could experience intensified marginalisation as the attention of policymakers and investors is directed by a media and technological imaginary that conceives of solutions that centre media or privilege access to the Internet (in education or welfare, for instance). There is also a need to look far beyond the limited media forms we have explored here—web content, theatre, comics, handheld games—these are all part of children's media worlds and need to be understood as part of their everyday practices.

Clearly, there is an interest in understanding children's worlds, and their many ways of sense-making and self-making, and how the media may be implicated in these processes. Our experience in creating this volume assured us that we need interdisciplinary perspectives and multiple theoretical and methodological approaches to bear on the many intersecting issues relating to children and media—education, psychology, anthropology, public health, cognitive and behavioural science, sociology and others. We hope the essays in this volume prompt readers to ask more questions and probe deeper into some of those explored here. The goal is to ensure that the world—mediated and otherwise—is a safe, happy, affirming and productive place for children.

Note

1. The popular app was banned by the Government of India in June 2020 citing security and data privacy issues. It was one of the 59 apps, mostly of Chinese origin, that were banned in the country (*The Times of India* 2020).

References

Altheide, D. L., and R. P. Snow. 1992. 'Media Logic and Culture: Reply to Oakes'. *International Journal of Politics, Culture, and Society* 5(3): 465–72.

Asthana, S. 2017. 'Translation and Localization of Children's Rights in Youth-produced Digital Media in the Global South: A Hermeneutic Exploration'. *New Media & Society* 19(5): 686–700.

Banaji, S. 2017. *Children and Media in India: Narratives of Class, Agency and Social Change*. New York: Routledge.

Basak, S. 2020. 'Why 8-Year-Old Manipuri Climate Activist Licypriya Kangujam Hates Being Called "Greta of India"'. News18, 28 January. Available at https://www.news18.com/news/buzz/why-8-year-old-manipuri-climate-activist-licypriya-kangujam-hates-being-called-greta-of-india-2476793.html (accessed on 28 August 2022).

BBC. 2020. 'India Climate Activist Licypriya Kangujam on Why She Took a Stand'. 6 February. Available at https://www.bbc.com/news/world-asia-india-51399721 (accessed on 28 August 2022).

Bhatia, K. V., and M. Pathak-Shelat. 2019. *Challenging Discriminatory Practices of Religious Socialization among Adolescents*. Springer International Publishing.

Block, L., and D. Buckingham. 2007. *Global Children, Global Media: Migration, Media and Childhood*. London: Palgrave Macmillan.

Bruns, A. 2008. *Blogs, Wikipedia, Second Life, and Beyond: From Production to Produsage*. New York, NY: Peter Lang.

Buckingham, D. 2007. 'Selling Childhood? Children and Consumer Culture'. *Journal of Children and Media* 1(1): 15–24.

_____. 2008. 'Children and Media: A Cultural Studies Approach'. In *The International Handbook of Children, Media and Culture*, eds K. Drotner and S. Livingstone, 219–36. London: Sage.

_____. 2013. 'Constructing Children as Consumers'. In *The Routledge International Handbook of Children, Adolescents and Media*, ed. D. Lemish, 80–86. New York, NY: Routledge.

Buckingham, D., and R. Willett, eds. 2013. *Digital Generations: Children, Young People, and the New Media*. Abingdon and New York: Routledge.

Carter, C. 2013. 'Children and the News: Rethinking Citizenship in the Twenty-first Century'. In *The Routledge International Handbook of Children, Adolescents and Media*, ed. D. Lemish, 255–62. New York, NY: Routledge.

Cole, D. 2017. 'Study: What Was the Impact of the Iconic Photo of the Syrian Boy?' NPR, 13 January. Available at https://www.npr.org/sections/goatsandsoda/2017/01/13/509650251/study-what-was-the-impact-of-the-iconic-photo-of-the-syrian-boy (accessed on 30 August 2022).

Cook, D. T. 2009. 'Children as Consumers'. In *The Palgrave Handbook of Childhood Studies*, eds J. Qvortrup, W. A. Corsaro, M. S. Honig and G. Valentine, 332–46. Basingstoke: Palgrave Macmillan.

Couldry, N. 2012. *Media, Society, World: Social Theory and Digital Media Practice*. London: Polity.

Couldry, N., and A. Hepp. 2017. *The Mediated Construction of Reality*. Cambridge: Polity Press.

Cunningham, H. 1995. *Children and Childhood in Western Society since 1500*. London: Longman.

Cvetkovic, V. B., and D. C. Olson, eds. 2012. *Portrayals of Children in Popular Culture: Fleeting Images*. Lanham: Lexington Books.

Davies, C., J. Coleman and S. Livingstone, eds. 2014. *Digital Technologies in the Lives of Young People*. New York and Abingdon: Routledge.

Deuze, M. 2006. 'Participation, Remediation, Bricolage: Considering Principal Components of a Digital Culture'. *The Information Society* 22(2): 63–75.

———. 2011. 'Media Life'. *Media, Culture & Society* 33(1): 137–48.

Drotner, K. 2013. 'The Co-construction of Media and Childhood'. In *The Routledge International Handbook of Children, Adolescents and Media*, ed. D. Lemish, 15–22. New York, NY: Routledge.

Du Gay, P., S. Hall, L. Janes, A. K. Madsen, H. Mackay and K. Negus. 2013. *Doing Cultural Studies: The Story of the Sony Walkman*. London, UK and Thousand Oaks, CA: Sage.

Fisherkeller, J. 2013. 'Young People Producing Media: Creating and Distributing Through Adult Sponsored Projects'. In *The Routledge International Handbook of Children, Adolescents and Media*, ed. D. Lemish. New York, NY: Routledge.

Giroux, H. A. 1994. 'Animating Youth: The Disneyfication of Children's Culture'. *Socialist Review—San Francisco* 24(3): 23–55.

———. 2020. *On Critical Pedagogy*. London, New York, Oxford: Bloomsbury Publishing.

Hepp, A., and F. Krotz. 2014. 'Mediatized Worlds—Understanding Everyday Mediatization'. In *Mediatized Worlds: Culture and Society in a Media Age*, eds A. Hepp and F. Krotz, 1–15. London: Palgrave Macmillan.

Herrera, L. 2012. 'Youth and Citizenship in the Digital Age: A View from Egypt'. *Harvard Educational Review* 82(3): 333–52.

Holland, P. 2004. *Picturing Childhood: The Myth of the Child in Popular Imagery*. New York, NY: IB Tauris.

Jenkins, H. 1998. *The Children's Culture Reader*. New York, NY: New York University Press.

Jenkins, H. 2006. *Convergence Culture: Where Old and New Media Collide*. New York, NY: New York University Press.

Jordan, A. 2004. 'The Role of Media in Children's Development: An Ecological Perspective'. *Journal of Developmental & Behavioral Pediatrics* 25(3): 196–206.

Kantar IMRB. 2018. 'Digital Adoption and Usage Trends'. Available at https://imrbint.com/images/common/ICUBE™_2019_Highlights.pdf (accessed on 4 June 2020).

Kasturi, S. 2002. 'Constructing Childhood in a Corporate World: Cultural Studies, Childhood, and Disney'. In *Kidworld: Childhood Studies, Global Perspectives, and Education*, Vol. 16, eds G. S. Cannella, J. L. Kincheloe and K. Anijar, 39–58. New York, NY: Peter Lang.

Kędra, J., and M. Sommier. 2018. 'Children in the Visual Coverage of the European Refugee Crisis: A Case Study of the World Press Photo 2016'. *Journal of Applied Journalism & Media Studies* 7(1): 37–58.

Krcmar, M. 2013. 'Examining the Assumptions in Research on Children and Media'. In *The Routledge International Handbook of Children, Adolescents and Media*, ed. D. Lemish, 65–71. New York, NY: Routledge.

Lemish, D. 2007. *Children and Television: A Global Perspective*. Hoboken, NJ: Blackwell Publishing.

____. 2019. '"A Room of Our Own": Farewell Comments on Editing the Journal of Children and Media'. *Journal of Children and Media* 13(1): 116–26.

Lester-Roushanzamir, E. P., and U. Raman. 1999. 'The Global Village in Atlanta: A Textual Analysis of Olympic News Coverage for Children in the Atlanta Journal-Constitution'. *Journalism & Mass Communication Quarterly* 76(4): 699–712.

Livingstone, S. 2009. 'On the Mediation of Everything: ICA Presidential Address 2008'. *Journal of Communication* 59(1): 1–18.

McDool, E., P. Powell, J. Roberts and K. Taylor. 2016. 'Social Media Use and Children's Wellbeing'. Sheffield Economic Research Paper Series. Available at https://eprints.whiterose.ac.uk/112696/1/paper_2016011.pdf (accessed on 28 August 2022).

McQuail, D. 2010. *McQuail's Mass Communication Theory*. Thousand Oaks, CA: Sage Publications.

Meenakshi, A. 2017. 'World of Chhota Bheem'. 27 August. Available at https://www.thehindu.com/opinion/open-page/world-of-chhota-bheem/article19566644.ece (accessed on 28 August 2022).

Montgomery, K. 2015. 'Children's Media Culture in a Big Data World'. *Journal of Children and Media* 9(2): 266–71.

Mosco, V. 1996. *The Political Economy of Communication: Rethinking and Renewal*, Vol. 13. London, UK and Thousand Oaks, CA: Sage.

Nolas, S-M. 2020. 'Childhood Publics'. In *The SAGE Encyclopaedia of Children and Childhood Studies*, ed. D. T. Cook, 337. London: Sage.

Olson, D., and G. Rampaul. 2013. 'Representations of Childhood in the Media'. In *The Routledge International Handbook of Children, Adolescents and Media*, ed. D. Lemish, 49–56. New York, NY: Routledge.

Paasonen, S. 2011. 'Online Pornography: Ubiquitous and Effaced'. In *The Blackwell Handbook of Internet Studies*, eds M. Consalvo and C. Ess, 424–39. Oxford: Blackwell.

Palfrey, J. G., and U. Gasser. 2008. *Born Digital: Understanding the First Generation of Digital Natives*. New York, NY: Basic Books.

Parameswaran, R. 2013. 'Media Culture and Childhood in the Age of Globalization'. In *The Routledge International Handbook of Children, Adolescents and Media*, ed. D. Lemish, 75–81. New York, NY: Routledge.

Postman, N. 1994. *The Disappearance of Childhood*. New York: Vintage.

Sarikakis, K., and Z. Shaukat. 2007. 'The Global Structures and Cultures of Pornography: The Global Brothel'. In *Feminist Interventions in International Communication: Minding the Gap*, eds K. Sarikakis and L. R. Shade, 106–26. Lanham: Rowman & Littlefield Publishers.

Sebastian, M. 2020. '"Boys Locker Room" Case: Delhi Police Apprehends Teen Boy, Investigates Online Chats'. 5 May. Available at https://www.huffingtonpost.in/entry/boys-locker-room-case-delhi-police-apprehends-teenager_in_5eb0df67c5b6a15b6f450eb2 (accessed on 28 August 2022).

Sengupta, M. 2009. 'Reductive Realities and Empty Humanism: A Critique of *Born into Brothels* and *Slumdog Millionaire*'. *Indian Journal of Human Development* 3(2): 367–78.

Singer, D. G., and J. L. Singer. 1990. 'The Popular Media as Educators and Socializers of Growing Children'. In *Handbook of Children and the Media*, eds D. G. Singer and J. L. Singer, 1–6. Thousand Oaks: Sage.

Sreenivas, D. 2011. 'Telling Different Tales: Possible Childhoods in Children's Literature'. *Childhood* 18(3): 316–32.

Statista. 2022. 'Proportion of Selected Age Groups of World Population in 2021, by Region'. Available at https://www.statista.com/statistics/265759/world-population-by-age-and-region/ (accessed on 28 August 2022).

Steinberg, S. R., and J. L. Kincheloe. 1997. 'Introduction: No More Secrets—Kinderculture, Information Saturation, and the Postmodern Childhood'. In *Kinderculture: The Corporate Construction of Childhood*, eds S. R. Steinberg and J. L. Kincheloe, 1–30. Boulder, CP: Westview Press.

The Indian Express. 2020. 'Bihar Girl Jyoti Kumari, Who Put Studies over Trial Offer, to Play Herself on Screen'. 4 July. Available at https://indianexpress.com/article/sports/sport-others/bihar-cycle-girl-turns-down-trial-6425115/ (accessed on 28 August 2022).

The Times of India. 2020. 'Centre Bans 59 Mobile Apps Including TikTok, UC Browser, Others'. 29 June. Available at https://timesofindia.indiatimes.com/business/india-business/centre-bans-59-mobile-apps-including-tik-tok-uc-browser-others/articleshow/76694828.cms (accessed on 28 August 2022).

The Week. 2019. '17-yr-old Payal Jangid gets Changemaker Award for Fight Against Child Marriage'. 26 September. Available at https://www.theweek.in/leisure/society/2019/09/26/17-yr-old-payal-jangid-gets-changemaker-award-for-fight-against-child-marriage.html (accessed on 28 August 2022).

Tsaliki, L. 2015. 'Popular Culture and Moral Panics about "Children at Risk": Revisiting the Sexualisation-of-Young-Girls Debate'. *Sex Education* 15(5): 500–14.

Wartella, E., and B. Reeves. 1983. 'Recurring Issues in Research on Children and Media'. *Educational Technology* 23(6): 5–9.

Weber, S., and S. Dixon. 2007. 'Reviewing Young Peoples' Engagement with Technology'. In *Growing Up Online: Young People and Digital Technologies*, eds S. Weber and S. Dixon, 249–62. New York: Palgrave Macmillan.

PART I

DISCOURSES

1

COMING OF AGE

Reviewing Research on Children and Media in India

*Manisha Pathak-Shelat**

I must begin by congratulating the volume editors for this much needed and timely initiative that fills a glaring gap in the literature on children and media in India. A collection that reflects the diversity and richness of children's experience with media in India is important from both theoretical as well as instrumental perspectives.

Though recent advancements in the field of theory and practice explore children's media engagements, most of these studies focus on young people in countries of the global North who primarily inhabit digital media ecologies. In contemporary academia, there is a predominant emphasis on exploring the potential of digital technologies, practices associated with digital media and their impact on young children (Craig and Cunningham 2017; Jenkins et al. 2016; Marsh 2015; Mihailidis and Cohen 2013). Though these studies provide crucial insights into media cultures of children with digital access, mainly in the global North, they seldom appreciate how social identities such as caste, class, gender and religion in vastly different geopolitical locations shape relations between children's media engagements, place, culture and lived realities.

*The author would like to acknowledge Kiran Bhatia, Saesha Kini and Hardik Shukla from MICA for their help with the review of literature and copy-editing.

In India, children (0–14 years) constitute 30.76 per cent of the total population, one of the highest in the world (Ministry of Statistics and Programme Implementation 2018). India's diversity and, unfortunately, inequalities are duly reflected in the way young people in India engage with media, ranging from those who have limited access to media and digital technologies to those who have easy access and use media to learn, innovate and create, and those who engage with media content for leisure, entertainment and community-building. Also, in many cases of ingenuity, young people in India have used media and digital networks to transcend their geographical limitations and forge online ties to support a social cause in and through their discursive engagement (Pathak-Shelat and Bhatia 2018; Praharaj et al. 2017; Roy and Sarkar 2016). As is evident and explained in detail by Nayar and Bhide (2008), children in India inhabit varied socio-cultural realities and their lived experiences influence the techno-mediated environments they participate in.

Representing children and their media cultures is a task inherent with a responsibility to uphold the agency and safety of children. This book is, therefore, a crucial contribution in the field of children and media studies because it presents cases and empirical insights from a subsection of children who have received limited attention from academics and policy researchers. Researchers must also articulate their authority over the representations and narratives they create. This will help them identify their stake in creating childhood discourses influencing policy, parenting, education and, consequently, real-life implications for various stakeholders in society. The narratives they choose to represent children and their media experience may either bring recognition to issues and population groups or push them into oblivion. In the absence of hard evidence, it is very common to resort to assumptions, myths, panic attacks and uncalled-for celebration, all of which can do much damage to our young people's lives.

It is, therefore, important to review how far we have accomplished the task of understanding Indian children's experience with media. It should be our constant endeavour to address crucial questions such as: What kind of stories are we telling? Whose voices are we privileging? Whose voices are being excluded? Whose voices need to be paid more attention to? What aspects need examination? How can we contextualise children's media experiences in relation to their social identities and dynamic lived realities?

In the following sections, I provide a broad topographical mapping of the terrain to draw our attention to accomplishments and gaps, concerns and challenges, and areas for future research. There are many conference papers and journal papers on the topic but, in this review, I focus on researchers who have consistently examined the field and created a body of work.

Tracing the Roots: From Influence to Engagement

Serious attention to children's engagement with media in India began with the introduction of television. The earliest children's programmes were produced and broadcast by Doordarshan in the 1960s. These shows were produced in collaboration with educators and practitioners to ensure that they could be used for classroom instruction in schools across the country. Agrawal and Aghi (1987), Agrawal (2000), and Agrawal and Sinha (1986), among others, conducted some of the earliest studies in India to examine the collocation of media and children in India. They emphasised the significance of and unpacked the role of government-led initiatives (like Doordarshan) in identifying ways of using media for children's informational and educational needs.

In 1975–76, the Government of India in collaboration with the Indian Space Research Organisation (ISRO) designed a first-of-its-kind media intervention programme—Satellite Instructional Television Experiment (SITE)—to educate, guide and help rural populations for development in the country. As a part of this project, several shows were produced to educate children and were deployed for classroom instructions in schools across the country (Agrawal et al. 1999). Various other such projects, including the Kheda Communications Project, were launched as experiments in rural development broadcasting where television sets were placed in open community areas designated for collective viewing (Agrawal and Malek 1986). As part of these projects, several programmes on science, history, language, social sciences, and so on, were produced to educate children. Early studies were focused on understanding the phenomenon of educational television.

As is evident, several studies conducted during the period of 1960s–1980s aimed to understand the role of television in the lives of children, identified media as a technology with the potential to uplift masses and develop societies. According to this approach, greater agency rests with technology, although audience demographics and psychographics are seen as playing an important role. Also, in most of these studies, media (here, television) are considered to have an undeniable influence on children's worldviews.

With the advent of commercial media in India in the 1980s, especially television advertisements, many scholars and researchers focused their attention on the commercial media landscape and its influence on children. Indian children's commercial television started in 1995 and was dominated by imported programmes and foreign channels in the first decade of the millennium. Das and Kini (2018) in their comprehensive overview of this landscape point out that despite the spurt in home-grown programming after 2008, there are serious issues with content of children's television such as 'lack of diversity in genres, inadequate educational programming, regressive character portrayals, stereotypical gender representation, and under-representation of India's cultural treasure-trove' (p. 335).

Apart from reviewing the media offerings (for example, Atre and Vaze 2013; Das and Kini 2018; Jaggi 2014; Joshi 2002), most studies addressed two core questions. First, market researchers and advertisers have been interested in examining if media narratives (mostly television advertisements) can be used to expand the customer base of companies by convincing children and through them adults to buy their products. For example, scholars such as Chadha et al. (2010) and Panwar and Agnihotri (2006) have conducted research to understand commercial media's appeal among children in order to devise effective advertising strategies for promoting products and services to children. Second, critical media and market research scholars have been inclined to understand the influence of media and technologies and protect children from negative influences. They wanted to establish a cause–effect relationship between media consumption and negative attitudes, especially those related to body image issues and gender roles. Several scholars (Jaggi 2013; Pollay and Mittal 1993; Raman 1988; Vaishnav 1989) argue that commercial media, curated to target children as potential audience/consumer base, have some detrimental impact on them. Commercial media for children in India have been criticised for publishing false and misleading information, promoting harmful ideas and values, increasing obesity and for encouraging materialism. In all these studies, children are considered to be more a passive than active audience and are seen as vulnerable to the influence of the media narratives (Agrawal and Raghaviah 2008; Kapoor and Verma 2005).

With the advancement in scholarship, many researchers have adopted a descriptive methodology in an attempt to understand children's media habits and practices, such as the time they spend consuming media, their preferences concerning media genres, the role of family and friends on their media consumption patterns, and so on. Several studies (Joshi 2002; Pathak-Shelat and DeShano 2013; Rangaswamy et al. 2008; Yadav 2016) use ethnographic probes and/or descriptive methods to collect data on how children and families consume media on a daily basis. The focus of these studies is on understanding children's media engagement patterns and how these influence their lived realities and everyday interactions with people, places, culture and identities. On the other hand, critical media scholars such as Chakraborty (2015) and Jaggi (2015) reveal how popular media texts interact with social discourse and practices in India thus impacting children and youth at a very local level. These media narratives either reinforce the dominant rationality of discrimination based on gender, religion and caste or create a rupture in the dominant discourses of suppression by creating alternative and progressive narratives. In either case, children find opportunities to question and challenge these texts, and in doing so, they enact their agency.

It is important to note, here, that these more recent studies were carried out in the new millennium at a time when digital technologies and networks had begun proliferating in the Indian mediascape. As a result, we notice a gradual shift towards examining how emerging digital media technologies are situated within the larger media mix of entertainment, education, leisure, information circulation and public opinion formation. The emergence of digital media technologies initiated friction in the centralised system of content creation and dissemination widely prevalent in and through the use of media such as newspaper, radio and television (Jenkins 2006). The Internet afforded the audience opportunities to speak to the structures of authorities, gave them resources required to create and circulate self-curated content, and encouraged them to develop new communities online (Coleman 2008; Jenkins et al. 2016; Livingstone and Haddon 2009; Pathak-Shelat and Bhatia 2019). Audiences were now not just receivers; they were being readily identified as editors, producers, content creators and prosumers. For example, Livingstone and Haddon (2009: 9) enlist the different capacities in which children explore online opportunities. They show that children are recipients, participants and actors. In these roles, children experience opportunities in the areas of education, learning and literacy; participation and civic engagement; creativity; and identity and social construction. The theoretical tenets of this argument had crucial significance for media studies and research in relation to children and their engagement habits. As a result, an increasing number of studies in India focused on how children use media for educational and/or entertainment purposes (Arora 2008; Garai and Shadrach 2006; Nedungadi et al. 2017; Tripathi and Sengupta 2011; Yadav 2016). Several of these studies, however, problematised children's engagement with media, especially digital technologies, by interjecting their findings with critical discourses related to the notions of personhood, agency, empowerment and development. For instance, Pathak-Shelat and DeShano challenged the technology-centric explanations with regard to children from small-town and rural India and their media cultures with empirical evidence arguing that new media technologies are 'one limited component of their otherwise rich lives and social experiences… new media are at the periphery of their lives, as these youths have strong interpersonal connections that are rooted in geographic proximity and active school experiences' (2013: 985). In another study conducted by Banaji et al. (2018), the authors scrutinise the dominant discourse in studies related to children and media in India to suggest that examining children's media cultures requires that we re-focus our approach towards understanding children accessing and using media from within the imaginaries of their social realities and cultural experiences.

By the time digital media entered India in the 1990s, globalisation had started to influence all aspects of life. We can clearly see the impact on research of global flows of media, people, ideas and funding. Not only did an increasing number of Indian researchers (Bhatia and Pathak-Shelat 2017, 2019a, 2019b; Narayan and Narayanan 2016; Rangaswamy and Arora 2016; Shah et al. 2015; Rangaswamy et al. 2013; Shah and Jansen 2011; Tripathi and Sengupta 2011; Shah and Abraham 2009) turn their attention to digital media, but also researchers trained and based in universities abroad started showing greater interest in Indian media and children (for example, Banaji 2016; Chakraborty 2015; Asthana 2012; Arora 2008). Besides exploring media cultures of children and how social identities and cultures influence the interpretive frames used to engage with popular texts and discourse, some critical scholars have also designed intervention projects and strategies to enable children with critical media skills. Kumar (1988, 1989, 2000) is one of the earliest voices in India to call for equipping children with critical thinking skills required to engage effectively with media. On the same lines, scholars such as Gonsalves (1999) and Yadav (2016) have developed media education exercises and modules for children. Most of these studies are developed on the premise that action-oriented research is required to guide children and young individuals to take an 'interpretive detour' (Ricoeur 1981) away from their biases and towards new and alternative perspectives based on liberal critical principles of co-existence and justice. The theoretical force of this argument has influenced several media education researchers in India who believe that media can be used as a site to enact resistance and challenge power hierarchies. For instance, Bhatia (2016) and Bhatia and Pathak-Shelat (2017) have developed media education curricula to help children question practices of religious discrimination in their communities.

These studies conducted by researchers in India are complemented by international collaborations between researchers in India and several universities across the world. Here, it is crucial to note that the proliferation of digital networks has increased opportunities for international collaborations and, as a result, comparative cross-cultural studies have gained momentum. An early collaboration based on which McMillin (2009) examines Indian youth's mediated identities investigated teens, identity and television in four distinct regions of the world. The empirical research for this collaborative project that explored youth agency amidst globalisation was carried out in Bangalore, India; Johannesburg, South Africa; Munich, Germany; and New York, USA. The collaboration among Pathak-Shelat, Kotilainen and Hirsjärvi (2015) focused on developing a polycentric approach to comparative research on young individual's media participation. The focus was on developing media literacies required to enable children and young individuals to participate in global networks emerging in their mediascapes. In the same cross-cultural study, Hirsjärvi et al. (2012) delineate the numerous ways in which young people use and engage with media in five countries: Egypt, India, Kenya, Finland and Argentina. This study also enlists resources developed by UNESCO and other international media organisations to help educators and scholars develop healthy media habits in young people. Many international media organisations have also collaborated with researchers to explore the relationship between childhood practices in India and media use. For instance, a report by Grizzle et al. (2014), *Media and Information Literacy: Policy and Strategy Guidelines*, explores media contexts of children in several countries with the objective of identifying media literacy needs of young individuals. Asthana (2012) has also authored *Youth Media Imaginaries from Around the World* that includes India as one of the sites. The European Research Council funded the Connectors Study (2014–19) which examines the relationship between childhood and public life in three cities: Athens, Greece; Hyderabad, India; and

London, UK. While not exclusively focusing on media engagement, the multi-modal ethnography touched upon several dimensions of media engagement (Nolas et al. 2016, 2017; Varvantakis 2015; Nolas 2015). Similarly, Global Kids Online is an international research project spearheaded by Innocenti, the UNICEF Office of Research, identifying risks and opportunities for children and young individuals inherent in online spaces. This global collaboration will generate a rigorous cross-national evidence base around children's use of the Internet by creating a global network of researchers and experts that also includes India.

Areas That Need Evidence-based Intervention

As is evident from the brief overview above, we can find a fairly large number of studies on children/young people's use of different media, predominantly television and mobile phones. There also has been much concern with media effect (advertising, cinema, mobile phones and the Internet). The focus of a large proportion of research, however, has been on young people's media practices mainly with reference to consumption and to a much lower extent to the contribution, creation and participation or the recent phenomenon of prosumption. There have been comparatively fewer studies on parenting, media literacy and media cultures such as gaming, fandoms or online civic cultures.

A large number of studies on children and media in India have shown concerns with young people's media use. It is understandable that adults are concerned about media influences on children and, to some extent, such concerns are desirable too, as adults still play a major role in shaping media experiences of children. Adults control important nodes such as production and circulation of media in the circuit of culture (Du Gay 1997); take important decisions about content and in many instances intervene in young people's reception experiences. There is, however, a need to move from the protection mindset to a participation mindset now. Fisherkeller pointed out way back in 2009, 'a good deal of the debates, research, and policymaking about youth and popular media tend to simplify situations, overlook the specificities of circumstance, as well as, patronise youth—and various regions of the world too. Simplification, disregard, and patronisation are represented in various scholarly discussions' (Fisherkeller 2009: viii). India is no exception and, even after a decade, Fisherkeller's observation stands true. India is a fertile ground for moral panic attacks and sensational headlines in popular media out of sporadic anecdotes. Popular media narratives on topics such as Blue Whale Challenge and PUBG have painted digital media and the Internet as monsters. In giving publicity to villages banning mobile phones for unmarried girls, media often ignores a large number of young Indian women who have been using digital media in innovative and empowering ways. We need research that examines this diversity of experience in a nuanced manner. Even if we want to focus on negative media impact as risks are real, we will have to reach out to embrace tough questions of radicalisation, hate speech and serious child abuse that are not easy or convenient to examine, and study them as issues that are, at the same time, local as well as global.

The debate over young people's agency is a crucial component of the participatory framework. Though many scholars have investigated the area of young people's experiences with media with a sense of urgency to limit the influence of media on children, it is important to recognise that young individuals are innovative thinkers who exercise autonomy while perusing, using and participating in media. It is, therefore, crucial that scholars and academics invest efforts in studies which identify children as active social actors who selectively construct the conditions of media ecologies (Sharma 2011). Many scholars such as Banaji (2016), McMillin (2009), Sharma (2011) and Pathak-Shelat and DeShano (2013) emphasise the need to critique studies and research which situate agency for social change in media and communication technologies. Children must be recognised as social actors who have the agency to decide if and how media and digital technologies can be deployed as a key dimension informing their personhood, community interactions, identities, rights and civic engagement. At the same time, it is rather utopian to regard children as fully autonomous or having uncompromised agency over their media appropriation. This is why researchers have to situate their investigation at the intersection of cultural and structural forces that shape young people's agency.

Addressing this gap in research, few scholars have undertaken studies to explore how children experience and enact agency while engaging with media from within the contours of the conduct approved by their communities. In one such ethnographic study (Bhatia and Pathak-Shelat 2019a), the researchers examine how social identities of gender, religion and caste fix the interpretive boundaries from within which children operate and engage with media. Similarly, based on her empirical work with children in urban areas in India, Banaji (2015, 2016) argues that most of the children identify moments in their media engagements where they can negotiate with the social limitations imposed on them to enact their agency in relation to interpretation and practice. Asthana (2006) is the author of the UNESCO project 'Innovative Practices of Youth Participation in Media', which included several initiatives from India along with countries such as Ghana, Haiti, Kyrgyzstan, Mexico, Mozambique, Nigeria, Somalia, South Africa, Vietnam and Zambia as case studies where young people are directly involved in creating, designing and producing media content: newspaper graphics work, page design and layout, radio broadcasts, television/video production and digital multimedia-based materials.

Privileging urban and educated youth in research creates another gap in the body of literature. Interestingly, early research on children and television in India had included rural children and young people with limited media access as key groups. In recent research, this focus has shifted. According to Banaji (2016), most research exploring children's engagement with media technologies and culture include a subsection of children who belong to middle-income groups in urban areas and have easy access to digital technologies. The unending emphasis on the technology-centred discourse draws attention away from the media ecologies and concerns of children whose access to media is shaped in and through the boundaries of their social identities and lived experiences. Studies on less privileged groups of young people like those residing in rural and tribal areas (Arora 2008;

Bhatia and Pathak-Shelat 2019a; Pathak-Shelat and DeShano 2013) or urban slums (Chakraborty 2015; Rangaswamy and Arora 2016), and those from minority communities (Chakraborty 2016) can be counted on the fingers of one's hand.

Finally, we address the gap in methodology. Though there is a welcome move away from surveys using convenience sampling and towards in-depth qualitative studies and triangulation, greater attention must be paid towards innovation in methodology and transparency in reporting the methodology. Consent, vulnerability, adult-centricity, etc., are some key areas requiring a fresh examination. Scholars following the cultural studies approach and those working in the area of child well-being have argued that childhood should be respected as a stage in its own right and not just as a passage to adulthood. According to Lemish (2015):

> [T]hese scholars highlight the need to allow children, in each stage of their development, to be fully recognised as having a unique personal voice that deserves to be listened to and understood with empathy. Such research advances studies that are as much with children and for children as they are on children (p. 3).

This would have implications for methodology. We have seen arguments in favour of involving young people in design, data collection and interpretation of findings, that is, letting them tell their own stories, for over a decade now, but few studies actually practice this approach (for example, Harcourt and Einarsdottir 2011; Kellett 2005) probably because logistically this approach would pose its own challenges or most research on children still follows an adult-centric approach.

This is a valid recommendation indeed. Few pieces of research writing, however, discuss, in detail, how to address the question of inherent vulnerability in involving children as research participants or the problems posed by the involvement of adults when it comes to analysing research on children's media engagement. Similarly, there is barely any discussion on challenges posed by ethical issues and what methodological interventions may be used to resolve these. These are some important gaps in conducting and reporting research that call for our attention.

In summary, I would like to point out three areas for researchers to pursue in order to address the gaps. One, moving from protection to participation and negotiation as the key frameworks in young people's media engagement and paying attention to how young people negotiate agency with respect to media engagement and other aspects of their lives. Two, conducting more nuanced research that is informed by young people's lived realities and situating media engagement within the complex web of cultures and structures that surround young people. Three, introducing fresh methodological approaches and interdisciplinary collaborations.

Future Directions

As we continue to expand the scope and scale of research on young people and media, ethical and methodological questions will keep emerging. For example, is the digital turn marginalising certain groups and is there a need to decentre the digital? If so, how should we ensure that these groups are not silenced? On the other hand, as the world becomes more and more transnational, how should we think about moving out of strict nationally bound thinking on media and include new kinds of audiences, creators and contributors or the new-age prosumers in our research? What new theories and methodologies can take us beyond uses and gratification and help us examine the many ways young people appropriate media in every aspect of their daily lives?

Based on the above broad review of research in India and the global scenario, I present some thoughts that might help shape research on young people and media that is more youth-centric, context-sensitive yet broadly relevant, and impactful.

First of all, our concern with media impact, especially negative media impact, has to be placed in a proper perspective. Again, our concern with the vulnerability of children is legitimate but it should not displace other important dimensions such as opportunities, participation, agency and negotiation. In short, our focus must shift from what media are doing to our children to what our children are doing with media.

Second, we cannot, anymore, neatly divide old media and new media. Few studies on digital/new media look at the commonalities that the thread of continuity between conventional and new media provides. Also, the continued all-pervasive influence of Bollywood, in India and on the vast Indian diaspora, and of every other genre of media—old and new—needs a nuanced examination.

According to Hoechsmann and Poyntz (2012), analysing children's media cultures as 'a site of pedagogy' is crucial to identifying ways of deploying mediascapes as resources for learning, healthy entertainment and civic engagement. For this, academics and practitioners must emphasise on unpacking how children consume, engage with and use media from within a complex network of ideas, conduct and practices related to access and interpretation. Also, critical research with children and media requires that the researchers acknowledge their stake in creating narratives used to represent children and their concerns.

Moving on, we will produce more meaningful findings by being sensitive to young people's specific lived contexts and linking media engagement with their life-worlds. In order to develop a comprehensive understanding of the experiences of children and media from around the world, we must pay attention to the dynamics of children–media–social identities collocation in countries of the global South. Understanding how children bring their social identities and lived experiences to influence their engagements in and through media will help various stakeholders such as parents, teachers, administrators, media practitioners and policymakers to develop youth-centric and sensitive intervention strategies to monitor and optimise children's use of media and digital technologies.

I acknowledge that researchers working in India face several challenges. Many struggle to find academic homes where there is a thriving research culture and matching research support. Not only that, the field of academic research and publication is still Eurocentric, that is, dominated by scholars and practices of the global North. Even when India is represented in global anthologies or edited volumes, the representatives are often chosen from those based in universities in North America or Europe and not in India. English is still the most dominant language for academic publishing and writing conventions differ in the global North and South.

Under these circumstances how does one create a higher uptake and use of one's research on India and in India? How does one strive for a stronger impact of research? One strategy could be to create stronger South–South networks. Such networks could bring to the forefront diverse academic traditions, theories and contexts, and make research on children and media more polycentric than Eurocentric. It will modify the existing theories to include experiences from the global South and diverse understandings of youth, childhood and media systems in vastly different locations. Collaboration—both South–South as well as North–South, and across disciplines—is key to greater impact, especially for qualitative researchers. As this review shows, there are many small and local attempts at research and they are by no means irrelevant or uninteresting. It is only through collaborations and connecting small individual attempts, however, that the larger picture emerges. As they say, we cannot miss out the forest for the trees.

Second, the academic institutions in India need to make greater investment in promising researchers. A few institutions in India have initiated programmes of facilitating seed grants, conference travel and training support for their faculty but this is yet to be a norm. If we want to create a thriving research culture in our institutions, then we need the following at the least: Researchers with solid theoretical grounding and methodological training, provision of dedicated research time in work plans, respect for research as a valuable academic activity, encouragement rather than punitive appraisal of research initiatives, and affordable venues and opportunities to share research. Researchers on their part also need to pay attention to rigour, research ethics and relevance of the research.

Fortunately, global exchanges have encouraged South Asian academia and industry to strengthen research output, improve quality and foster competitiveness. We have also seen a surge in the number of South Asian scholars looking at their own scholarly and folk traditions to get new insights on diverse themes. I would end my review on a positive note, with the hope that with proper support, the direction of research can only be 'upwards and onwards'.

References

Agrawal, B. 2000. *Statistics on Children's Media Access and Media Use.* Nordicom: The UNESCO International Clearinghouse on Children and Violence on the Screen (ICCVOS), 4(1).

Agrawal, B., and A. Sinha. 1986. *SITE to INSAT: Challenges of Production and Research for Women and Children.* New Delhi: Concept Publishing Company.

Agrawal, B., K. Karnik, C. Lal, and K. Vishwanath. 1999. *Children's Television in India: A Situational Analysis.* New Delhi: Concept Publishing Company.

Agrawal, B., and M. Aghi. 1987. *Television and the Indian Child.* New Delhi: United Nations Children's Fund Regional Office for South Central Asia.

Agrawal, B., and M. Malek. 1986. *Television in Kheda: A Social Evaluation of SITE.* New Delhi: Concept Publishing Company.

Agrawal, B., and S. Raghaviah. 2008. 'India: A Quarter Century of Children's Television'. *Media Asia* 35(1): 9–16.

Arora, P. 2008. 'Instant-messaging Shiva, Flying Taxis, Bil Klinton and More: Children's Narratives from Rural India'. *International Journal of Cultural Studies* 11(1): 69–86.

Asthana, S. 2006. *Innovative Practices of Youth Participation in Media.* Paris: United Nations Educational, Scientific and Cultural Organization.

———. 2012. *Youth Media Imaginaries from Around the World.* New York: Peter Lang.

Atre, S., and A. Vaze. 2013. 'Children's Programming in India: An Analysis of Trends and Evolution in Programming'. Paper presented at National Seminar on Contemporary Media Issues and Themes, Garden City College, Bangalore.

Banaji, S. 2015. 'Behind the High-tech Fetish: Children, Work and Media Use across Classes in India'. *International Communication Gazette* 77(6): 577–99.

———. 2016. *Children and Media in India: Narratives of Class, Agency, and Social Change.* New York: Routledge.

Banaji, S., S. Livingstone, A. Nandi and M. Stoilova. 2018. 'Instrumentalising the Digital: Adolescents' Engagement with ICTs in Low-and Middle-income Countries'. *Development in Practice* 28(3): 432–43.

Bhatia, K. 2016. 'Understanding the Role of Media Education in Promoting Religious Literacy: A Critical Pedagogy for Primary School Students in Rural India'. *Media Education Research Journal* 7(2): 11–28.

Bhatia, K., and M. Pathak-Shelat. 2017. 'Media Literacy as a Pathway to Religious Literacy in Pluralistic Democracies: Designing a Critical Media Education Pedagogy for Primary School Children in India'. *Interaction: Studies in Communication and Culture* 8(2–3): 189–209.

____. 2019a. 'Media Experiences in Community-Driven Rural Areas: Exploring Children's Media Cultures in Rural Gujarat, India'. *Journal of Children and Media* 13(3): 260–75.

____. 2019b. 'Using Applied Theater Practices in Classrooms to Challenge Religious Discrimination Among Students'. *Journal of Adolescent and Adult Literacy* 62(6): 605–13.

Chadha, R., R. Bhatiani and S. Dutta. 2010. *Opportunities in the Packaged Food Market in India*. Available atwww.technopak.com/images/TPK-perspectives-vol3.pdf (accessed on 19 October 2019).

Chakraborty, K. 2015. *Young Muslim Women in India: Bollywood, Identity and Changing Youth Culture*. London: Routledge.

____. 2016. 'Eve-Teasing and Education Mobility: Young Women's Experiences in the Urban Slums of India'. In *Identities and Subjectivities*, eds N. Worth, C. Dwyer and T. Skelton, 269–92. Singapore: Springer.

Coleman, S. 2008. 'Doing IT for Themselves: Management versus Autonomy in Youth E-citizenship'. In *Civic Life Online: Learning How Digital Media Can Engage Youth*, ed. W. L. Bennett, 189–206. Cambridge, MA: MIT Press.

Craig, D., and S. Cunningham. 2017. 'Toy Unboxing: Living in a(n Unregulated) Material World'. *Media International Australia* 163(1): 77–86.

Das, S., and S. S. Kini. 2018. 'Children's Entertainment Television in India: The Changing Scenario and the Indian Child'. *Interactions: Studies in Communication & Culture* 9(3): 335–52.

Du Gay, P., ed. 1997. *Production of Culture/Cultures of Production*. London: Sage.

Fisherkeller, J. E. 2009. 'Foreword'. In *Mediated Identities: Youth, Agency, & Globalization*, Divya McMillin, Vol. 6, vii–ix. New York: Peter Lang.

Garai, A., and B. Shadrach. 2006. *Taking ICT to Every Indian Village: Opportunities and Challenges*. New Delhi: One World South Asia.

Gonsalves, P. 1999. *Exercises in Media Education*. Delhi: Don Bosco Communications.

Grizzle, A., P. Moore, M. Dezuanni, S. Asthana, C. Wilson, F. Banda and C. Onumah. 2014. *Media and Information Literacy: Policy and Strategy Guidelines*. Paris: United Nations Educational, Scientific and Cultural Organization.

Harcourt, D., and J. Einarsdottir. 2011. 'Introducing Children's Perspectives and Participation in Research'. *European Early Childhood Education Research Journal* 19(3): 301–07.

Hirsjärvi, I., S. Tayie and M. Pathak-Shelat. 2012. 'Young People's Interaction with Media in Egypt, India, Finland, Argentina and Kenya'. *Comunicar* 39(20): 53–63.

Hoechsmann, M., and S. Poyntz. 2012. *Media Literacies: A Critical Introduction*. Oxford, UK: Wiley-Blackwell.

Jaggi, R. 2013. 'Women in Indian TV Advertising: The Discourse in the Fair & Lovely Ad Campaign'. *IMS Manthan* 8(2): 181–84.

———. 2014. 'An Overview of Japanese Content on Children's Television in India'. *Media Asia* 41(3): 240–54.

———. 2015. 'Deconstructing Gender in Cartoon Programming on Children's Television Channels in India—A Textual Analysis'. *IMS Manthan* 10(1): 123–30.

Jenkins, H. 2006. *Convergence Culture: Where Old and New Media Collide*. New York, NY: New York University Press.

Jenkins, H., S. Shresthova, L. Gamber-Thompson, N. Kligler-Vilenchik and A. Zimmerman. 2016. *By Any Media Necessary: The New Youth Activism*. New York, NY: New York University Press.

Joshi, S. 2002. *Children's Fare: Indian Media*. Ahmedabad, Gujarat: The Development and Educational Communication Unit, Indian Space Research Organisation.

Kapoor, N., and D. P. S. Verma. 2005. 'Children's Understanding of TV Advertisements: Influence of Age, Sex, and Parents'. *Vision: The Journal of Business Perspective* 9(1): 21–36.

Kellett, M. 2005. *Children as Active Researchers: A New Research Paradigm for the 21st Century?* UK: Economic and Social Research Council.

Kumar, K. J. 1988. 'Communication and Development'. *Communication Research Trends* 1988–1989. Santa Clara, US: Centre for the Study of Communication and Culture.

Kumar, K. J. 1989. 'Media Education: A Historical Analysis'. *The Media Education Journal* 1989(1).

_____. 2000. 'Media Education and Development in the Context of "Globalization": Asian Perspective'. *SPIEL* 19(2): 251–60.

Lemish, D. 2015. *Children and Media: A Global Perspective*. West Sussex, UK: John Wiley & Sons.

Livingstone, S., and L. Haddon. 2009. 'Introduction'. In *Kids Online: Opportunities and Risks for Children*, eds S. Livingstone and L. Haddon, 1–18. Bristol, UK: The Policy Press.

Marsh, J. 2015. '"Unboxing" Videos: Co-construction of the Child as Cyberflâneur'. *Discourse: Studies in the Cultural Politics of Education* 37(3): 369–80.

McMillin, D. C. 2009. *Mediated Identities: Youth, Agency, & Globalization*, Vol. 6. New York: Peter Lang.

Mihailidis, P., and J. N. Cohen. 2013. 'Exploring Curation as a Core Competency in Digital and Media Literacy Education'. *Journal of Interactive Media in Education* 2013(1), Art. 2.

Ministry of Statistics and Programme Implementation. 2018. *Children in India 2018—A Statistical Appraisal*. New Delhi: Government of India.

Narayan, S. S., and S. Narayanan. 2016. *India Connected: Mapping the Impact of New Media*. New Delhi: Sage.

Nayar, U. S., and A. Bhide. 2008. 'Contextualizing Media Competencies among Young People in Indian Culture: Interface with Globalization'. In *The International Handbook of Children, Media and Culture*, eds K. Drotner and S. Livingstone, 328–35. London: Sage.

Nedungadi, P., K. Mulki and R. Raman. 2017. 'Improving Educational Outcomes & Reducing Absenteeism at Remote Villages with Mobile Technology and WhatsApp: Findings from Rural India'. *Education and Information Technologies* 23(1): 1–15.

Nolas, S-M. 2015. 'Children's Participation, Childhood Publics and Social Change: A Review'. *Children & Society* 29(2): 157–67.

Nolas, S-M., C. Varvantakis and V. Aruldoss. 2016. '(Im)possible Conversations? Activism, Childhood and Everyday Life'. *Journal of Social and Political Psychology* 4(1): 252–65.

_____. 2017. 'Talking Politics in Everyday Family Lives'. *Contemporary Social Science* 12(1–2): 68–83.

Panwar, J., and M. Agnihotri. 2006. 'Advertising Message Processing amongst Urban Children: An Indian Experience—with Special Reference to TV Advertising'. *Asia Pacific Journal of Marketing and Logistics* 18(4): 303–27.

Pathak-Shelat, M., and C. DeShano. 2013. 'Digital Youth Cultures in Small Town and Rural Gujarat, India'. *New Media and Society* 16(6): 983–1001.

Pathak-Shelat, M., and K. Bhatia. 2018. 'Young People as Global Citizens: Negotiation of Youth Civic Participation in Adult-managed Online Spaces'. *Journal of Youth Studies* 22(1): 1–21.

———. 2019. 'Examining the Significance of Online Discursive Engagement as a Form of Civic Participation'. *Global Media Journal* 11(1): 2–19.

Pathak-Shelat, M., S. Kotilainen and I. Hirsjärvi. 2015. 'A Polycentric Approach to Comparative Research: Reflections on an International Youth Media Participation Study'. *Journal of Children and Media* 9(3): 386–93.

Pollay, R., and B. Mittal. 1993. 'Here's the Beef: Factors, Determinants, and Segments in Consumer Criticism of Advertising'. *Journal of Marketing* 57(3): 99–114.

Praharaj, S., J. H. Han and S. Hawken. 2017. 'Innovative Civic Engagement and Digital Urban Infrastructure: Lessons from 100 Smart Cities Mission in India'. *Procedia Engineering* 180: 1423–32.

Raman, A. 1988. 'Targeting the Tots'. *India Today*, 30 September, pp. 102–04.

Rangaswamy, N., G. Challagulla, M. Young and E. Cutrell. 2013. 'Local Pocket Internet and Global Social Media Bridging the Digital Gap: Facebook and Youth Sub-Stratum in Urban India'. IFIP WG 9.4, 12th International Conference on Social Implications of Computers in Developing Countries, Ocho Rios, Jamaica, 19–22 May.

Rangaswamy, N., and P. Arora. 2016. 'The Mobile Internet in the Wild and Every Day: Digital Leisure in the Slums of Urban India'. *International Journal of Cultural Studies* 19(6): 611–26.

Rangaswamy, N., S. Nair and K. Toyama. 2008. '"My TV Is the Family Oven/Toaster/Grill": Personalizing TV for the Indian Audience'. In *Proceedings of the 1st International Conference on Designing Interactive User Experiences for TV and Video—UXTV'08*, eds J. Masthoff, S. Panabaker, M. Sullivan and A. Lugmayr, 19–22. New York: Association for Computing Machinery (ACM).

Ricoeur, P. 1981. *Hermeneutics and the Human Sciences: Essays on Language, Action and Interpretation*. Cambridge: Cambridge University Press.

Roy, D., and J. D. Sarkar. 2016. 'Social Media: The New Weapon in Indian Democracy'. In *Role of Media in Nation Building*, ed. A. S. Singh, 98–107. Newcastle upon Tyne: Cambridge Scholars Publishing.

Shah, N., and F. Jansen. 2011. *Digital AlterNatives with a Cause?* Bangalore: Centre for Internet and Society.

Shah, N., P. P. Sneha and S. Chattapadhyay. 2015. *Digital Activism in Asia Reader*. Lüneberg: Meson Press.

Shah, N., and S. Abraham. 2009. *Digital Natives with a Cause? A Knowledge Survey and Framework*. Hivos Publications: The Hague.

Sharma, A. 2011. 'Role of Family in Consumer Socialization of Children: Literature Review'. *Researchers World—Journal of Arts, Science & Commerce* 2(3): 161–67.

Tripathi, P., and A. Sengupta. 2011. 'Increasing Role of Children in Family Purchase Decisions'. *Indian Journal of Marketing* 41(6): 29–35.

Vaishnav, M. 1989. 'TV Ads: Hypnotizing Children'. *Eve's Weekly*, 14–18.

Varvantakis, C. 2015. 'Like the Palm of My Hand: Children and Public Space in Central Athens'. In *Digital Proceedings of the Symposium with International Participation: Places for Learning Experiences. Think, Make, Change*, eds D. Germanos and M. Liapi, 152–63. Athens: Greek National Documentation Centre.

Yadav, A. 2016. 'ICT and the Indian Education System: Challenges and Possibilities'. In *India Connected: Mapping the Impact of New Media*, eds S. Narayan and S. Narayanan, 171–91. New Delhi: Sage.

2

WHAT'S THE STORY HERE?

Children in the Digital Media Landscape

Devina Sarwatay

Children from middle- and upper middle–class families in India often have easy access to digital and social media. Scholarship regarding children's access, usage and its effects on identity formation and social interactions has been equivocal and often polarised. Discussions in mainstream media have reiterated concerns articulated in research and policy circles about children's digital access and parental cautions about appropriate use. Multilateral agencies like UNICEF have attempted to define and advocate 'Children's Rights in the Digital Age', but these efforts are based on understandings of children's lives in Western contexts. While moral panics surrounding children's digital media use are just as pervasive in India and the global South, there has been little empirical work to inform a possible articulation of children's digital media use, their digital rights and literacies. This preliminary study seeks to map the discourse on these issues in the Indian media space. Based on newspaper coverage related to children and social media, this analysis will help uncover major themes that have played a role in shaping popular narrative on children's digital lives, and offer a starting point from which to develop a more pointed inquiry.

The Complicated World of Digital and Social Media

It was not very long ago that audiences were considered an invisible, indivisible mass (Livingstone 2015). However, the Internet and social media arguably generated a greater level of engagement and participation in the public sphere (Mascheroni and Murru 2014). With time and technology, the notion of audiences has evolved from a passive, mass-bundled-together entity to differentiated and segmented groups and active engagers and participants in this digital/social media world. In fact, Papacharissi (2012), in her study of bloggers, considers (a section of) audiences today as media producers. Young people are especially likely to be enthusiastic adopters of new media because they offer opportunities for interpersonal communication, mass self-communication[1] and new ways of presenting, representing and mediating (Buckingham 2002, 2010).

While some welcome these developments as opportunities for children to learn and grow, others fear the risks of exposure to a world we do not fully know and understand (Livingstone and Helsper 2007). There is also the anxiety of the older generations (parents, teachers, etc.) of being left behind due to their lack of understanding and ability to effectively use these media, as compared to those from the younger generation who are identified as 'digital natives' (Burn et al. 2010). Some also question the skills of these natives in navigating the complicated world of social media and social network sites (SNSs) given their vulnerability as children and the possibility of cyber crimes and other risks in this new media environment. This, to some extent, takes forward a media literacy movement that emerged in the wake of the spread of television, but incorporates an active audience perspective from more recent scholarship (see Livingstone 2015; Mascheroni and Murru 2014; Kwak 2012). The emergence of literature around literacy—ranging from information literacy to media literacy and digital literacy to social media literacy—has led to interventions that have enabled children to skilfully and safely engage with this virtual environment (Buckingham 2010; Bennet et al. 2008; Livingstone 2014). This is one of the ways in which children can be made aware of the risks and opportunities online and how to deal with them as active audiences, users and prosumers.

Children from middle- and upper middle–class families in India often have easy access to digital and social media these days. An ASSOCHAM (*Business Standard India* 2015) survey found that children with both parents working were more prone to being addicted to technology like smartphones and social media. Scholarship regarding children's access to and usage of technology and its effects on identity formation and social interactions, among other things, has been equivocal and often polarised. Dr Jean Twenge's book, *iGen: Why Today's Super-Connected Kids Are Growing Up Less Rebellious, More Tolerant, Less Happy—And Completely Unprepared for Adulthood* (2018) based on research in the US, where she posits that an entire generation has been lost to smartphones, sparked off a contentious debate across academia and popular media (Livingstone 2018; Twenge 2017; Lumby 2017; Rideout 2017), with some scholars taking issue both with Twenge's findings and her interpretation of children's media use and, more broadly, the consequences of screen time. This discussion reiterated concerns articulated in research and policy circles about children's digital literacies, digital rights and parental cautions about appropriate and productive digital media use/participation.

Against this backdrop, multilateral agencies like UNICEF have attempted to define and advocate 'Children's Rights in the Digital Age', drawing on research-based inputs from activists and academics (Livingstone and Third 2017). However, these frameworks and analyses are almost all based on understandings of children's lives in Western contexts, with some work coming from Latin America and Central Europe. While the moral panics (as seen in the works of Bennet et al. 2008; Cassell and Cramer 2008; Marwick 2008; Tripp 2011) surrounding children's digital media use are just as pervasive in India and in other parts of the global South, there has been little empirical work that can inform a possible articulation of children's digital rights and digital literacies in these contexts. These moral/technopanics, however, do find a place in mainstream media discourse in India, which we uncover in this chapter.

As part of a larger project that aims to understand how children in media-rich environments in India interact with digital technology and make meaning of their digital lives, this chapter seeks to map the discourse on these issues in the Indian media space, based on newspaper coverage and analysis of topics and events related to children and social media. It is expected that this analysis will help identify the major themes that have played a role in shaping the popular narrative on children's digital lives in India. Some questions that emerge from the exercise offer a starting point from which to develop a more pointed inquiry and imagine future research.

How Did We Get Here?

New media have not only been studied extensively for their interactive nature, but also been critically investigated for their impact on children and youth (see Figure 2.1 for a diagrammatic representation of the research trajectory). In fact, so great is the interest generated in studying the young generation in and through these new media that Buckingham (2006: 1) lists a whole range of terms used to describe them:

> ...'the Nintendo generation'...'the Playstation generation'... and the 'net generation'...; as well as related constructions such as 'cyberkids'..., 'bionic children'...and even 'cyborg babies'.... Meanwhile in Japan, there has been considerable discussion of the 'thumb generation'—young people who have apparently developed a new dexterity in their thumbs as a result of their use of games consoles and mobile phones....

Essentially, the new generation[2] is seen to have been as deeply impacted by the Internet as older ones were by television. In his book *Growing Up Digital: The Rise of the Net Generation*, Tapscott (1998) makes the point that the Internet is an important force in the lives of those who grew up in this era. Early on in the era of Internet, it was found that children who lived in multimedia environments had access to computers and Internet easily if their parents were comfortable around these technologies and their attitudes were moulded by those of their parents (Livingstone 2007).

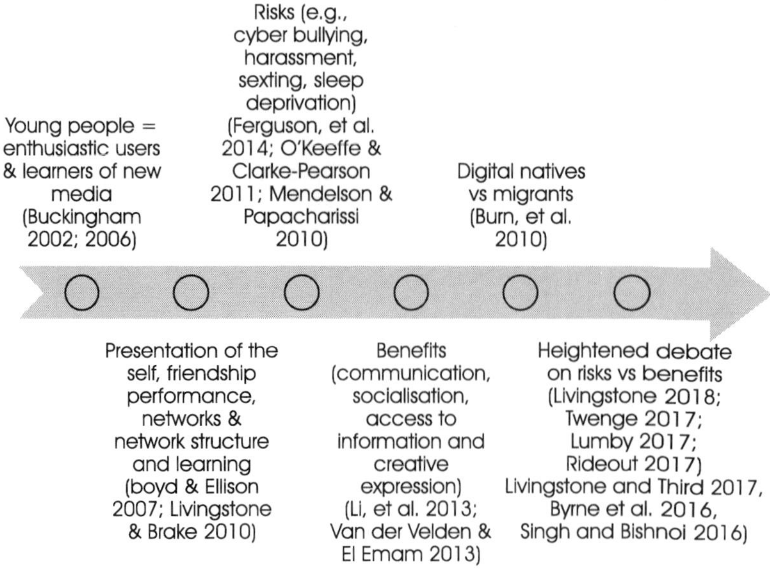

FIGURE 2.1 Research Discourse in the Global North

Source: Author.

Gradually, computers, Internet and online gaming overtook children's lives so far as to affect their sleep due to night-time usage (Eggermont and Van Den Bulck 2006), eliciting concerns regarding exposure to inappropriate content (boyd and Marwick 2009) and having parents mediate their Internet use to reduce risk (Livingstone and Helsper 2008). While the moral panics around Internet were still raging, SNSs and social media came into the picture to further 'complicate' matters. boyd and Ellison (2007: 211) define SNSs as follows:

> ...web-based services that allow individuals to (1) construct a public or semi-public profile within a bounded system, (2) articulate a list of other users with whom they share a connection, and (3) view and traverse their list of connections and those made by

others within the system. The nature and nomenclature of these connections may vary from site to site.

boyd (2015) offered some further insight into social media and said that it was more about cultural positioning and took the discourse further from just about the platforms' affordances. They insisted that ordinary people used social media to reimagine how information was shared, community was developed and communication was undertaken.

Early scholarship regarding SNSs and social media was centred on impression management and friendship performance, networks and network structure, online/offline connections and privacy issues (boyd and Ellison 2007). Naturally, children and youth were not far behind in adopting the exciting SNSs and social media for their own use. Scholarship surrounding children, especially teenagers, and young people concentrated on presentation of the self, learning, relationships, privacy, etc. (Livingstone and Brake 2010).

Gradually, the narrative shifted to risks encountered by children using social media. In a clinical report for the American Academy of Pediatrics, O'Keeffe and Clarke-Pearson (2011) recount how children are increasingly facing risks like cyber bullying and online harassment, Facebook depression, sexting, along with concerns around privacy issues, influence of social media advertising, peer pressure to join social media despite age restriction, Internet addiction and concurrent sleep deprivation.

While there were many discernible benefits of children using social media like communication, socialisation, access to information, learning and creative expression, there was also concern regarding appropriate usage. For instance, young people—who could use social media for positive self-expression and identity creation—were also using Facebook with narcissistic ambitions (Mendelson and Papacharissi 2010). Teen dating violence was being perpetrated online (Korchmaros et al. 2013); the Internet was being used for youth sexual solicitation and harassment (Ybarra and Mitchell 2008) and social media had indirect effects on body-related outcomes and life satisfaction in adolescent girls (Ferguson et al. 2014).

At the same time, one strand of both academic and media discourse also focused on the positive outcomes of digital and social media use. The American Heart Association, in a statement, commented on the scope of using these technologies for specific content to address healthy lifestyles and scale up for broad implementation because of features like targeting, data collection and relative inexpensiveness (Li et al. 2013). Van der Velden and El Emam (2013) found that social media enabled young patients with chronic ailments to be 'regular' teenagers online and that it gave them a sense of freedom/ escape by allowing them to behave normally on their profiles.

Despite the relative recency of digital and social media, considerable scholarship has already been generated. For instance, a simple Google Scholar search[3] using the term 'social media' throws up more than 3.6 million results from varied fields like management studies, communication and media studies, and computer sciences. By changing the search term to children and social media, we get about 3.8 million results from disciplines like (paediatric) medicine, communication and media studies, and management studies. Similarly, a search for the term 'social media' on online research databases like IndianJournals.com and JSTOR led to thousands of articles from areas like women's studies, political science, and communication and media studies. When searching for children and social media on JSTOR, we get a plethora of papers from children's studies, communication and media studies, and visual studies, among others. However, the search on IndianJournals.com for children and social media did not yield any results. This certainly does not suggest that no work has been done in India; although nothing is available specifically on this particular database and very little of the so far limited work that is done is available online.[4]

While polarised opinions will continue to exist, current scholarship has paved the way for future research that seeks a more nuanced understanding. Unfortunately, most of the studies come from the US and the UK, with a few from Europe and Australia, and some of them featuring to a limited extent data from Asian countries like China and India. The author could only find limited industry research done on this topic (from organisations like ASSOCHAM [*Business Standard India* 2015],[5] Tata Consultancy Services [TCS] [Pednekar 2015], McAfee [*Mint* 2014], Intel Security [*Hindustan Times* 2017a]), research conducted by teachers and students[6] and some mainstream media[7] research around sensational stories like addiction, underage use, the 'Blue Whale' game and tips to parents plus some positive stories of Internet use benefits. Nimmi Rangaswamy has studied youth in the slums of urban India to uncover how this group (especially young boys) uses mobile Internet. In a co-authored paper with Arora (Rangaswamy and Arora 2016), she uses an ethnographic approach to understand the use of Facebook on mobile phones among a young population whose digital lives and cultures are largely ignored. In another article with Cutrell (Rangaswamy and Cutrell 2013), she presents an anthropological study of teenagers in slums adopting mobile Internet. Payal Arora's book *The Next Billion Users* (2019) was featured in *The Economist* (2019) as she wrote on how people in the global South are increasingly going online for leisure. Nonetheless, compared to the research and media attention given to this topic in the global North, these endeavours are but a start to focusing on an increasingly important topic.

Breaking the News!

The background of academic and mainstream media discourse in the West, as we saw earlier, is quite polarised. Children in the digital and social media landscape in India have not been studied in as much detail as the global North. Hence, it would be interesting to see how media discourse in India shapes up in this context. The author looked at newspaper coverage on children, the Internet and social media from *Hindustan Times*—headquartered in Delhi—and *The Hindu*—headquartered in Chennai—for a five-year period, that is, 2013–17. These newspapers were selected because (a) they are two of the largest circulated English-language newspapers in India as per the Audit Bureau of Circulations (2019) (as per the 2018 report) and (b) they cover the country's length and breadth, and hence have the potential to impact academic and public discourse as well as policy. Seventy articles (inclusive of news and press reports, features and opinion-editorials) were found by using the search function on the websites of *Hindustan Times* and *The Hindu* and by excluding duplicate results. These dealt directly with the topic of children, the Internet and social media in the title and the lead paragraph. After a casual reading of the articles, a coding frame for content analysis was constructed to analyse aspects of manifest content regarding the topic of interest. This was later examined closely to classify articles into the following thematic categories of 'risks', 'addiction', 'problems', 'monitoring', 'action taken' and 'learning', essentially answering the following questions about newspaper coverage regarding children, the Internet and social media in India:

- Which risks do children face online and on social media?
- Which kinds of addiction plague young people, what are the reasons and ways out?
- What problems do children face online and on social media?
- Who can monitor children and how? What restrictions have been imposed so far?
- What can parents and schools do and what should be avoided?
- What are the positive learning experiences of children online?

Each main thematic category (refer to Table 2.1) had three sub-categories; for example, 'risks' was further categorised into 'cyber crime', 'bad online experience' and 'children and risky behaviour', and so on with the others, after a closer reading of the articles. Each sub-category was then populated by illustrations that unfolded from the media discourse. For instance, 'cyber crime' had cyber bullying, cyber stalking, sexual abuse, etc., as themes emerging from the analysis. Similarly, 'bad online experience' consisted of humiliation, targeting of girls, cruel behaviour, trolling, among others. 'Children and risky behaviour' highlighted the Blue Whale Challenge (BWC) and how children were vulnerable.

Table 2.1 Categories from Newspaper Coverage on Children, Internet and Social Media in India

	Risks	
Cyber crime	***Bad Online Experience***	***Children and Risky Behaviour***
Children unaware	70% teens have had one	Underage use violating laws
Cyber bullying	Use of Social Media (SM) to embarrass, humiliate	40% believe home address should not be shared but still do
Cyber safety	Facebook 'other' folder used to send lewd messages	Children are vulnerable
Cyber stalking	Girls targeted	Blue Whale Challenge (BWC) issues
Sexual abuse	40% witnessed cruel behaviour online	BWC ban won't work
25% children in metros bullied	Trolling	No clarity about how BWC works
	Addiction	
Types	***Reasons***	***Ways Out***
Smartphone/ Tablet/ Computer	Internet penetration at a younger age	Digital detox
Internet	Younger children hooked to online games	Hospital in Pennsylvania first to offer de-addiction
Gaming	Just like gambling	Several hospitals and NGOs now across India
Social Media		E.g., NIMHANS, CCITD
	Problems	
Physical	***Psychological***	***Others***
Sleep disturbed	iDisorder = caused by Internet addiction	Threats made
Weak immune systems	Depression	Shaming, slut shaming, etc.
Health being affected	Distress due to prolonged use	Identifiable features of girls described
Self-harm	Irritability	Working families = more time online

(Contd)

Table 2.1 (Contd)

Problems		
Physical	***Psychological***	***Others***
Suicides	Concentration problems	If intent is misuse, nothing is safe
	Brain development hampered	Studies being affected
	Negativity affects children	
Monitoring		
Parents	***Schools***	***Restrictions***
Access under supervision	Children monitored	Ban online games in school
Computers in living rooms	CCTV in computer labs	Age appropriate sites should be accessed
Parents ask for passwords	Software to monitor grades, homework, attendance, etc.	Online helicopter parenting
Use parental controls	Talk about Internet habits	Communication with strangers online is a strict no
Apps to monitor children online		No sharing personal info online
Action Taken		
Parents' Dos	***Parents' Don'ts***	***Schools***
Inform and interact with children	Respond aggressively	Colleges crackdown on confession pages
Limit screen time	Take hasty decisions	Parents informed and instructed
Set a positive example	Be a satellite parent hovering over your child	Discuss pros and cons of SM with children
Help children rediscover joys of real interaction	Forget to prevent misuse	Install firewalls, filtering and monitoring software and review everything periodically
Report cyber safety issues	Forget to fix family time	Stress on Internet safety must
Limit access to sensitive sites		Counselling sessions organised

(Contd)

Table 2.1 (Contd)

Learning		
Digital Literacy	***Education***	***Others***
Safe Internet use essential	50% use SM for assignments	Facebook used by children for games, learning, networking, etc.
Schools should educate children and parents	Online tuition	SM can help students relieve stress and learn better
Online storytelling	Self-organised learning environment	Apps and websites help young and restless connect with tradition
Internet will change the way we learn	Sex education	Students use video chat for learning new hobbies, tutorials and chatting with parents/grandparents

Source: Author's analysis of articles from *Hindustan Times* and *The Hindu* (2013–17).

Risks

The main category of 'risks' was further classified into 'cyber crime', 'bad online experience' and 'children and risky behaviour'. General media discourse regarding cyber crime drew from the coverage of different kinds of crime and how children were unaware of them. Cases of cyber bullying, stalking, abuse and harm were also covered. Many children had bad experiences online and more often than not, they did not tell anybody about them. For example, in one of the newspaper articles analysed for this study, Bhandary (2017) reported a survey conducted by two students of a Mumbai college that recounted low awareness regarding cyber crime and cyber safety among children with the young researchers finding that 'less than 40% students knew about cyber bullying', and that they were not sure who to share problems with when they came across something alarming online. Another article titled 'Confessions or cyber bullying?' dealt with 'confession pages' on social media and how they are often used for cyber bullying, and serious confessions—which should get attention and action—as well as cases of bullying online often remain anonymous or go unreported as young people do not come forward. A student was quoted, 'Most confessions target the girls which are highly abusive and bullying, even the words that are used in the post are disgusting. Most take it as a chance to make fun of girls in their institution' (Gowri 2013). The Blue Whale Challenge (BWC) was covered widely, receiving seven articles in 2017, most of them being featured in *Hindustan Times*. These articles (Arshi 2017; *Hindustan Times* 2017b; *The Hindu* 2017b) had descriptions of alleged cases of the fatal game, sharing tips and guidelines, and commenting on legal and other aspects of it.

Addiction

Online addiction has come a long way from being 'discovered' as a 'thing now' (Goswami 2013) to overtaking other priorities in the lives of children and becoming a genuine cause for concern by, for example, distracting children from their exam preparation (Dutt 2017). Different types of addiction were found: smartphone addiction, Internet/online addiction, gaming addiction, social media addiction, etc. Media discourse, as mentioned earlier, went from dismissing it as over-dependency to actively talking about reasons and de-addiction methods. Articles were littered with anecdotal evidence and among the reasons identified were engagement and pleasure that stimulates a dopamine spike getting young people hooked (ibid.) and Internet penetration at a younger age (Sharma 2014; Kumar 2015). Articles also went on to suggest ways to battle addictions like 'digital detox' and de-addiction centres across India.

Problems

Various physical, psychological and allied problems were reported due to excessive use of digital and social media. From disturbed sleep (Dutt 2017) to suicide and distress to depression (*Hindustan Times* 2017c), children were reported as having experienced an array of problems due to overuse of technology. Media coverage in the newspapers studied reported everything from children's sleep being disturbed at night due to smartphones, Internet, social media and gaming to their health being affected because of compromised immune systems caused by long-term overuse and alleged self-harm cases and suicides (Dutt 2017; *Hindustan Times* 2017c). Dutt (2017), like many other reporters/authors, also came up with a checklist for online addiction, red flags and tips for parents, and dos and don'ts for children and parents. Some articles also threw light on problematic behaviour like shaming, slut shaming, bullying and showing off weapons on social media (Sandhu 2015). One article (*Hindustan Times* 2017c) spoke ominously about the BWC and its links to alleged suicides and self-harm along with helpline numbers for psychological support to teenagers. It also highlighted other cons of smartphones like 'lower academic performance, fear of missing out, weak eyesight, disturbed sleep cycle, headaches and fatigue' and touched on the Central Board of Secondary Education's (CBSE) 18-point guideline for safe and effective use of Internet and digital technologies in schools and school buses. For its part, CBSE (2017) in its official communications hails the Internet as a 'valuable learning resource' but also warns children to use it with 'safety awareness' to avoid falling prey to cyber bullying, online fraud, etc., and highlights the schools' role to control and monitor children's use in schools and school buses. To this end, they have advised schools to take certain measures for children's education, awareness and monitoring.

Monitoring

The need for parents and schools to monitor children's smartphone and Internet usage was a topic that was widely discussed in newspapers. Several methods ranging from technological interventions to communication were cited as ways to combat these problems. 'Supporting them by talking to them, spending more time with them, making them understand the pros and cons can help children develop a better understanding about smartphone usage,' according to a New Delhi–based psychiatrist who offered tips that went beyond monitoring (*Hindustan Times* 2017c). This seems to follow the broad approach taken by the education sector, with the CBSE (2017) guidelines also including pointers like having CCTVs in computer labs, softwares to monitor and alert administration about attendance, homework and grades, and holding sessions on Internet habits and dos and don'ts. Parents were advised to keep children under supervision while accessing smartphones, computers, social media, Internet and games. However, they were also discouraged from helicopter parenting and advised instead to form a mentor–mentee bond with children rather than restricting it to strict monitoring.

Action Taken

Action taken, in terms of dos and don'ts by parents and steps taken by schools, was the next thematic category observed. Articles reported on some of the best ways to help young people navigate through the virtual world with tips like informing and interacting with them, limiting screen time and setting up other activities like reading and playing instead, setting a positive example for them, reporting cyber crime and safety issues, and helping children rediscover the joys of face-to-face interaction. Dutt (2017) quoted a psychiatrist in her report who advised, 'The best antidote for online addiction is real face-to-face communication. Talk to your child; encourage him to visit friends or family members. Encourage them to step out and participate in group activities like various outdoor games, dancing or singing.' Guidelines by institutions like CBSE (2017) were also put to action by schools and several steps were taken to safeguard children from harm like keeping parents informed of their wards' performance, discussing the pros and cons of technology, installing firewalls, filtering and monitoring software use and periodically reviewing their online presence. Some schools and colleges also cracked down on confession pages (Gowri 2013) that acted as spheres of cyber bullying and slut shaming, and organised counselling for their students.

Learning

Not everything about digital and social media was seen negatively in the newspaper coverage. These technologies and environments were used positively for education and learning as well. School assignments, online tuitions and even sex education were accessed online. It was found that effective usage of social media over a short duration actually boosts students' performance (Sandhu 2017). A village student who travels quite the distance daily to attend school interviewed by Sandhu (2017) said, 'This is for the first time that I am using these social networking platforms for study. Best part is that you can instantly exchange notes and clear any doubts. Luckily, in my WhatsApp group, there are classmates who are top scorers and their guidance is very helpful.' Students also mentioned a sense of freedom in asking questions online versus in class where they might feel shy and nervous as well as how positive use of technology helps in saving time and other resources and aids learning. For some children, experiencing Internet for the very first time was also their doorway to learning as they watched math and science videos online (*The Hindu* 2017a). These technologies are also used to keep in touch with one's traditions and families (Murali 2015), and many youngsters are using them to question stereotypes and parody clichés using humour (Sengupta 2015).

Overarching Themes

In this analysis of media discourse surrounding children and social media, two overarching themes were noticed: 'technopanics' and 'digital literacy'. A large part of the media narrative is constantly making Internet and allied technologies look like the villain and how our children are vulnerable and helpless and need to be taken care of at home and school. Marwick (2008) elaborates:

> Technopanics have the following characteristics. First, they focus on new media forms, which currently take the form of computer-mediated technologies. Second, technopanics generally pathologize young people's use of this media, like hacking, file-sharing, or playing violent video games. Third, this cultural anxiety manifests itself in an attempt to modify or regulate young people's behavior, either by controlling young people or the creators or producers of media products.

Like every other technology around us, there are pros and cons to social media as well. It is our engagement with them and our children that determines what use they will be put to. One might argue that large-scale technopanics have led to a digital literacy movement that has directly or indirectly become part of children's, parents' and teachers' lives. Gilster (1997: 1) defines digital literacy as 'The ability to access networked computer resources and use them… [to] understand and use information in multiple formats from a wide range of sources when it is presented via computers.' This can be extended to the world of smartphones and social media, and has been alluded to in newspaper coverage by means of tips and lists of dos and don'ts for parents and guidelines to schools, urging them to become more digitally literate and ensure that young people are mindful of the same too.

It was interesting to note that there was a deep chasm between Western and Indian media discourse regarding social media platforms' abuse of personal data and monetisation via tracking and advertising. Children's datafication and active targeting as an emerging market is a cause for growing concern in the global discourse (Mascheroni and Holloway 2019; Lupton and Williamson 2017) but newspapers in India have not touched on this topic in as much detail as might have been expected. Guidelines from the CBSE (2017) also do not specifically address this issue. This is an important theme that is absent from media discourse and, while the profit-making aspect of social media may not be the focus of this chapter, it certainly is one of the most significant topics that is not being discussed in media, schools or among parents, teachers and young people.

The Way Ahead

Technopanics are visible in Indian media discourse surrounding children and social media. Social media platforms are technologies we put to use and when it is for the good, they could augur positive outcomes. While the same technologies can be used to keep a hawk eye on our children, research in other contexts has shown that it is much better if we communicate with them, show them the pros and cons, set a positive example and trust them to make the right choice. In a world that is increasingly becoming technology-based, it is difficult to pry children away from screens. It is up to us to ensure they are digital literates, know their digital rights and feel free to communicate with their peers, siblings, parents, teachers and others in their circle about their experiences online and, if needed, be able to confide their problems and look for solutions to them together. Children might inherently also be more or as digitally literate as adults and might navigate through opportunities and risks online better than or as well as 'digital migrants' and need guidance from time to time for new challenges coming their way, as highlighted in studies conducted by Livingstone (2007, 2014), Livingstone and Helsper (2008), Bennet et al. (2008) and Burn et al. (2010).

As the Indian user base increases, we will find newer and many more challenges in ensuring the digital rights of our children and that they have a safe and enriching experience online. Further research and input to policy and practice is something we all owe to our next generation, the 'digital natives', who should be digital literates as well. While digital and media literacy is also about safekeeping from manipulation of social media's affordances for profit, this essay does not deal with that aspect, and that debate needs its own investigation. However, it is curious how mainstream media in India does not reflect these apprehensions in the context of children and social media. Western media have often dealt with the topic of social media companies targeting children as a market for apps and/or sales (Obordo 2017; Tsukayama 2017). This not only leads us to asking questions about but also serves as a guide for possible future research on media framing regarding children and social media, political economy of social media, young people's digital labour, and youth as a commodity for targeted advertising, surveillance and datafication, among other concerns.

There is already demand for a separate law in India to regulate children's social media exposure (Dutta 2018). While the Information Technology Act, 2000, exists to protect Indians from cyber crimes,

UNICEF India's 'Child Online Protection in India' report (Singh and Bishnoi 2016) stated an urgent need to have a legal framework to protect young people from crimes on social media given the rapid proliferation of cheap smartphones and access to Internet through mobile data plans. This report helps understand online risks faced by children, identify the legislative gaps and how they can be filled, including a stakeholder analysis that can help guide and implement the process. Their categorisation of online child abuse into two kinds—harmful and abusive online behaviour between children, and online sexual exploitation of children—is a great start towards guiding further action. While the former kind of abuse could presumably be tackled by ensuring we become and enable others (especially young people) to become digitally literate, among other solutions, the latter definitely requires legal action. UNICEF already has a team of experts working on these issues.

Research based on children's practices and experiences is the need of the hour to approach these issues from evidence- and child rights–based perspectives. We now need guided efforts into mapping existing ecosystems of children and digital and social media in the country: (a) What kind of research and advocacy is getting generated around this issue? (b) What are the thoughts and concerns of practitioners, policymakers and civil society members working for children? We also need to hear children's voices in the matter: (a) How do they access and use the Internet and social media? (b) What are their practices, experiences and perceptions? Armed with all this information and research, we need to find a way to weave the insights into our policies and practices impacting young people across the country because access to smartphones, Internet and social media is on the rise and a part of our lives. Media coverage also needs to ideally shift in the direction which pushes discourse further by asking tough questions, leaning towards a rights-based approach for children's digital and social media lives, and spurring policy and regulatory frameworks to move at the desired pace.

Notes

1. A term coined by Manuel Castells (2007): Using digital and social media to create self-directed, self-selected and self-defined messages which have the potential to reach masses.

2. New generation comprises millennials, who are generally understood to be born between 1980 and 1995 (also known as Gen Y), and those born between 1995 and 2010 known as Gen Z.

3. Search engine results as on 21 November 2019.

4. Gleaned from conversations during conferences and workshops held at SNDT Women's University, Mumbai, and Sri Padmavati Mahila Visvavidyalayam, Tirupati, among others in India.

5. Report based on survey conducted in major metropolitan cities of India of 4,750 parents of children in the age group of 6–13 years under ASSOCHAM's Social Development Foundation (ASDF).

6. These were part of students' requirement for a degree. For example: Jadav (2014) wanted to examine the effect of social media on and its role in attitude formation of those between the ages of 15 and 35 years. Another study (Bhandary 2017) was about levels of awareness among children regarding cyber safety that was conducted in three phases of pre-test, intervention and post-test which mapped awareness before and after conducting sessions on cyber safety.

7. For instance 'Addicted to You(Tube)' in *The Hindu* takes on toddlers going crazy about cartoons on the site (Kumar 2015).

References

Arora, P. 2019. *The Next Billion Users: Digital Life Beyond the West.* Cambridge: Harvard University Press.

Arshi, A. 2017. 'Chandigarh Education Dept Issues Advisory on Blue Whale Game; Instructions for Teachers, Parents'. *Hindustan Times,* 25 September. Available at https://www.hindustantimes.com/punjab/education-dept-issues-advisory-on-blue-whale-game-instructions-for-teachers-and-parents/story-Xgs5AmxOTOaT9YFcV0BciN.html (accessed on 22 October 2022).

Audit Bureau of Circulations. 2019. 'Highest Circulated amongst ABC Member Publications (across Languages) as Certified upto 22nd February, 2019'. Audit Bureau of Circulations. Available at http://www.auditbureau.org/files/JJ2018%20Highest%20Circulated%20amongst%20ABC%20Member%20Publications%20(across%20languages).pdf (accessed on 22 October 2022).

Bennet, S., K. A. Maton and Kervin Lisa. 2008. 'The "Digital Natives" Debates: A Critical Review of the Evidence'. *British Journal of Educational Technology* 39(5): 775–86.

Bhandary, S. 2017. 'Awareness about Internet Safety Very Low among Mumbai School Kids: Survey'. *Hindustan Times*, 3 July. Available at https://www.hindustantimes.com/mumbai-news/awareness-about-internet-safety-very-low-among-mumbai-school-kids-survey/story-Wb0t9qjlMXs3rbUlHMQmoM.html (accessed on 20 July 2019).

boyd, d. 2015. 'Social Media: A Phenomenon to be Analyzed'. *Social Media + Society* 1(1): 1–2.

boyd, d., and A. Marwick. 2009. 'The Conundrum of Visibility'. *Journal of Children and Media* 3(4): 410–14.

boyd, d., and N. Ellison. 2007. 'Social Network Sites: Definition, History, and Scholarship'. *Journal of Computer-Mediated Communication* 13(1): 210–30.

Buckingham, D. 2002. *Children and Media Overview*. UNESCO.

———. 2006. 'Is There a Digital Generation?'. In *Digital Generations: Children, Young People and the New Media*, eds D. Buckingham and R. Willett. Mahwah, NJ: Erlbaum.

———. 2010. 'Defining Digital Literacy: What Young People Need to Know About Digital Media'. In *Medienbildung in neuen Kulturräumen* [Media Education in New Cultural Spaces], ed. B. Bachmair, 59–71. VS Verlag für Sozialwissenschaften [VS Verlag for Social Sciences].

Burn, A., D. Buckingham, B. Parry and M. Powell. 2010. 'Minding the Gaps: Teachers' Cultures, Students' Cultures'. In *Adolescents' Online Literacies: Connecting Classrooms, Digital Media & Popular Culture* (Vol. 75), ed. D. E. Alvermann, 183–201. New York: Peter Lang Publishing.

Business Standard India. 2015. '76 Percent Kids Below Age 13 Hooked to YouTube: Assocham'. 21 December. Available at https://www.business-standard.com/article/news-ians/76-percent-kids-below-age-13-hooked-to-youtube-assocham-115122100769_1.html (accessed on 22 October 2022).

Byrne, J., D. Kardefelt Winther, S. Livingstone and M. Stoilova. 2016. Global Kids Online Research Synthesis, 2015–2016. *Innocenti Research Report*, No. IRR_2016_01. UNICEF Office of Research-Innocenti, Florence. Available at https://www.unicef-irc.org/publications/869-global-kids-online-research-synthesis-2015-2016.html (accessed on 22 October 2022).

Cassell, J., and M. Cramer. 2008. 'High Tech or High Risk: Moral Panics about Girls Online'. In *Digital Youth, Innovation, and the Unexpected*, ed. Tara McPherson (The John D. and Catherine T. MacArthur Foundation Series on Digital Media and Learning), 53–76. Cambridge, MA: The MIT Press.

Castells, M. 2007. 'Communication, Power and Counter-power in the Network Society'. *International Journal of Communication* 1(1): 238–66.

Central Board of Secondary Education (CBSE). 2017. 'Guidelines for Safe and Effective Use of Internet and Digital Technologies in Schools and School Buses'. New Delhi: Central Board of Secondary Education. Available at http://cbse.nic.in/newsite/circulars/2017/32_Circular_2017.pdf (accessed on 23 November 2018).

Dutt, A. 2017. 'Are You Easily Distracted? Put Your Phone Away While Studying'. *Hindustan Times*, 3 March. Available at https://www.hindustantimes.com/delhi-news/are-you-easily-distracted-put-your-phone-way-while-studying/story-LcEMzNNDSgmCZWS3nsFmGN.html (accessed on 20 July 2019).

Dutta, P. 2018. 'Safer Internet Day: Should India Have Law to Regulate Children's Social Media Exposure?' *India Today*, 6 February. Available at https://www.indiatoday.in/india/story/safer-internet-day-should-india-have-law-to-regulate-children-s-social-media-exposure-1162516-2018-02-06 (accessed on 23 July 2019).

Eggermont, S., and J. Van Den Bulck. 2006. 'Nodding Off or Switching Off? The Use of Popular Media as a Sleep Aid in Secondary-School Children'. *Journal of Paediatrics and Child Health* 42(7): 428–33.

Ferguson, C. J., M. E. Muñoz, A. Garza and M. Galindo. 2014. 'Concurrent and Prospective Analyses of Peer, Television and Social Media Influences on Body Dissatisfaction, Eating Disorder Symptoms and Life Satisfaction in Adolescent Girls'. *Journal of Youth and Adolescence* 43(1): 1–14.

Gilster, P. 1997. *Digital Literacy*. New York: Wiley Computer Pub.

Goswami, S. 2013. 'Internet Addiction?' *Hindustan Times*, 7 September. Available at http://www.hindustantimes.com/brunch/internet-addiction/story-MltEDkpd7zOMyWw3a1Y9SJ.html (accessed on 20 July 2019).

Gowri, G. 2013. 'Confessions or Cyber Bullying?' *The Hindu*, 4 July. Available at http://www.thehindu.com/features/metroplus/society/confessions-or-cyber-bullying/article4880962.ece (accessed on 20 July 2019).

Hindustan Times. 2017a. 'Harassment Not Confined to Schools, Online Bullies Are at Work at All Places'. 9 February. Available at https://www.hindustantimes.com/india-news/harassment-not-confined-to-schools-online-bullies-are-at-work-at-all-places/story-Irs4N6UvMrFyOmYVWPOD8M.html (accessed on 22 October 2022).

———. 2017b. 'What Is the Blue Whale Challenge?' 31 August. https://www.hindustantimes.com/india-news/what-is-the-blue-whale-challenge/story-nfCbTOR9ta9x6HT0SfkrcO.html (accessed on 22 October 2022).

———. 2017c. 'Are Your Children Addicted to Smartphones? It Can Be Injurious to Their Mental Health'. 14 September. Available at https://www.hindustantimes.com/fitness/are-your-children-addicted-to-smartphones-it-can-be-injurious-to-their-mental-health/story-vl5e5QbMWX6IE8aG5YyeYJ.html (accessed on 20 July 2019).

Jadav, S. 2014. 'An Analytical Study on Influence of Social Media Pertaining to Youth'. Ph.D. diss., Shri Jagdish Prasad Jhabarmal Tibrewala University.

Korchmaros, J. D., M. L. Ybarra, J. Langhinrichsen-Rohling, d. boyd and A. Lenhart. 2013. 'Perpetration of Teen Dating Violence in a Networked Society'. *Cyberpsychology, Behavior, and Social Networking* 16(8): 561–67.

Kumar, D. 2015. 'Addicted to You(Tube)'. *The Hindu*, 26 January. Available at http://www.thehindu.com/features/metroplus/society/toddler-talk-addicted-to-youtube/article6823872.ece (accessed on 19 July 2019).

Kwak, H. 2012. 'Self-disclosure in Online Media: An Active Audience Perspective'. *International Journal of Advertising* 31(3): 485–510.

Li, J. S., T. A. Barnett, E. Goodman, R. C. Wasserman and A. R. Kemper. 2013. 'Approaches to the Prevention and Management of Childhood Obesity—The Role of Social Networks and the Use of Social Media and Related Electronic Technologies: A Scientific Statement from the American Heart Association'. *Circulation* 127(2): 260–67.

Livingstone, S. 2007. 'Strategies of Parental Regulation in the Media-Rich Home'. *Computers in Human Behavior* 23(3): 920–41.

———. 2014. 'Developing Social Media Literacy: How Children Learn to Interpret Risky Opportunities on Social Network Sites'. *Communications* 39(3): 283–303.

———. 2015. 'Active Audiences? The Debate Progresses But Is Far From Resolved'. *Communication Theory* 25(4): 439–46.

Livingstone, S. 2018. 'Book Review: "iGen: Why Today's Super-Connected Kids are Growing Up Less Rebellious, More Tolerant, Less Happy—and Completely Unprepared for Adulthood"'. *Journal of Children and Media* 12(1): 118–23.

Livingstone, S., and A. Third. 2017. 'Children and Young People's Rights in the Digital Age: An Emerging Agenda'. *New Media & Society* 19(5): 657–70.

Livingstone, S., and D. R. Brake. 2010. 'On the Rapid Rise of Social Networking Sites: New Findings and Policy Implications'. *Children and Society* 24(1): 75–83.

Livingstone, S., and E. J. Helsper. 2007. 'Taking Risks When Communicating on the Internet: The Role of Offline Social-Psychological Factors in Young People's Vulnerability to Online Risks'. *Information Communication and Society* 10(5): 619–44.

____. 2008. 'Parental Mediation of Children's Internet Use'. *Journal of Broadcasting and Electronic Media* 52(4): 581–99.

Lumby, C. 2017. 'Enough With the Moral Panic over Smartphones. The Kids are All Right'. *The Guardian*, 10 August. Available at https://www.theguardian.com/commentisfree/2017/aug/10/enough-with-the-moral-panic-over-smartphones-the-kids-are-alright (accessed on 17 July 2019).

Lupton, D., and B. Williamson. 2017. 'The Datafied Child: The Dataveillance of Children and Implications for Their Rights'. *New Media and Society* 19(5): 780–94.

Marwick, A. E. 2008. 'To Catch a Predator? The MySpace Moral Panic'. *First Monday* 13(6). Available at https://doi.org/10.5210/fm.v13i6.2152 (accessed on 22 October 2022).

Mascheroni, G., and D. Holloway. 2019. 'IoToys Are Here to Stay, and It's Time We Moved Beyond Media Panics and Hype'. 3 July. https://blogs.lse.ac.uk/parenting4digitalfuture/2019/07/03/iotoys-are-here-to-stay-media-panics-and-hype/ (accessed on 7 November 2019).

Mascheroni, G., and M. F. Murru. 2014. 'Digital Literacies and Civic Literacies: Theoretical Issues, Research Questions and Methodological Approaches'. *Medijska Istraživanja* 20(2): 31–53.

Mendelson, A. L., and Z. Papacharissi. 2010. 'Look at Us: Collective Narcissism in College Student Facebook Photo Galleries'. In *A Networked Self: Identity, Community, and Culture on Social Network Sites* (1st edn), ed. Z. Papacharissi, 251–73. New York: Routledge.

Mint. 2014. 'Indian Teenagers Show Risky Behaviour Online: McAfee'. 10 November. Available at https://www.livemint.com/Industry/t7jUP4dxW2P9r9lCDNANHP/Indian-teenagers-show-risky-behaviour-online-McAfee.html (accessed on 22 October 2022).

Murali, A. 2015. 'Networked to Tradition'. *The Hindu*, 9 June. Available at http://www.thehindu.com/features/metroplus/having-a-taste-of-different-cultures-with-social-networking/article7298488.ece (accessed on 21 July 2019).

Obordo, R. 2017. 'Their Childhoods Shouldn't Be Owned': Readers on Children and Social Media'. *The Guardian*, 5 January. https://www.theguardian.com/society/2017/jan/05/their-childhoods-shouldnt-be-owned-readers-on-children-and-social-media (accessed on 9 December 2018).

O'Keeffe, G. S., and K. Clarke-Pearson. 2011. 'The Impact of Social Media on Children, Adolescents, and Families'. *Pediatrics* 127(4): 800–804.

Papacharissi, Z. 2012. 'Audiences as Media Producers: Content Analysis of 260 Blogs'. In *Self-Mediation: New Media, Citizenship and Civil Selves* (1st edn), ed. L. Chouliaraki, 21–38. New York: Routledge.

Pednekar, P. 2015. '60% Parents in Mumbai Have Access to Children's Social Media: Survey'. *Hindustan Times*, 20 May. Available at https://www.hindustantimes.com/mumbai/60-parents-in-mumbai-have-access-to-children-s-social-media-survey/story-CA3r4sYzTDDROcUaPwXA1M.html (accessed on 22 October 2022).

Raina, R. (n.d.) 'Engaging Indian Millennial @Workplace'. Amdocs (India). Available at https://www.shrm.org/shrm-india/Documents/EMAW8.pdf (accessed on 19 December 2018).

Rangaswamy, N., and E. Cutrell. 2013. 'Anthropology, Development and ICTs: Slums, Youth and the Mobile Internet in Urban India'. *Information Technologies & International Development* 9(2): 51–63.

Rangaswamy, N., and P. Arora. 2016. 'The Mobile Internet in the Wild and Every Day: Digital Leisure in the Slums of Urban India'. *International Journal of Cultural Studies* 19(6): 611–26.

Rideout, V. 2017. 'Some Thoughts on the Atlantic's "Have Smartphones Destroyed a Generation?"'. 11 August. Available at https://blogs.lse.ac.uk/parenting4digitalfuture/2017/08/11/some-thoughts-on-the-atlantic/ (accessed on 17 July 2019).

Sandhu, R. 2015. 'Youngsters Take to Flaunting Weapons on Social Media'. *Hindustan Times*, 20 July. Available at https://www.hindustantimes.com/punjab/youngsters-take-to-flaunting-weapons-on-social-media/story-ID1xWzaITvoFwWGNks6vFP.html (accessed on 21 July 2019).

———. 2017. 'Social Media Use for Exam Preparation a Hit Among Students in Ludhiana'. *Hindustan Times*, 3 March. Available at https://www.hindustantimes.com/punjab/social-media-use-for-exam-preparation-a-hit-among-students-in-ludhiana/story-11UXzC3b5LJPCy2J1noXOJ.html (accessed on 21 July 2019).

Sengupta, A. 2015. 'Parodying Gender Cliches'. *The Hindu*, 16 May. Available at http://www.thehindu.com/features/magazine/parodying-gender-cliches/article7209411.ece (accessed on 21 July 2019).

Sharma, M. 2014. 'Delhi's First Internet De-Addiction Centre Helps Children Log Out of the Virtual World'. *Hindustan Times*, 3 August. Available at https://www.hindustantimes.com/delhi-news/delhi-s-first-internet-de-addiction-centre-helps-children-log-out-of-the-virtual-world/story-o5QwvVWdP3LxlPaANW3IAI.html (accessed on 20 July 2019).

Singh, N., and K. Bishnoi. 2016. 'Child Online Protection in India' (No. 115). New Delhi: UNICEF. Available at https://www.icmec.org/wp-content/uploads/2016/09/UNICEF-Child-Protection-Online-India-pub_doc115-1.pdf (accessed on 9 December 2018).

Tapscott, D. 1998. *Growing Up Digital: The Rise of the Net Generation*. New York: McGraw-Hill.

The Economist. 2019. 'How the Pursuit of Leisure Drives Internet Use'. 8 June. Available at https://www.economist.com/briefing/2019/06/08/how-the-pursuit-of-leisure-drives-internet-use (accessed on 21 February 2020).

The Hindu. 2017a. 'Taking the Web to Children in India's Remote Salt Desert'. 11 April. Available at http://www.thehindu.com/news/national/other-states/taking-the-web-to-children-in-indias-remote-salt-desert/article17924310.ece (accessed on 21 July 2019).

———. 2017b. 'Remove Links to Blue Whale Challenge or Face Action, Minister Tells Social Media Firms'. 16 August. https://www.thehindu.com/news/national/will-act-against-social-media-firms-on-blue-whale-game-ravi-shankar-prasad/article19503064.ece (accessed on 1 February 2023).

Tripp, L. M. 2011. '"The Computer Is Not for You to Be Looking Around, It Is for Schoolwork": Challenges for Digital Inclusion as Latino Immigrant Families Negotiate Children's Access to the Internet'. *New Media and Society* 13(4): 552–67.

Tsukayama, H. 2017. 'Facebook's New Messaging App Deepens Debate Over Kids' Social-Media Use'. *The Washington Post.* Available at https://www.washingtonpost.com/news/the-switch/wp/2017/12/04/facebook-now-has-a-messenger-app-just-for-kids/?noredirect=on&utm_term=.bb66d5190229 (accessed on 19 December 2018).

Twenge, J. 2017. 'Have Smartphones Destroyed a Generation?'. *The Atlantic*, September. Available at https://www.theatlantic.com/magazine/archive/2017/09/has-the-smartphone-destroyed-a-generation/534198/ (accessed on 17 July 2019).

———. 2018. *iGen: Why Today's Super-Connected Kids Are Growing Up Less Rebellious, More Tolerant, Less Happy—And Completely Unprepared for Adulthood—And What That Means for the Rest of Us.* New York: Simon & Schuster.

Van der Velden, M., and K. El Emam. 2013. '"Not All My Friends Need to Know": A Qualitative Study of Teenage Patients, Privacy, and Social Media'. *Journal of the American Medical Informatics Association* 20(1): 16–24.

Ybarra, M. L., and K. J. Mitchell. 2008. 'How Risky Are Social Networking Sites? A Comparison of Places Online Where Youth Sexual Solicitation and Harassment Occurs'. *Pediatrics* 121(2): e350–e357.

PART II

REPRESENTATIONS

3

TRANSGRESSING 'INNOCENCE'

Childhoods from the Margins

Deepa Sreenivas

Can there be a children's story that does not, in any recognisable fashion, address children, or is conspicuous by their absence? This is an unsettling question, especially when one is accustomed to the normative idea of children's literature, premised upon an idealised notion of childhood—as a sheltered, happy place, full of innocence and spontaneity. Stories about non-mainstream childhoods and experiences can only be designated as a 'lack' by such standards—forever falling short of the aesthetic or moral norm of the 'children's story'. Worse, they appear burdened by an 'unseemly politics' inappropriate and possibly dangerous for young minds. However, as several scholars have pointed out, the concept of an ideal childhood is deeply exclusionary—delegitimising and rendering invisible the lives, families, struggles, games and joys of large groups of children from marginalised classes and communities.[1] This calls for an expansion and, indeed, re-imagination of the field of children's literature—providing space for stories from/about marginalised childhoods.

Perry Nodelman (2008) has discussed how producers of children's literature must make judgements about what to produce based, not on what they believe will appeal to children but rather, on what they believe adult consumers (parents, teachers, librarians, etc.) believe will appeal to children (or perhaps what should appeal to them, or what they need to be taught). He observes, 'Whether or not child readers do match how adults think about them, the children in the phrase "children's literature" are most usefully understood as the child readers that writers, responding to the assumptions of adult purchasers, imagine and imply in their works' (ibid.: 5).

Clearly the idea of the children's book is embedded in a set of familial, cultural and economic relations that are interdependent and consolidate one another. Looking at a range of children's books in the UK and the US, published in the nineteenth and twentieth centuries, aimed at different age groups, Nodelman argues that while it is important to locate these texts in their divergent times and places, underlying each text there is 'a consistent sense of how young human beings differ from older ones' (ibid.: 7). His analysis demonstrates that the presumed homogeneity of childhood is ideologically produced and implicated in questions of race, caste and gender. Contemporary theories of education and culture have thrown into sharp relief the urban, upper-caste and middle-class address of standard reading materials. Children from non-mainstream settings do sometimes appear in these stories, but they have to strive to establish their exceptionality. A blind boy might have to make up for his lack of sight by demonstrating his musical talent; an *adivasi* (tribal) girl must prove that her knowledge of the forest is relevant to the modern world.[2] Such images have a disabling impact, undermining self-worth and making it impossible for 'different' children to think of themselves as part of the nation-world.[3] Concomitantly, middle-class children too grow up without the ethical and cultural education necessary to engage with others in a complex, democratic society.

In this essay, I look at tensions between the hegemonic notion of children's literature and narratives emerging from within the lives and experiences of children from marginalised communities. When and if the latter find a place in children's writing, they are often re-mediated ideologically and aesthetically through several registers (language, tone, address, illustration, among others). The rawness is toned down; the hard parts of life are simplified, if not prettified. As Stuart Hall (1991: 118) has said: 'the event must become a story before it can become a communicative event'. For a story to communicate to the child reader (according to normative adult perception), issues of pain, sexuality and violence need to be sanitised.

As I have discussed elsewhere (Sreenivas 2010), the comic series, *Amar Chitra Katha* (Immortal Picture Stories, henceforth ACK)—hugely popular in the 1970s and 1980s and regarded as the repertoire of Indian mythology and culture by middle-class parents—routinely depicted violence (against *rakshasas* [demons] and Muslims, for instance). However, this violence was reconfigured as justice, tying up with an already existing hegemonic common sense. Notably, the series promised to be a substitute for the 'story-telling grandmother' who was becoming increasingly absent in children's lives with the break-up of joint families. By taking on this role, ACK tasked itself to act as a cohesive agent in a society that was marked by radical movements for socio-economic justice in the 1970s.[4] However, as Susie Tharu points out, children deviating from 'this governing idea are presumed to be inferior or even pathological, as somehow not yet freed to be natural. Various forms and grades of violence, ranging from disapproval and disregard, to humiliation, failure, and punishment are involved in the correction and disciplining of deviations' (2009: 281).

In recent years, one notes a small but significant drive within nationally circulated English language children's publishing invested in bringing out unusual stories and experiences, spearheaded by publishing initiatives like Tulika Books, Tara Books and Puffin Books. These publishers have consistently produced books that break away from folk or heroic themes, and initiate a different imagination of what might/should appeal to children. I briefly refer to a few such narratives which I hope will point to the spirit of this trend. This by no means sums up the wide range of themes and books introduced by publishers mentioned earlier, but aims to understand the tensions and blind spots involved in the process of re-telling non-mainstream stories.

Tulika Books' *Kali and the Rat Snake* (Whitaker 2000) engages with the persistent isolation faced by Dalit/tribal children in school—demonstrating a critical awareness of a theme that routinely surfaces in Dalit writing. Kali, a first-generation tribal school-goer from the Irula community in Tamil Nadu, hates his school because of the torment he faces at the hands of his middle-class, urban classmates. As Nodelman (2008: 18) has argued, however apparently simple a story appears, the 'implied reader' is someone with a certain pre-existing knowledge to comprehend its overt and underlying meanings: 'The simpler it is, the more obviously will it say less than it hints at, demand an implied reader who knows more—and therefore, the more likely it will be that child readers who can make sense of it will understand more than is actually said.'

For Kali to be comprehensible/acceptable to his implied middle-class child reader, he needs to become a 'recognisable' hero in the conventional mode of a children's story. Thus, in the end, he finds many friends but only after fearlessly catching a rat-snake that accidentally enters the classroom. But this act remains disconnected from the occupational (snake-catching) practices of his family/ community. The book aims to sensitise the middle-class child reader about the inequalities/prejudices within a classroom (and the larger society by extension), but gets locked into the stereotype of the tribal—Kali's flat nose, wild curly hair, swarthy complexion and the act of catching the snake fix him into a timeless ethnic identity. The project of sensitisation can be risk-laden, as pointed out by Wendy Brown (2006: 16):

> When…middle and high schoolers are urged to tolerate one another's race, ethnicity, culture, religion, or sexual orientation, there is no suggestion that the differences at issue, or the identities through which these differences are negotiated, have been socially and historically constituted and are themselves the effect of power and hegemonic norms, and even of certain discourses about race, ethnicity, sexuality, and culture. Rather, difference itself is what students learn they must tolerate.

Let me quickly refer to two stories from Tara Books—*Ponni the Flower Seller* (Rao 2000a) and *Babu the Waiter* (Rao 2000b)—from their much acclaimed *People Around Us Series*. Addressed to very young children, the books are evocatively designed as family albums except that they narrate the lives of working class people. As the blurb states: 'Each story features the world of a real-life working person, who is familiar to the child.'

This is indeed a critical gesture towards inclusion because children's books hardly ever have a working class protagonist. But we also need to ask, 'familiar in what sense?' As members of the family/community, who are the ones that generally feature in family albums? Or, as those who are visible to the child every day, carrying out certain chores/labour, yet invisible and hence need an introduction. It is this mode of introduction that calls for further engagement. In these two books, photographs are chosen as the visual medium—meant to capture 'reality'. However, the images and one-line captions below freeze Babu and Ponni into their identities as waiter and flower-seller, respectively. They appear self-conscious, their bodies 'posed' for the camera's gaze. Extending Laura Mulvey's (1989) analysis in the context of cinema, one might say that the middle-class producer/consumer becomes the 'bearer of the look'.[5] What if the story called for a disruption of the middle-class gaze itself? What kind of mediations would then be necessary at both the visual and verbal levels? To take one particular photograph, Ponni awkwardly stands beside a male customer buying flowers, the latter appearing smug, smirking and towering over her. The photograph is coded through markers of gender/class/caste hierarchy. Let us pause to imagine if these codes could be subverted if Ponni were to haggle and negotiate and even have an upper hand (if only momentarily) as many women of her caste/class do? What if she were to look back at the camera defiantly/actively? The following section may lead us to think about how the world might appear if the gaze was (re)turned, if one were to 'see' from a non-mainstream location.

Telling Different Tales

In this section, I draw on my insights while working with a team on a project titled 'Different Tales: Stories from Marginal Cultures and Regional Languages', at the Anveshi Research Centre for Women's Studies. Funded by Sir Ratan Tata Trust, it entailed collecting children's stories from Dalit and other marginalised groups, outside the normative middle-class setting. The objective was to make visible stories that are rarely seen in print. Written in Telugu and Malayalam originally, these stories were translated into English and into both the regional languages. The initiative took shape within a larger critique of dominant representations of childhood in children's literature, textbooks, consumer culture and popular media as a period of play and vulnerability, demarcated from adult anxieties and responsibilities. As pointed out before, narrative worlds are routinely deployed around the everyday lives, economic resources, familial bonds, beliefs, food habits and emotions of children from privileged backgrounds. Different Tales marked a search for stories that mirrored the lives and aspirations of children from marginalised contexts in enabling and nurturing ways, while introducing middle-class children to a range of settings, dilemmas, characters as well as to new sources of enjoyment and strength.

However, as we would soon discover, there was no such children's story simply waiting to be picked up by us. It was a long-drawn and sometimes disheartening process. We would slowly find stories that circulated orally from generation to generation in communities. There were also those written by accomplished Dalit/Muslim writers, which resonated with themes that we were searching for, but published in magazines or collections meant for a general readership. When these writers were requested to contribute their stories for publication in the Different Tales initiative, some wrote new stories for us, many rewrote stories that were already published. Significantly, we noted that many of the writers were intrigued by the idea of the 'children's story' as a separate category. They were not invested in the anxious maintenance of the adult–child boundary. To bring in just one example, Gogu Shyamala, who had already published 'Tataki' in a small Telugu magazine meant for a more general audience, felt it was important to retain the Telangana *Madiga* register which was so integrally enmeshed with the occupational/specific histories of her community that she chronicled. We had several discussions revolving around the hegemony of standard coastal Andhra dialect in textbooks, school and the public sphere of the Andhra Pradesh/ Telangana region. One needed to seriously address this existing inequality even as one attempted to reach her story to a wider group of children, many of whom would be unfamiliar with the register the author used. Shyamala would agree that many children from her community might have lost touch with the occupational registers (linked to agriculture/leather-curing, and so on) she used. However, she also felt that the task of the story was to retrieve buried histories for the children of the community. The author eventually agreed to make a few changes, without compromising the politics and regional specificities of the story. When 'Tataki' was translated into English ('Tataki Wins Again'; Shyamala [2008]), the publisher insisted that the word 'bitch' (which is how its 11-year-old heroine is addressed by the landlord when he tries to rape her) be changed to 'witch'. This was clearly an out-of-place phrase aimed at sanitisation, but we had to comply in order to ensure its publication. As Shyamala would point out, abuses such as *lanjha* (which would translate as slut/bitch in English) were an everyday part of the feudal land/spatial relations inhabited by Dalit girls/women of her community. The task of mediation thus was a difficult one—on the one hand, one needed to respect the perspective of the author and, on the other, facilitate publication in a market guided by dominant cultural norms and concerns of profit.

The stories published in the series titled *Different Tales* have received the attention of scholars, educationists and groups committed to the production of textbooks and other pedagogic material with an inclusive focus.[6] For the purposes of this essay, I would like to draw attention specifically to a particular strand of criticism of the series accusing it of dealing with subjects inappropriate and incomprehensible for young readers (Rammohan 2008). This response resonates with the fundamental tenet of children's literature—that it must depict a 'simple' world, uncomplicated by 'grown up issues'. Most important, certain themes should be avoided—sexual assault or discrimination based on caste or religion, for example, as these would contaminate its 'innocence'.[7]

Let me approach this problematic through Jacqueline Rose's ground-breaking analysis of the 'Peter Pan' phenomenon that disrupts the carefully guarded boundary between adult desires and childhood innocence. Rose (2004) argues that children's fiction constructs the 'child' inside the book in order to secure and contain the child outside it. The eternal youth/innocence of Peter Pan is in fact an adult fantasy, a projection and effect of adult desire. J. M. Barrie's *Peter Pan* (1928), and by extension children's fiction, is marked by an elision of material and cultural differences underlying the universal category of 'children'. Children's fiction, Rose points out, is engendered within the Rouseauvian frame constructing the child as one who has direct access to the material world, unmediated by contradictions of the real world. The myth of the innocent child is crucial for maintenance of the 'fiction' that there is indeed a pristine world outside and prior to political and sexual corruptions.

Against this backdrop, it is significant that most of the writers of *Different Tales* come across as unencumbered by the desire to construct the child as distanced from adult concerns. Most of the writers draw on their own childhoods, which were not insulated from the everyday struggles of the adult members of their families/communities. This essay takes a close look at a few stories from the series in trying to understand how they reframe the norms of childhood as well as children's literature. I start with 'Beloved Spirits'—a story without any substantive presence of children/childhood. I follow it up with 'Tataki Wins Again' (henceforth referred to as 'Tataki') which deals with the life of a child but draws her into 'adult' conflicts. Finally, I look at 'My Friend, the Emperor'—a story that complicates an ideal that is a given in most textbooks and children's writing of post-Independence India, 'unity in diversity'.

Land, Dispossession, Alienation and Spectres of Resistance

Rekha Raj's 'Beloved Spirits' translated from the Malayalam 'Njaaru' (a literal albeit inadequate translation into English would be 'transplantation') confounds all pre-conceived notions of the children's story. It is sombre, anchored by the haunting visuals of K. P. Reji. The author re-tells a story she heard from her grandmother in her childhood, but the storytelling grandmother here is very different from the 'grandmother' that ACK stood in for. She does not serve as a link with a monolithic Indian past. Looping back to the question I raised at the beginning of the essay, this story has no apparent traffic with childhood; if we discount incidental appearances, there are no child protagonists in this story. Yet, clearly such stories have been part of the oral traditions of Rekha Raj's community, forming a critical part of growing up. As the story unfolds we see how the tropes of land, oppression, death, resistance and local histories animate the interconnected fates of the members of the community. The oral narration forms part of the 'subjugated knowledges' that are passed on to children, teaching them community histories and modes of survival.[8] Rekha Raj's experience as a Dalit activist invested in the land struggles of Kerala animates the story with contemporary resonances.[9]

The story is about Mathai Appachan, a Dalit Christian farmer well into his seventy-fifth year, and his heart-breaking struggle to cultivate a small piece of land bought with his son's hard-earned money. Mathai has spent the best part of his life taking care of large tracts of land owned by different landlords for the meagre compensation of split, soil-mixed grains left on the threshing floor after the harvest. But he had educated his children with a dogged determination, and as he puts it: 'That's why our boy can give us money to live with a little extra, for a tot of toddy for me and hymn books for Anna. Imagine! She now wears clothes made of *malmal* (muslin)' (Rekha Raj 2008: 3). However, despite paying for the land, 'he had to beg and plead before the landlords allowed him to buy even these one and a half acres' (ibid.: 5). The story takes us through the various stages of farming woven into the very idiom, skill and emotional turmoil of a dispossessed farmer who dares to stake a claim to a piece of earth despite all odds. Yet, at a crucial juncture when the saplings are to be transplanted, the landlords threaten the women workers of his community with no work if they dare to show up in 'that Pulaya's field'. A desperate Mathai works ceaselessly with his fever-wrecked wife Anna, trying to replant the saplings before the water from the dam is released into the agricultural fields the following day. However, by late evening he realises the futility of this effort. Alternating between anger and despair, he invokes his ancestors to stand by him. That night, when he goes back to the field for one last look before the seedlings perished, he finds his desolate plot full of people (ibid.: 15): the women transplanting the seedlings, and the men repairing the ridges:

> God! Some of the women are in the ninth month, their bellies so large that they touch the earth as they bend over, transplanting the seedlings.... There are some children too. Whose children could they be? And some very old women. They are all at work, transplanting the seedlings, row after row! As each row is done, exhausted they drag themselves painfully away... Oh my God! It is to the burial ground that they are going!

The 'ancestors' are repeatedly invoked in the story, not as the pre-modern, irrational belief of an illiterate farmer but as a trope that infuses the present with a subaltern historical consciousness. In his crisis-laden life, Mathai makes offerings to them and prays to the 'flame of the burial place'. His memory of the untimely deaths of his young aunts recalls the historical wrongs done to his community. Satyanarayana and Tharu (2011: 62) speak of the many spirits that populate Dalit writing: 'Bodies that have not been put to rest with the rituals of property/propriety; such unrecognised and unrequited beings haunt and destabilise the living.'

The ghost story is a popular genre within children's literature. However, it is most often framed as folklore or legend—the Vikram and Vetala narratives are a case in point.[10] Another example is the well-known children's book author Ruskin Bond (1989) who has written about the endearing exploits of mischievous ghosts. Simon Hay (2011: 146) suggests that the ghost in Rudyard Kipling's stories set in the barracks and cantonments of British India gestures to the limits and uncertainties of imperialist knowledge about the native and his land.

Rekha Raj's re-telling of her grandmother's story resurrects the ghost as the bearer of subaltern history. Does it qualify as a children's story? In a reading of the ghost story as a genre, Hay (2011: 145) suggests that it is concerned with historical trauma: '[The] ghost is something that returns from the past, something that erupts into the present, disrupting both the present's presumed separateness from the past, as well as its stable inheritance of that past.' In 'Beloved Spirits', the ghosts are not creatures of horror, nor are they funny. They recall the ghost stories of the Caribbean. Hay speaks of the dual purpose of the ghost stories in the Caribbean:

> They [the ghosts] revive in order to dispel the ghosts of a past conceived by Europe, a history couched in the paralysing terms of dispossession and defeat.... At the same time, they reclaim a past anterior to European conquest, a history whose outlines blend with those of the originary myth, and whose ghosts are not horrifying apparitions from another, unwanted era but welcome catalysts for the recovery of a buried ancestral consciousness (2011: 129).

Similarly, the ghosts in Rekha Raj's narrative are not unwelcome to Mathai/his community; they are 'beloved guests'.

Gogu Shyamala's 'Tataki' is once again built around the struggles of a Dalit family around land. Eleven-year-old Balamma must water her family's tiny plot of land at the crack of dawn, before the supply from the canal dries up. This draws the wrath of the *karnam* (landlord) as the child unknowingly flouts the incontrovertible law of the village—the landlord's land must receive water before anyone else's.

The story could have been told as a conventional children's story built around an irrepressible, adventurous little girl. Also, being an unlettered working girl child, Balamma might be perceived as in need of reformist intervention—by the state, by the school or by the middle-class activist/citizen.[11] But both frames would grossly misrepresent its spirit. As Ann Arnet Ferguson (2000) has argued with respect to the African American context, it is impossible for black children to stay removed from the daily struggles of their parents; children learn to support or even switch roles with their parents on occasion. Balamma's father can undertake wage labour only because she waters the fields. But play and work are not two opposing categories in her life. She is the natural leader among her friends, beating the boys in every game. She can swim against the strong currents of the lake to catch a fleeing rabbit, so her family can enjoy a rare meal of meat. Shyamala draws on her own childhood, set in the lower caste Madiga quarters of a small village in Telangana. Balamma's character is closely modelled after her older sister whom the writer, with a sense of pride, recalls as physically strong, excelling in agricultural work.[12] The autobiographical aspects of 'Tataki' have a critical function; to tell one's story from a marginalised location is also to stake a claim to a public voice. As Sharmila Rege (2006: 13) contends, Dalit life narratives are testimonies which 'forge a right to speak both for and beyond the individual and contest explicitly or implicitly the "official forgetting" of histories of caste oppression, struggles, and resistance'. Shyamala challenges the terms within which Balamma's childhood may find a space—in other words, the story poses a fundamental critique of the normative and epistemological frames of 'recognisability' that Judith Butler (2001: 23—24) has critiqued: '[U]nder what conditions do some individuals acquire a face, a legible and visible face, and others do not? There is a language that frames the encounter, and embedded in that language a set of norms concerning what will or will not constitute recognisability.'

Set against the alarming statistics of children who drop out of school, 'Tataki' may lead one to question if schooling can be viewed as a haven for marginalised children, without addressing larger questions of hegemony and cultural alienation.[13] Most poor Dalit families need to make a hard call in deciding which one among their children is best suited for school. Shyamala recalls that she was the one who her family had decided to send to school while her sister was marked for agricultural work due to her physical stamina.[14] In 'Tataki', Shyamala pays tribute to her sister and the community that are invisible in mainstream discourse of childhood.

It is noteworthy that for the powerful karnam, Balamma's 'childhood' does not provide her with immunity—she is guilty of transgressing the boundaries of caste as well as gender. He abuses her as 'Tataki' (the name of a female demon from the Hindu mythology of *Ramayana*) and attempts to rape her as an act of punishment: 'You *mala*s and *madiga*s don't even know that girls have to be kept at home!' (Shyamala 2008: 41). In upper-caste mythology and in children's literature such as ACK, 'Tataki' is represented as the wicked *rakshasi* (she-demon) killed by Rama and his brother Lakshmana at the behest of the sage Vishwamitra so that the brahminical order is restored in the forests. Shyamala stands the myth on its head. Balamma, disadvantaged as she is by her childish frame and social location, remembers the collective wisdom of the women of her community during her crisis (ibid.): 'Balamma trembled all over. Her mouth went dry. One corner of her mind recalled the women in the *mala* and *madiga* settlements whispering about how the landlord had taken one woman or another. Then it struck her, "This swine is going to do something awful!"'

At this moment, Balamma truly becomes Tataki—a characterisation intended to degrade her—assuming both her proportions and her insurgent politics—she 'took aim and kicked him as hard as she could on the groin with both her legs' (Shyamala 2008: 42). As the karnam collapses in pain, Balamma escapes. The final lines of the story defuse the power of the landlord, choosing to focus on the irreverent banter among the women of the community: 'In the village the *mala* and *madiga* women giggled through their *pallu*s (a part of the *sari*) as they shared the news, "The landlord wanted to catch our Balamani. She kicked him in the groin!"' (ibid.: 43).

'Tataki' redraws the boundaries of children's literature by bringing into its orbit subjects such as sexual violence and caste-based violence, which are regarded as a threat to 'innocence'. Notwithstanding the criticism from certain quarters of the Telugu public sphere that 'sexual assault' might not be appropriate for children (Rammohan 2008), Shymala has reiterated that such encounters/struggles formed part of the reality of growing up within her community.

Shefali Jha's 'My Friend, the Emperor', the last story that I discuss here, is about the identity crisis of a Muslim child, a subject rarely addressed in mainstream children's writing. This is not surprising since the project of children's literature, right from its inception in India, has been largely tied to nationalism and citizen-building. Children are routinely introduced to the idea of Islam through the trope of a festival such as Eid-ul-Fitr which is placed alongside Diwali or Christmas, reinforcing the trope of 'unity in diversity'.[15] In children's writing, certain stock characters/narratives function as the metonyms of Muslimness. *Alibaba and the Forty Thieves*, the *Arabian Nights* or the stories of *Mullah Nasruddin* are examples. Muhammad Khadeer Babu, a Muslim writer from the Nellore district in Andhra Pradesh, writes:

> The stories my grandmother told me in my childhood, and her stories retold by her daughter, my *Phuhpu* (aunt), and the stories told by my maternal aunt, and the stories told by our women folk to our children—when I looked at them carefully, I noticed something. In our homes, only these stories are told. However popular the other stories are in the outside world, some stories are never told in our homes... You don't hear even names like Allauddin, The Thief of Baghdad, or Alibaba. If you ask them [our people] for a story, they start with *Ek gaon mein ek basha tha* [In a village, there was a king][16] (2004: 9).

Khadeer Babu's own stories published in *Different Tales* and in several other collections locate the Muslim not as a pan-Indian abstraction but rooted in regional/familial practices.[17] Nuaiman (2008) also addresses the question of Muslim identity in his 'Textbook', depicting a Muslim child's puzzlement upon not finding a single Muslim name in his textbook. When the teacher asks him to list the characters in a lesson, the child invents a Muslim name, inviting the chagrin of the teacher who accuses him of 'communalism'.

'My Friend, the Emperor' is a story of a Muslim child who grows up believing that he is part of a seamless nation until he is rudely pulled out of this faith. Twelve-year-old Adil is the son of a *maulvi* (cleric), Ali Musaliyar, who lives in Changanacherry in Kerala, removed from the acrimonious Hindu–Muslim conflicts of the northern part of India. His father, who never remarried after his mother died, looks after his son, subverting the stereotype of the hyper-masculine Muslim patriarch. Adil attends an English-medium school and has a Christian family for neighbours with whom his family shares close ties. Jessy Aunty teaches History at his school and her son Abby is Adil's closest friend.

However, during a lesson on the legendary battle of Khanua,[18] between Babur and Rana Sanga, Adil feels uncomfortably implicated.

Jessy Teacher, through her remarkable narrative skills, makes the children feel as though the battle between the great Rana Sanga and Babur had 'taken place right in the classroom' (Jha 2008: 13). Each one of them had wanted the old Rajput king to win:

> But why had she kept looking at him like that? She always looked at everyone while telling stories, but this was different. Her look would rest on him, wander off, and then come back to rest on him again. The more exciting the story got, the more the look seemed to rest on him. It had seemed to seek him out, from every corner of the room, until he was forced not to look at Jessy Teacher... Babur had won, with a far smaller army than the Rana's, but it was clear who the hero of the story was. But that is not what he remembered from the class—he remembered the look. He could not understand it, but it made him want to stay away from class, even from school (ibid.).

Adil's sense of alienation is not attributed to any readymade reason—the distorted representation of the Muslim in the textbook or to the prejudice of a biased teacher. 'My Friend, the Emperor' gestures to a deeper norming of the classroom; while there is no ambiguity for the other children in the class as to who the real winner of the battle of Khanua is, Adil alone feels called upon to adjudicate. He has to bear the representational burden of the Muslim (child)—through repeated avowals of his Indianness. Aamir Mufti (1995: 84) captures this conundrum, 'For the representational burden that falls on the figure of the Muslim is precisely that of being the *other* within the modern nation, the continually repeated, *negative* reminder of the national(ist) self's modernity' (emphasis in original).

'My Friend, the Emperor' uses fantasy—a popular genre in children's literature—to resurrect a new history. As Adil sits forlornly in the garden of the mosque that evening, a stranger in magnificent clothes approaches him. Introducing himself as a king, he recounts his extraordinary childhood. At the age of 11, he was forced to leave the beautiful city of Samarkand, following battles and bloodshed over the throne. Feeling a strange bond with the stranger, Adil asks a question he could not voice even to his father: 'Do you think Babur was braver than Rana Sanga?' The king replies that in a battle, even among those who are equals in terms of strategy, experience and bravery, the results are always unpredictable. One can only do one's best and 'leave the rest to Allah'. The emperor disappears but Adil is left feeling much less embattled. Later in the evening, when he sees a portrait of Emperor Babur in his father's copy of the *Baburnama* Adil realises who his new friend was. 'Babur' from his dream/fantasy re-connects him to his Muslim identity in an affirmative mode.

Disseminating New Ideas of Childhood: Challenges and Possibilities

I would like to recall a book that challenged the idea of childhood innocence in the early 1970s, in the midst of the Chilean revolutionary process—*How to Read Donald Duck: Imperialist Ideology in the Disney Comic* by Armand Mattelart and Ariel Dorfman (1975). While the book went on to be a runaway success among the people in Chile, the fascist government of Chile and the American critics accused it of grossly misrepresenting the innocent exploits of Donald Duck and poisoning young minds with 'subtle ideological contraband' (Mattelart and Dorfman 1975: 13). Switching to the African American context, Ferguson (2000) speaks of the ideological underpinnings of 'innocence' itself. During her fieldwork in a public school in a black, poor neighbourhood in Michigan, she found that African American male students are routinely classified as prone to criminality; and the female students sexualised. In contrast, white children were viewed 'naughty by nature'—their mistakes or violations indulgently viewed by teachers as youthful exuberance or as plain mischief.

The stories from *Different Tales* discussed above reflect similar contradictions and contestations over the idea of childhood in Indian contexts. The perspective/commitment of the writers and artists, several of them well known regionally/nationally, greatly contributed to the imagination of the project. Yet, the circulation and dissemination of the books has been a slow process. DC Books of Kerala, the publisher of the Malayalam and English books, has largely chosen to sell the books online. Often sets of books are sold by word of mouth to scholars/students within the field of childhood studies/children's literature. But a rewarding outcome, about eight years after the publication of the books, is Eklavya's[19] decision to bring out the books in Hindi.

I feel that while the Anveshi team was initially very particular about the quality of paper, colour and design during the first round of publication in 2010, perhaps it has since rethought that position. It is more open to cost-effective modes of publication while retaining the politics and language of the stories. As I spent a lot of time at a printing press during the first round of publication, I learnt that it could be expensive to reproduce an artist's image on paper, replicating the exact tones and positioning it within the text in a particular way, even though the artists themselves charged us nothing for their artwork. The artists, most of them trained in the renowned Fine Arts School of M. S. University of Baroda, had been involved in the project right from the beginning. This was very unlike the typical children's book illustrator whose job would begin once the story was ready. The artist-illustrators attempted to work with the gaps in the text, without simply mirroring it. Thus the cover page of 'My Friend, the Emperor' is very different from, say, ACK's *Babur* which shows the emperor in full warrior gear, dwarfing the soldiers engaged in war all around him. Chinnan, the artist of 'My Friend, the Emperor', shows Babur on a horse with a spear and Rana Sanga on an elephant but a miniature-like, two-dimensional style brings in many other elements: banana plants, boats with people, water bodies, thus displacing both space and context. 'Head Curry', which is about the cooking of a ram's head in a Telangana Muslim family, is illustrated by the celebrated artist Ghulam Muhammad Sheikh. With the use of muted shades of maroon, brown and green, the illustrations have a range of vantage points, allowing the eye (coinciding with the point of view of the child protagonist) to discover the houses, relationships and activities of the community, thus locating 'head curry' in the regional and community context. Designing such artworks in a book meant that the text would have to be part of the illustration, rather than the other way around.

The project resulted in some beautiful and unusual books, thanks to meaningful play between artwork and text. As we know, illustrations are an integral part of a children's story, enhancing its historical functions to 'instruct and delight'. Illustration is not a mere embellishment to the text, but a part of its ideological structure. It does not mirror the text; it enhances, legitimates or sometimes undercuts the verbal meaning. To bring in a telling example, in ACK's *Padmini* (Sharma 1973), there are six panels depicting Khilji in his harem while there is no reference to the harem in the speech balloons. But the images powerfully reinforce the Orientalist/Hindu nationalist stereotype of the sexually perverted Muslim sultan. Thus, pictures can endow even an overtly simple text with ideological meanings. Similarly, as Nodelman (2008: 19) has pointed out, texts in picture books often function as anchoring labels: Even the simple sentence 'This is a cat' allows us to see the accompanying picture differently from the label 'This is my friend, Peter, who is a cat…'.

Coming to the Different Tales project, as Deeptha Achar and I have discussed elsewhere (Sreenivas and Achar 2010), the questions before the artist-illustrators were: 'How may non-normative childhoods be understood visually? What are the modes of representing this visually? How can one set up visual modes of address in the context of the non-normative?' The artists figured out that it was in these invisible spaces that illustrations can both open out the text, offering possibilities and nuances that are flattened out by the text while, on the other hand, they can also close off and limit the potential of the text. An image from 'Textbook' shows the central figure trudging to school with a bag and umbrella. There is no particular mark that indicates that the child is Muslim. It is only through the loading of detail in the landscape, mosque as much as school, grandmother rolling beedis, friends and siblings, in which he walks, that the viewer locates the child. The realist language familiarises what is a less common image—a Muslim boy whose world is constituted equally by the stories told by his grandmother, experiences at school, prayer and play. The local flavour of the buildings, the trees and plants in the picture subtly suggests the central role of region in making the life-world of this boy.

But, if one were to think about continuing and broader dissemination of these and similar books, funding, printing costs and, most of all, circulation channels emerge as important factors. How might one make unconventional children's books accessible to a large number of children? Paper, design and colours might be re-adjusted keeping in mind costs even as one remains alert to possible trivialisation of a complex reality. This would entail working with the constraints of the market even while pushing the boundaries, with every resource and partnership that one can muster. Ultimately it would surely help to work with like-minded institutions/organisations that already have a large reach in regional medium schools. Anveshi has, in the recent past, started a collaboration with Eklavya and the latter has translated and published six of the *Different Tales* books in Hindi. While Anveshi has been hard pressed to find channels for circulation of the books, given its primary thrust is research and activism, Eklavya's well-established networks such as the Pitara initiative, the online bookstore and regular stalls at book fairs have opened important channels of dissemination. I might add that this was not feasible in an earlier tie-up with a more commercial publisher. Looking at the back and forth emails between the Anveshi and the Eklavya teams, one finds a more engaged conversation that is rare to find between a children's story author/producer and a typical publisher. Surely this emerges from a shared history of engagement with questions of school education and the local realities of the children from rural/marginalised backgrounds. While stories from *Different Tales* or similar initiatives will not find it easy to become popular in the 'mainstream' sense, surely there are spaces that open out possibilities and unanticipated connections. It is worth the labour if low-priced editions reach children who find some parts of their lives—agriculture/occupation, familial connections, food practices, and so on—mirrored in these narratives.

I feel that children's literature can look to biographies and other narratives emerging from Dalit and other marginalised groups for a productive and radical re-imagination of the field. This would not entail the abandonment of enjoyment; but perhaps new pleasures will emerge.[20] Most stories in *Different Tales* are about children faced with discrimination and difficult circumstances. But they are not framed within the victim mode; instead, the narration highlights their capacity to negotiate and discover sources of friendship and happiness. In such stories, childhood is perhaps displaced from the haven of innocence, but may provide children—from all classes—with tools to deal with that which cannot be voiced or lacks 'authenticity'. That indeed is a future to look forward to.

Notes

1. See Bissell (2003), Vasanta (2004) and Sreenivas (2010).

2. For example, in *Kali and the Rat Snake* (Whitaker 2000), Kali, a boy from the Irula community in Tamil Nadu, is carefully refigured as heroic and 'also' human in order to find the approval of his classmates. Similarly, in *Mumtaz Embroiders Her Dreams* (Rahtogi and Soni 2005), a disabled Muslim girl displays exceptional creativity and talent—smoothing over the plural axes of marginalisation within which its disabled Muslim girl protagonist is placed. For a longer analysis, see Sreenivas (2011).

3. Krishna Kumar (1989) has discussed, in depth, how a tribal student may choose to stay silent because the pedagogic transactions in the classroom (teacher, textbook, fellow classmates) are inherently exclusionary and even humiliating towards her community.

4. Sreenivas (2010) points out that the 1970s witnessed an explosion of popular radical protests and movements—the great railways strike, the anti–price hike protests, the women's movement and the peasant/tribal movements against feudal exploitation. Important in the context of this essay is the rising sense of failure, frustration and disconnect among the youth in schools/colleges with growing competition and stress.

5. See Mulvey (1989). According to her, the camera in cinema projects the male protagonist as the bearer of the look and the mover of the narrative, while the woman's body is coded through its to-be-looked-at-ness.

6. Pratham, Eklavya and Teacher Plus are some of the initiatives that have critically engaged with *Different Tales* to address the critical gaps in pedagogic/reading material for children.

7. As several scholars have pointed out, childhood is fraught with insecurities, anxieties and 'adult' responsibilities. Children's literature itself has evolved to address this more complex notion of childhood. Jacqueline Wilson, the popular British writer of children's books, explores the difficult

yet caring relationship between a mother with bipolar disorder and her two young daughters in *The Illustrated Mum* (1999). 'The Sackclothman' (Kalathil 2008) published as part of the *Different Tales* series takes up a similar issue—a child dealing with the loss of a sister, father's alcoholism and mother's depression, and forming an unusual, sustaining friendship with the village 'madman'—*Chakkupranthan* (Sackclothman).

8. I use Michel Foucault's idea of 'subjugated knowledges': 'a whole set of knowledges that have been disqualified...located low down on the hierarchy, beneath the required level of cognition and scientificity...it is through the re-emergence of...these local popular knowledges...that criticism performs its work' (1980: 82).

9. In the late 1990s, Rekha Raj was part of the protests against the raising of an 11-KV power line over hutments in Kurichi and the setting up of an engineering college on tribal lands in Kundara. She has also been associated with the historic agitation for land by tribal people under the leadership of C. K. Janu (Satyanarayana and Tharu 2011: 570–72).

10. In Hindu legend and folklore, the vetala is a spirit/vampire that haunts cemeteries and takes possession of corpses. For my purposes here, I have on mind the stories set within the never-ending story of King Vikramaditya and Vetala, an adaptation of the ancient Sanskrit text *Baital Pachisi*, in the widely circulated children's magazine *Chandamama*, and subsequently featured in a popular TV serial in India. In this story, a sorcerer asks King Vikramaditya to capture a vetala who lives in a tree in the middle of a cremation ground. Each time the king catches the vetala, the latter presents him a story that ends with a question involving a moral dilemma. The wise king would always provide the correct answer, but the breaking of his silence would also enable the vetala to slip back to his tree. In the manner of folk tales, the emphasis is on the 'wisdom' (as prudence/ common sense that has a timeless character) of the king and a showcasing of his moral authority. The vetala, despite his recalcitrance, is not subversive, and appears duly placated by the king. I would suspect that this entity has a more complex history in tantric and subaltern cults/legends.

11. For instance, in 'Anita: A Working Schoolgirl', Kaul (1989) links the struggles of young Anita, from a washer-person's family, to the reality that she must shoulder responsibilities beyond her years, thus missing out on a proper childhood. However, the analysis does not connect with the larger struggle of the family to survive and educate the two daughters—which, in turn, is implicated in contemporary relations of power and unequal access

to education and rights. For detailed engagement, see Bissell (2003), Probe Team (1999) and Vasanta (2004).

12. Susan Bissell (2003) argues that 'ideal childhood' is a global social construction with an underlying middle-class bias. It is built around a normative child who is 'in school, not at work, playing, carefree, and sheltered from the wicked, sordid facts of adult life' (ibid.: 56). Childhoods that do not conform to this construction are described as 'lost' or 'stolen'.

13. Vasanta (2004) makes a critical distinction between child labour and child work. She argues that while a majority of children in India balance school and work, neither the curriculum nor mainstream culture acknowledges their lives in a positive manner. This has a damaging impact on the self-worth and confidence of such children, leading many of them to drop out. See also Anveshi (2003).

14. Personal interview with author, Hyderabad, 2014.

15. See Amin (2005) for an insightful discussion of how the 'unity in diversity' ideology in post-Independence India resulted in stereotypical representation of the members of minorities in India in various popular cultural genres such as advertisements and calendars.

16. This is a rough translation of the phrase from Khadeer Babu's *Phuppujaan Kathalu* (2004).

17. I have discussed elsewhere how Khadeer Babu's 'Head Curry' (2008) is built around the pleasure of eating the ram's head curry in his family. It is firmly set in a region-specific context and has the idiosyncrasies of an affectionately drawn family portrait. In the process, it subtly shifts away from the hegemonic vegetarian imaginary. See Sreenivas (2011).

18. The story of the battle of Khanua (1527) is often narrated as a Hindu versus Muslim story, where the strength, courage and heroic Rajput values of Rana Sanga are highlighted. Babur, on the other hand, is projected as the Muslim invader.

19. Eklavya is a non-governmental foundation based in Bhopal, Madhya Pradesh, with years of involvement in the field of school education. The organisation is linked to an earlier programme in Madhya Pradesh, widely known as the Hoshangabad Science Teaching Programme (HSTP)—one that emphasised learning by doing. Eklavya began its Social Science Programme in 1986 in eight schools of Madhya Pradesh. As Balagopalan has pointed out, this programme may be regarded as 'a landmark effort to make social studies more interesting through its focus on causality rather than facts' and for making abstract concepts accessible by linking them to the child's local realities (2003: 97).

20. To bring in an inspiring example, W. E. B. Du Bois, a leading figure of the Harlem Renaissance, wielded enormous influence in the re-imagination of the black child in black children's literature of the 1920s. As Katharine Capshaw Smith (2004) writes, his enormously influential *Crisis* editorials, annual *Crisis* Children's Number (1912–34) and the children's magazine *The Brownie's Book* changed/ushered in a new writing for and about black children. 'In contrast to the primitivistic images of black childhood like the pickaninny stereotype of nineteenth century minstrelsy, Du Bois reimagined the black child as culturally, politically and aesthetically sophisticated' (Capshaw Smith 2004: 1). While some of the writers for adults in the *Crisis* were deeply affected by the harsh racial relations that forced an early maturity on black children, in *The Brownie's Book* 'such awareness allowed its writers to address its child audience on a range of topics' (ibid.: 25). I refer to this history to bring out the crisscrossing between adult concerns and children's worlds that every publisher and writer of 'new' children's writing that is not distanced from contemporary questions must face.

References

Amin, S. 2005. 'Representing the Musalman: Then and Now, Now and Then'. In *Subaltern Studies*, Vol. XII, *Muslims, Dalits, and the Fabrications of History*, eds S. Mayaram, M. S. S. Pandian and A. Skaria, 1–35. Delhi: Permanent Black.

Anveshi. 2003. *Curricular Transaction in Selected Government Schools in A.P.* Unpublished report submitted to Sir Ratan Tata Trust, Mumbai.

Babu, M. K. 2004. 'Kathala Mundari Katha'. In *Phuppujaan Kathalu*, 8–10. Hyderabad: Asmita.

____. 2008. 'Head Curry'. In *Different Tales*, ed. D. Sreenivas. Kottayam: DC Books.

Balagopalan, S. 2003. 'Understanding Educational Innovation in India: The Case of Eklavya. Interviews with Staff and Teachers'. *Contemporary Education Dialogue* 1(1): 97–121.

Barrie, J. M. 1928. *Peter Pan: Or, The Boy Who Would Not Grow Up*. New York: Charles Scribner's Sons.

Bissell, S. 2003. 'The Social Construction of Childhood: A Perspective from Bangladesh'. In *Child Labour and the Right to Education in South Asia: Needs versus Rights?* eds N. Kabeer, G. B. Nambissan and R. Subrahmanian, 47–72. New Delhi: Sage.

Bond, Ruskin. 1989. *Ghost Trouble*. New York: Random House Children's Books.

Brown, W. 2006. *Regulating Aversion: Tolerance in the Age of Identity and Empire*. Princeton, NJ, and Oxford: Princeton University Press.

Butler, J. 2001. 'Giving an Account of Oneself'. *Diacritics* 31(4): 22–40.

Capshaw Smith, K. 2004. *Children's Literature of the Harlem Renaissance*. Bloomington: Indiana University Press.

Ferguson, A. A. 2000. *Bad Boys: Public Schools in the Making of Black Masculinity*. Ann Arbor: University of Michigan Press.

Foucault, M. 1980. 'Two Lectures'. In *Power/Knowledge: Selected Interviews and Other Writings 1972–1977*, ed. C. Gordon, 78–108. New York: Pantheon Books.

Hall, S. 1991. 'Encoding/Decoding'. In *Culture, Media, Language: Working Papers in Cultural Studies, 1972–79*, ed. Stuart Hall, 117–27. London and New York: Routledge.

Hay, S. 2011. *A History of the Modern Ghost Story*. New York: Palgrave Macmillan.

Jha, S. 2008. 'My Friend, the Emperor'. In *Different Tales: Spirits from History*, ed. D. Sreenivas. Kottayam: DC Books.

Kalathil, J. 2008. 'The Sackclothman'. In *Different Tales*, ed. D. Sreenivas. Kottayam: DC Books.

Kaul, P. 1989. 'Anita: A Working Schoolgirl'. *Manushi* 53 (July–August): 30–35.

Kumar, K. 1989. 'Learning to be Backward'. In *Social Character of Learning*, 59–78. New Delhi: Sage.

Mattelart, A., and A. Dorfman. 1975. *How to Read Donald Duck: Imperialist Ideology in the Disney Comic*. New York: International General.

Mufti, A. R. 1995. 'Secularism and Minority: Elements of a Critique'. *Social Text* 45: 75–96.

Mulvey, L. 1989. 'Visual Pleasure and Narrative Cinema'. In *Visual and Other Pleasures*, eds Stephen Heath, Colin MacCabe and Denise Riley, 14–26. London: Palgrave Macmillan.

Nodelman, P. 2008. *The Hidden Adult: Defining Children's Literature*. Baltimore: Johns Hopkins University Press.

Nuaiman. 2008. 'Textbook', trans. M. T. Ansari and L. Varghese. In *Different Tales: Untold School Stories*, ed. D. Sreenivas. Kottayam: DC Books.

Probe Team. 1999. *Public Report on Basic Education in India*. New Delhi: Oxford University Press.

Rahtogi, J., and R. Soni. 2005. *Mumtaz Embroiders Her Dreams*. New Delhi: Puffin Books.

Rammohan, G. S. 2008. 'Big Stories for Small Children?' *Andhra Jyoti*, 22 December.

Rao, Sirish. 2000a. *Ponni the Flower Seller*. Chennai: Tara Books.

_____. 2000b. *Babu the Waiter*. Chennai: Tara Books.

Rege, S. 2006. *Writing Caste, Writing Gender: Reading Dalit Women's Testimonios*. New Delhi: Zubaan.

Rekha Raj. 2008. 'Beloved Spirits'. In *Different Tales: Spirits from History*, ed. D. Sreenivas. Kottayam: DC Books.

Rose, J. 2004. 'The Case of Peter Pan or the Impossibility of Children's Fiction'. In *The Language, Discourse and Society Reader*, eds Stephen Heath, Colin MacCabe and Denise Riley, 62–72. New York: Palgrave Macmillan.

Satyanarayana, K., and S. Tharu (eds). 2011. *No Alphabet in Sight: New Dalit Writing from South India*. New Delhi: Penguin.

Sharma, Y. 1973. *Padmini*. Amar Chitra Katha, ed. Anant Pai. Bombay: India Book House.

Shyamala, G. 2008. 'Tataki Wins Again'. In *Different Tales: Tataki Wins Again and Braveheart Badeyya*, ed. D. Sreenivas. Kottayam: DC Books.

Sreenivas, D. 2010. *Sculpting the Middle Class: History, Masculinity and the Amar Chitra Katha in India*, 1st edn. New Delhi: Routledge.

_____. 2011. 'Telling Different Tales: Possible Childhoods in Children's Literature'. *Childhood: A Journal of Global Child Research* 18(3): 316–32.

Sreenivas, D., and D. Achar. 2010. 'Beyond the "National Child": How to Create Storybooks for a Plural World'. *Himal Southasian*, 1 May. Available at https://www.himalmag.com/author/deepa-sreenivas-and-deeptha-achar/ (accessed on 24 October 2022).

Tharu, S. 2009. 'Different Tales for Children'. *Contemporary Education Dialogue* 6(2): 279–84.

Vasanta, D. 2004. 'Childhood, Work and Schooling: Some Reflections'. *Contemporary Education Dialogue* 2(1): 5–29.

Whitaker, Z. 2000. *Kali and the Rat Snake*. Chennai: Tulika Books.

Wilson, J. 1999. *The Illustrated Mum*, 1st edn. London: Doubleday.

4

JUXTAPOSITIONS AND TRANSFORMATIONS

Children, Gaming and Society

Aditya Deshbandhu

Children are generally considered to be the future of the human race, a section of society that is always viewed in terms of the potential and promise they hold. All societies hope that the world will be better for future generations, and have thus invested in children their hopes for solutions to persistent problems of hunger, poverty and inequality, the expectation for them to someday discover cures for intractable diseases and conditions, and the belief that along the way they will find unique ways to combat climate change. In short, from the future generations we expect the capability to right all things wrong plaguing the world.

However, for a section of the society from which much is expected, the role of children in history has often been limited to the re-telling of feats of mythological heroes, rulers and people of historical consequence in their childhood (Carr 1964). The role of children in erstwhile feudal societies can be considered to have been limited as they grew up to become subjects and, with the lack of civil society in autocracies, it is unlikely that they enjoyed rights. However, the focus on children changes with the rise of capitalism and what Engels calls monogamous nuclear families. It is in the context of capitalism that concepts like private ownership and personal wealth emerge (Engels 2010). It is only in the capitalist framework that inheritance and familial well-being began to take concrete shape as societies moved from a primitive classless communism to organised self-serving societies as subjects transformed into citizens (ibid.).

In today's capitalist framework, children are key to maintaining the status quo as they are viewed as the human resource of the future to keep the capitalist machinery running. The development and careful implementation of specific apparatuses (Althusser 2006) coupled with their inheritances and the expectations from civil society ensure their willingness to comply with the perpetual cycle of want fulfilment (Gagnier 2000; Folbre 1982). The interest in such a society then is to ensure that children are optimally trained for the demands of the market economy they live in. An observation that is reinforced by Buckingham's assessment when he says the dominant way to examine childhoods, the sociology of childhood approach, overlooks the role of media and commercial culture in favour of what he calls a 'welfarist perspective' (Buckingham 2000).

While UNICEF, World Bank and other child-welfare agencies define children to be vulnerable, lacking adequate care and protection, when they are under the age of 18 years, there seems to be no definition for a child who is not at risk. Neil Postman in his book *The Disappearance of Childhood* (Postman 1985) laments the loss of the child's protected and carefree dependency owing to the proliferation of electronic media. While acknowledging the limitations of Postman's work, especially the impact/effects-based approach or his use of the frame of a mass passive audience to make his claims (Hoikkala et al. 1987), I would still like to extend his fundamental argument. If children of the media age have become aware of the secrets of the adult world, then they lack any form of agency to negotiate, actively engage with or challenge these secrets. How are we to expect a section of society to remain passive and indifferent when they have the mental and physical capabilities to act upon these issues?

The purpose of this chapter is to contrast the general role of children in society and their representation in traditional media forms with their depiction in video games. Video games being one of the most 'postmodern' media forms prevalent today (Lister et al. 2008; Deshbandhu 2016) are characterised by their high levels of fluidity and scope of engagement (Juul 2011; Deshbandhu 2016). In video games—owing to their postmodern form (Deshbandhu 2016)—there is a relationship between the fluidity of the narration and the presence of characters as instrumental parts of the game. Thus, child characters in video games are in contrast to society's laid out roles for them. Due to their in-the-moment style of building narratives, video games also tend to refrain from the well-established Bildungsroman approach, where readers and viewers wait for the child protagonist to come of age and then affect the circumstances around him/her.

This chapter then uses the characters and circumstances on offer in video games as a frame of reference to juxtapose against cases from Indian society and mediated content for general audiences made in India to highlight the argument being made. While media for children initiatives and content specifically created for children allow for actively involved children characters, they are a specific genre where content is specifically crafted for young audiences.

This chapter examines three 'child' video game characters, namely, Atreus ('God of War', 2018), Ellie ('The Last of Us', 2013) and The Kid ('Bastion', 2011) to try and understand their role and importance in the plots of their respective games. By unravelling the narrative text and studying it concurrently with the experiential effect on the gamer, I explore how these child characters challenge the general understanding of children in Indian society.

Marxist critiques of children's media often take the view that media content for children is less about entertainment and more about grooming young viewers into efficient consumers who then take up the mantle of feeding the ever-hungry global capitalist machinery. This analysis takes a different approach and argues that video games, like those discussed here, offer a different view of what it means to be a child.

By also challenging the established trope of a Bildungsroman-styled narrative these characters allow us to peel off several layers of context from the worlds they inhabit and view children as not merely passive affectees but also individuals willing to react or seize initiative when the situation arises. This viewing of child characters as having both agency and being able to influence important events in narratives by rising to the occasion is in stark contrast to general mediation in the Indian context—a discrepancy this chapter seeks to lay out.

Thus, this essay, at the outset, is a comparison of the representation of children's experience and agency in traditional media forms versus how children are construed in video games. The latter half of this essay then addresses this difference at a deeper level by raising questions about how media-like games are created and consumed by their player bases.

Method

This chapter critically examines three cases in detail: the first two from real life based out of India that differ from each other in terms of circumstance, class and gender as they played out in diametrically opposing sides of the social spectrum; the third case is drawn from an Indian film made in 2002. The case from mediated content is chosen because it is representative of the circumstances and social contexts of production and draws as much from these contexts, if not more, as it lends to them (Livingstone 2005).

The mediated case serves two purposes in this study. First, it allows us to understand how children/child characters are constructed and perceived by the media (a lacuna in childhood studies) as a suitable counter to Buckingham (2000) and Livingstone's (1998) contention that existing childhood studies is disinterested in the role of the media. The use of a mediated case here is suitable because it allows us to address this issue in a somewhat retrospective manner. Second, it also provides us with an instance that typifies the young Indian adolescent from the turn of the millennium who was conceived to be well versed with technology, but unaware of the potential ramifications their abilities could bring about. This chapter then uses the fictional case from the film as a bridge to the three specific cases from video games. The three cases chosen here are textually analysed by performing close reading while the cases from real life were re-constructed and understood based on media reportage (Boyles 2012; Lehman and Roberts 2013).

The cases from video games chosen here are challenging to analyse as they serve two purposes: one in the narrative plot of the game, and the other in the overall game experience that a player engages with. It is not only enough that a character is written in a specific way in the plot, he/she must also exude the same feel and personality when engaged within the game world. The three cases analysed here are chosen for their importance to the plot as well as their contributions in playtime. In other words, these characters were crucial to both the story and the way the games are played. The ludic (derived from the Latin *ludus*, that is, play) cases chosen were not only analysed textually with regards to the narratives of the games but the analysis also accounted for the intended experience for the players.

This chapter draws parallels and contrasts between these specific cases by juxtaposing findings from traditional textual analyses with the analyses of game environments. The discussion is then carried forward by examining various possibilities of what happens to children's attitudes as they engage with virtual worlds. Children's attitudes and psyches are thus understood in a frame where they experience levels of agency, choice and decision-making that they are otherwise not used to in offline scenarios.

Cases

Budhia Singh[1]

Budhia Singh was a prodigious long-distance runner who in 2005 ran 65 km (the distance between Puri and Bhubaneshwar) in the heat of May as a four-year-old. The run made him the youngest to ever run a marathon, becoming a record listed in the *Limca Book of Records*, 2006 (Rediff 2006). Budhia, born after the death of his father, was sold to a contractor for Rs 800 by his mother in order to make ends meet. On hearing about the transaction, Biranchi Das, the president of Saliasahi Slum Dwellers' Association (where Budhia lived), decided to repay the purchaser and bought Budhia back (Mohanty 2016).

Though popular media coverage talks of Das' adoption of Budhia Singh, there are no official records to prove the same (ibid.). Das, a trainer of judo (a martial art form), discovered Budhia's ability to run long distances when he reprimanded him for the use of inappropriate language by asking him to run laps. Once aware of the talent, Das claimed to have nurtured it as Budhia began to run marathons regularly and his ability began to be discussed worldwide (Atwal 2011). However, as the runs became more common and Budhia's penchant for running began to be discussed, child welfare committees and the Government of Odisha stepped in for the fear of Budhia's burnout and the adverse effects it could have on his young body. Budhia was banned from running marathons by the Khurda district child welfare committee in 2006 (Mohanty 2016).

After the ban, Das was murdered (in an unrelated incident) and Budhia was admitted in a Sports Authority of India (SAI) hostel in 2007 (Atwal 2011; Mohanty 2016). The ban on long-distance running still stands as the discussions about him are no longer about the prodigious talent but about whether the talent has been wasted.

Aarushi Talwar

Aarushi Talwar is better known as the one of the victims of a double-murder that occurred in Noida, Uttar Pradesh. She, along with a household worker, Hemraj, was found murdered in the early hours of 16 May 2008. While the police investigations were not able to find enough evidence to convict the perpetrators, the case was heavily discussed in mainstream media (a suitable example of 'trial by media') as both the modus operandi and the motive of the murders remained elusive to investigative agencies and the public at large. The information used to recreate this case is drawn from a combination of academic and mass media–based sources.

The inability to solve the murder mystery and the various possible scenarios offered by the investigative agencies only skewed general perspectives, as theories like wife-swapping, extramarital affair and sexual relations between the two victims were suggested (Dutta and Dubey 2008; *Mumbai Mirror* 2008; Sen 2015). While the case has several facets, the matter of interest to this analysis relates to the way Aarushi was portrayed in the media by investigating agencies.

Further sections of this chapter will explore Aarushi's rights as a child and how specific members of investigating agencies attempted to character-assassinate the victim and her family by questioning her morals on the basis of her conversations on social media (Jaamun 2015). This will be achieved in conjunction with examining the role of the other child in the equation, Aarushi's friend, Anmol, who was supposedly a key informant in the case (*Mumbai Mirror* 2008).

Raju

Raju, unlike Budhia and Aarushi, is a fictional character in the 2002 Indian film *16 December*.[2] The choice of Raju as a specific case helps bridge the gap with characters from video games as, like them, Raju is set in an alternate reality albeit one that closely resembled India in 2002. Raju, in his mediated form, while fictional in existence, imbibes the contextual and social values of the time when the movie was made. In a way, thus, Raju is representative of the young Indian urban adolescent of 2002 (Livingstone 2005). The movie was made in the aftermath of the Kargil conflict, and thus the premise and plot are centred around a potential nuclear attack in New Delhi, the Indian capital.

A pre-pubescent Raju is supposed to be representative of the 1990s' tech-savvy generation; a happy-go-lucky child who is being raised by his uncle, a private investigator by profession and a former intelligence officer. Raju is well versed with computers and is portrayed as an extremely skilled hacker who has the ability to design decryption software that is not only voice controlled but also resembles a floating genie.

The movie is set in a digitally connected world where nuclear warheads are listed by rogue agencies on web platforms that resemble Amazon (not something Poster [2001] had in mind), and Raju is key in helping track the warhead once it reaches India. Raju's scope for this chapter, however, is limited to how his role as both a child and a hacker is facilitated by his legal guardian and how he fits in the larger frame of counter-intelligence and national security that the movie tries to erect.

By contrasting these three specific cases of Budhia, Aarushi and Raju with characters from video games, this chapter highlights issues of agency, choice and purpose that need to be explored in greater detail.

Ludic[3] *Profiles*

Atreus: The 'God of War' (GoW) franchise has established itself as an extremely successful series of titles in the hack 'n' slash genre of video games. Most GoW games involve a lot of action, repetitive violence and are often described as gore-filled spectacles where the narrative leads the player to seek vengeance for the protagonist Kratos. However, things changed considerably with the latest iteration in the franchise of GoW (2018)[4] with the addition of Kratos' son Atreus into the plot of the game. Atreus causes Kratos to shed his usual 'devil-may-care attitude' as for the first time he has someone to protect. The premise of the game involves the father–son duo journeying through the Norse realms as they find the ideal resting place for Atreus' mother. Atreus, through the journey, gets to know his father by initially learning to hunt and then provides some much-needed support to players in sticky situations. Throughout the narrative, Kratos' attitude towards Atreus changes from disdain to fatherly admiration as Atreus transforms from being a burden to a worthy ally.

The focus of the game, however, is Atreus, for in the narrative he begins as a timid boy in pain and with a strong dislike for his father to someone who watches Kratos in awe. The narrative progression allows for Atreus to face revelations about himself and then shows how he struggles to come to grips with it. Throughout the game, though Atreus might seem the deuteragonist or the secondary focus in terms of ludic action, from a narrative perspective it is his journey of self-realisation. The unique mix of challenges, emotions and experiences that he goes through is what makes GoW the compelling ludo-narratological experience that it is.

Ellie: Ellie, like Atreus, is the deuteragonist (second lead) of the highly acclaimed title 'The Last of Us'[5], a zombie apocalypse survival game. The story is set in a world where a mutated fungal infection reduces human hosts into flesh-eating zombies. Released in 2013, at a time when cannibalistic zombies were beginning to make waves in mainstream popular culture,[6] 'The Last of Us' stood out with its incredibly difficult survivalist gameplay and extremely well-defined characters.

The plot goes into how the protagonist, Joel, loses his daughter, Sarah, when the infection strikes and he is left to survive the zombie apocalypse as a smuggler. Joel is tasked to escort a girl, Ellie, and smuggle her to a specific place with humanity's survival in the balance. The alliance is uncomfortable at first as Joel fails to warm up to Ellie and views her just like any of his prior contracts.

The journey to smuggle Ellie is long and arduous and the relationship between the two lacks trust as Ellie lands Joel in a few uncomfortable situations. However, in time Joel begins to see in Ellie the daughter he lost and starts to care for her. The transformation for Ellie, however, is when she overcomes all odds to single-handedly rescue Joel and, soon, he begins to see her as a worthy ally and partner. The relationship between Joel and Ellie is shown to mature in innocuous places with doses of wry humour and emotional cut-scenes (the dilapidated hotel and the giraffes, in particular) as the narrative reaches a crescendo where Joel must make the ultimate decision.

The Kid: 'Bastion' is an unconventional game set in a world where a calamity struck and destroyed everything. The Kid is the playable protagonist in the game where he never utters a word and a narrator describes everything from the in-game action to key elements of the plot and premise. The Kid is also the epicentre of the narrative as his actions determine everything in the gameverse.

The game is designed such that the players have no inkling of who The Kid is and what his past was unless they play a specific level.

It is while playing that level that the narrator informs the players that The Kid never knew his father and his mother was frail. In order to help her and to keep food on the table, he left school and began to work for the army on the border. After his term, he came back to find his mother dead and all the money he sent gone, so he re-enlisted till the calamity struck.

The Kid in 'Bastion' has a persona characterised by extreme stoicism as he withstands all that the calamity throws at him. His journey is a solitary one as he overcomes numerous challenges to rebuild the Bastion; as the narrator puts it, 'through twisted streets he ran with nothing but the city crest and an old stranger's voice to guide him'. The narrative leads to a point where The Kid is betrayed by someone he saved, but despite that he relentlessly gets back to undoing the damage and moving on. As the protagonist of the 'Bastion', he personifies a silent being of action who is not only fearless but also aware of what is morally right and what needs to be done. Throughout, he simply goes about his business, guided by someone who 'never even asked his name'.

The use of children from specific cases from real and reel life along with those from ludic frames as representational figures is key to the next section of this chapter. However, it is also important to note that in four out of the six cases these figures belong to mediated products for which children were consumers. Children, for the purposes of this discussion, then need to be understood at both levels as representational figures as well as consumers in tandem.

Analysis

An analysis of Budhia's case is primarily indicative of the fact that he was born in a family where his mother was struggling to make ends meet. The chance encounter with the judo coach and the discovery of his innate ability to run long distances enabled him to find a place where he could express his talent to the fullest. The roads where he ran were where he felt revered and acknowledged, and the rewards of his running were recognition, food and possibly the consequential financial benefits. While at that age he was not in control of the other aspects of his life, his guardian and well-wishers were aware of the immense value in the success of his dream to run. Budhia's exponentially long runs were the proverbial golden goose and no one in his immediate family circle was likely to inhibit that.

On comparing what Budhia remembers from those early years to his life at the SAI hostel, media interactions depict him as an extremely dissatisfied individual lamenting the route his life has taken:

> I believe I am born to run marathons. Even now, I can run for more hours without being tired. I am neither getting the required coaching nor the food. I get just about 3–4 pieces of chicken while I was being fed more by Biranchi sir when I was four years old. I feel like I am in a jail (Budhia Singh, in Mohanty [2016]).

While the concerns voiced by the various bodies were both relevant and cautionary, as burn-out seems a legitimate concern for young athletes, the steps taken to separate a young protégé from his first coach and placing him in an alien environment amongst coaches unaware of his raw potential and ability appear to be counterproductive at best. The phenomenon of athletes undergoing rigorous training regimes at very young ages is not uncommon for prospects pursuing hopes to make it at the highest level. Michael Phelps was swimming at seven and was at his first Olympics in Sydney at the age of 15 years (Phelps and Cazeneuve 2012: 16). Similarly, closer to home, Saina Nehwal was playing badminton at the age of 8 years (International Olympic Committee 2018).

However, what separates Budhia from the other elite athletes are the circumstances. Adopted by a judo coach with no legal record and in a country where government facilities that foster sport and athletic achievements are subpar, his path to the top was riddled with challenges structured by class, caste and bureaucratic red tape. In this unyielding quagmire, he was enrolled in a place where he lost his identity (and probably his dream) in others' hope for him to be normal.

The closest parallel for Budhia can be drawn with The Kid from 'Bastion'. He too is a silent brooding spectator with nothing to say. Both have never known their fathers and their mothers were struggling with problems. While Budhia was sold to a hawker, The Kid had to leave school in order to provide for his ailing mother. However, the circumstances for The Kid in a virtual world were better than for Budhia in the 'real world'. The Kid, in his stoic existence, could still act and do what he felt was right. It may be considered a shame that Budhia was banned from running, the one key at his disposal that could help him unlock the barriers of class and caste that shackle him (Bourdieu 1991).

The case of Aarushi Talwar stands out for the inability of investigating forces to ascertain both the cause and the perpetrators of the murder. However, what needs to be examined from this case is its handling by the investigative agencies. Their understanding into the psyche of a 13–year-old girl by taking her messages to friends on social media at face-value seems baffling (Jaamun 2015). This chapter only focuses on the handling of Aarushi as an individual by investigating agencies and their depiction of her to society at large through mediated channels.

The use of the word 'slut' in one of the messages to describe herself implied that she was deemed characterless and this was then used as a foundation to call the entire family shady and to accuse it of impropriety. The investigating team went on to suggest that Aarushi's father was having an extramarital affair and Aarushi turned to the house-help (the other victim) seeking solace, which eventually turned into a sexual relationship (*Mumbai Mirror* 2008). The basis for all this information was Aarushi's 15-year-old friend Anmol (Sen 2015).

The challenges faced by Aarushi and her family are very different from those faced by Budhia because of the vast difference in class; the other major issue that also needs to be considered is that of gender. It is surprising that Aarushi sending a message can deem her characterless but when the same message is received by someone like Anmol, they are deemed to be worthy enough to be key informants in the case. Suddenly, judgements of a person's integrity and honesty are based not on their actions in requisite situations but rather on the basis of superficial elements like the clothes they wear, the slang they use and the language they use in personal conversations. Lastly, throughout the handling of the incident, Aarushi's role is never thought to be larger than that of either an innocent victim or someone killed in a fit of rage. Her dreams, ambitions and aspirations were completely forgotten as her portrayal in mass media—served to quench the metaphorical nation's unending desire to know—reduced her to a two-dimensional caricature.

The case of Ellie from 'The Last of Us' is in contrast to that of Aarushi as she begins her journey as a victim but then goes from strength to strength by learning to live with it. Ellie is the cause and source of all the action that is often accompanied by her witty and sarcastic remarks. Her story is also in stark contrast as she begins her journey as an orphan who can barely trust anyone as opposed to Aarushi who was with her family and surrounded by loved ones and trustworthy people.

Although it would be improper to draw too many parallels between a ghastly murder and a video game narrative, it is important to point out that an adolescent girl traversing the entire breadth of the country with an unknown stranger, fending for their lives together, does not really fall within the gendered social mores of Indian society, especially in a climate where girls/women can be targeted, victimised or killed in the safety of their rooms or on public transport. The challenges of girls and women using public transport services in India were made evident by the highly publicised gang-rape of a medical student in New Delhi in December 2012 or the increasing number of molestation and rape cases with regards to ride-sharing platforms like Uber or Ola (Ola 2019). A Thompson Reuters foundation report called Delhi the most dangerous capital city to travel in using public transport facilities (John 2018). Similar findings were also reported by a survey conducted by Ola where 91 per cent of women (from a sample of 9,935 women respondents across age groups) perceived public transport systems in India to be unsafe (Ola 2019).

While this argument can be whittled down to the simple fact that a fictional character can find scope for growth and realising her potential in a post-apocalyptic world infested by zombies, sadly an adolescent Indian girl of the same age cannot be afforded the same luxury in our system. On the contrary, adolescence/pre-pubescence is the age when most girls in the Indian context begin to see their freedoms be curtailed as physical activity, sport and other activities of leisure make way for learning 'wifely' skills that fit in the classic gendered roles that need to be performed in a societal setting where it is the job of women to provide nourishment to the workforce. Thus, the potential of growth for children in Indian settings is skewed with regards to gender, class and access.

The final case of Raju moves away from real life incidents to a fictional 2002 India where the potential of Internet as a communication platform is just being realised. Raju is created as a boy who is not only comfortable traversing the World Wide Web but is also proficient enough to manipulate its architecture for his benefit. He is shown to hack bank accounts with ease, but at the same time unaware of abiding by ethics. At the start of the movie, he sits at his personal computer and offers his uncle Rs 1 crore (approximately US$ 1.42 million) from the account of a certain 'Ambani' only to be slapped and told that money needs to be earned the right way. Throughout the movie, however, the same skills are utilised by the Indian intelligence services to hack into the terrorists' plot. Leaving aside the hypocrisy garbed in the shroud of nationalism, the movie is made in a way that undermines what Raju offers to the plot. Despite his unique skill set, the final scenes of the movie give him no credit whatsoever.

Off the screen, for the purpose of this chapter, tracing both Raju and Sajeel Parakh (the actor who essayed the role) was extremely difficult. They are listed neither on IMDb nor on Google (in the summation of the cast); two of the most reliable sources for information on movies today. For people who have not watched the movie, there is no way to know that an adolescent boy is key to foiling a possible nuclear attack on Indian soil in the story.

Raju and Atreus are very different characters but for the fact that both are, for all practical purposes, orphans. One lives with his uncle and the other is just meeting his father for the first time. However, Raju seems to have no connection or trust or angst or any emotion that conveys the loss he has endured as his character seems shallowly written. Atreus, on the other hand, experiences a wide range of emotions on his journey as he expresses fear, awe, angst, loss, anger, arrogance and pride as his understanding of the self evolves from that of an orphaned boy to that of a young god fighting by the side of his father and finally belonging somewhere. Raju, conversely, experiences no such thing because the writers of the film could not make a tiny sliver of screen space for a young boy to experience joy, wonderment and emotion amongst a group of people who all seem to be heavily dependent on him to achieve the suitable objectives in the film.

What video games seem to do better than society or conventionally mediated content is to primarily think of children as being instrumental. None of the games would have even existed without Ellie, Atreus or The Kid as these child characters are the soul of both the narrative and the gameplay experience. The use of these ludic cases allows for us to imagine possibilities where children can be viewed without burdening them with the perspectives of adulthood. By using these cases, this chapter argues for the need to examine child-centred interactions and cultural productions in the context in which they are performed rather than understanding childhood as a transitional stage of becoming. Sadly, neither Budhia nor Aarushi were deemed worthy to be protagonists of their own stories as they remained victims at best. Things happened to them while their corresponding ludic characters acted and reacted. Thus, leaving scope for introspection, virtual worlds not only offer children a wider range of participation and engagement but also provide them with agency, identity and a better understanding of the self.

Discussion

The final part of the chapter uses the findings from the analysis to understand what children experience and imbibe when they interact with the virtual. Video games specifically are often understood to be a magical space at the boundaries of which the real and the virtual coalesce, but not in a seamless fashion. Researchers in game studies have attempted to use concepts like magic circle, magic cycle, puzzle piece and recursive space (Salen and Zimmerman 2004; Arsenault and Perron 2008; Juul 2008; Wood 2012) to try and explain the magic in the sites of play once the act of play begins. The boundaries between the real and the in-game never truly disappear. This discussion section of the chapter veers away from children being representational figures to viewing children as consumers of mediated content. Thus, it takes into account how children engage with their media as well as social constructs once they have become aware of the secrets of the adult world (Postman 1985).

Janet Murray in her work identifies the power of games and playful activity in enabling children to understand how society and societal constructs function. She focuses on the potential of mimesis (mimicry/imitation) (Murray 2017), and in her cultural understanding of gaming as an activity, she labels them as a spatial and temporal construction (Murray 2006) which are joint attentional scenes, and thus bring about a co-evolution of media, mind and culture (Murray 2006, 2007). Thus, for children of today who play video games, their numerous cycles of play innately affect and shape their psyche, perceptions and understanding of the world they live in. The best way to understand ludic experiences would be to chart the gamer's journey as 'he/she oscillates in between the game world and the real, each time leaving a bit more of themselves in the game, and while logging out or taking with them a few things to the offline world, leaving both worlds forever changed' (Deshbandhu 2020: 38). This would mean that children imbibe the postmodern, fluid nature of their identities as well as (very likely) critically question the roles that the society has clearly laid out for them.

The manifestation of the aforementioned trend is clearly visible from the rise of new ways of making money that include making of user-generated content, live streaming of gaming action, and adolescents and teens becoming key fixtures on the pro-gaming circuit. The e-sports economy is slowly taking shape and suddenly it seems to be a possible career option. Children who have actively engaged with these platforms are now viewing them as offering viable career prospects.

Two recent examples stand out. First, Siddh Chandarana, who goes by the gamertag Jenasid, was signed as a professional e-sports player of FIFA by M10 Esports (Sen 2018). Second, 17-year-old Ajey Nagar quit school because he was making enough money from his twitch stream that has 8,50,000 followers (Hemrajani 2017). For both Siddh and Ajey, these are steps that will shape their lives ahead and are not decisions that were taken lightly. However, these decisions are indicative of the extent of agency that was available to them.

For Siddh, going professional as an e-sports player implies that playing FIFA will be his career for the foreseeable future. The requisite number of simulated football matches he needs to play every week to compete at the highest level as well as stay primed is an incredibly high number. As an 18-year-old, making that decision could not have been easy. Similarly, for Ajey to drop out of school in the pursuit of new subscribers and make it big in the world of online streaming indicates that these soon-to-be-young adults have re-imagined their roles in society.

This also implies that the society must re-think its definition of both labour and skill. Playing close to 90 games of competitive FIFA every week is definitely hard labour when the results desired in that environment are clear and well-defined. Also, streaming content close to seven to eight hours a day is nothing short of a full-time job as well. However, the act of playing games has always been about fun and leisure, and thus there is a need for these definitions to evolve now. In cases when childhood ceases to remain a site of realising one's potential but becomes a time when children are achieving goals and objectives reserved for adults, parenting, education and childcare will begin to take new forms. Emerging research in this regard could look at how parents prepare players of e-sports to balance education, handle life and find newer avenues for growth. While such examples will allow for other children to hope and view their lives as trajectories they are likely to have more autonomy over, society could begin to view them as intelligent individuals who can make decisions for themselves and shape their lives with their decisions.

But these two urban Indian boys and the career decisions made by them are only handpicked examples at best: they have access to high-end gaming equipment, the best infrastructure and a background that helps them challenge the status quo. For the rest of the children in the country, challenges of class, caste and gender will continue to persist. With regards to the empowering self-decisions and unique career choices made by Siddh and Ajey—afforded to them due to the immense amount of privilege they enjoy—it will be interesting to see if they are forging new paths or merely identifying a vacuum in the market economy that will quickly reshape itself by consuming them in the grand narrative.

Notes

1. A film on Budhia's life titled *Budhia Singh—Born to Run* was released in August 2016. The film directed by Soumendra Padhi won the National Film Award in the Best Children's Film category.
2. *16 December* is a film produced by Anjali Joshi and Arunima Roy, directed by Mani Shankar, and starring Milind Soman and Dippanita Sharma in lead roles. The film was a commercial success.
3. Ludic, Ludo and Ludological are all derivatives of Ludology, the study of video games. *Ludus* is the Latin word for play.
4. 'God of War' 2018 won the 'Game of the Year' for 2018, making it one of the best ludic experiences available for gamers on the current generation's gaming platforms.
5. Naughty Dog's PlayStation exclusive 'The Last of Us' with over 240 awards received is one of the most awarded games in the history of the gaming industry.
6. Since the release of the 2009 hit film *Zombieland* and the TV series *The Walking Dead*, content with infected humans with cannibalistic tendencies has enjoyed a renaissance and consequently received significant traction from the audience.

References

Althusser, L. 2006. 'Ideology and Ideological State Apparatuses (Notes Towards an Investigation)'. *The Anthropology of the State: A Reader* 9(1): 86–98.

Arsenault, Dominic, and Bernard Perron. 2008. 'In the Frame of the Magic Cycle: the Circle(s) of Gameplay', in *The Video Game Theory Reader 2*, eds B. Perron and Mark J. P. Wolf, 109–31. New York: Routledge.

Atwal, G. 2011. 'What Happened to Budhia Singh, India's Marathon Boy?' BBC South Asia, 16 March. Available at https://www.bbc.com/news/world-12745490 (accessed on 6 February 2020).

Bourdieu, P. 1991. *Language and Symbolic Power*. Boston: Harvard University Press.

Boyles, N. 2012. 'Closing In on Close Reading'. In *On Developing Readers: Readings from Educational Leadership*, ed. M. Scherer, 89–99. Alexandria, VA: ASCD.

Buckingham, D. 2000. 'Studying Children's Media Cultures: A New Agenda for Cultural Studies'. In *Children and Media: Multidisciplinary Approaches*, eds B. Van den Bergh and J. Van den Bulck, 49–66. Leuven, Belgium: Garant.

Carr, E. H. 1964. *What Is History?* London: Macmillan.

Deshbandhu, A. 2016. 'Player Perspectives: What It Means to Be a Gamer'. *Press Start* 3(2): 48–64.

____. 2020. *Gaming Culture(s) in India: Digital Play in Everyday Life*. London and New York: Routledge.

Dutta, A., and A. Dubey. 2008. 'Wife Swap Twist in Aarushi Case'. *Mid-Day*, 26 June. Available at https://archive.mid-day.com/news/2008/jun/260608nation2.htm (accessed on 6 February 2020).

Engels, F. 2010. *The Origin of the Family, Private Property and the State*. London: Penguin.

Folbre, N. 1982. 'Exploitation Comes Home: A Critique of the Marxian Theory of Family Labour'. *Cambridge Journal of Economics* 6(4): 317–29.

Gagnier, R. 2000. *The Insatiability of Human Wants: Economics and Aesthetics in Market Societies*. Chicago: University of Chicago Press.

Hemrajani, N. 2017. 'The Indian Gaming Stars Who Catch Your Eye'. *Livemint*, 1 April. Available at https://www.livemint.com/Leisure/kykh1oRK0b28ICVsZAD95N/Indias-young-gaming-stars.html (accessed on 6 February 2020).

Hoikkala, T., O. Rahkonen, C. Tigerstedt and J. Tuormaa. 1987. 'Wait a Minute, Mr Postman! Some Critical Remarks on Neil Postman's Childhood Theory'. *Acta Sociologica* 30(1): 87–99.

International Olympic Committee. 2018. 'The Olympics' Dossier on Saina Nehwal and Her Achievements'. Available at https://www.olympic.org/

news/get-to-know-indian-badminton-star-saina-nehwal (accessed on 6 February 2020).

Jaamun. 2015. 'Trial by Error: The Aarushi Files'. Arré. Available at https://www.arre.co.in/series/aarushi/ (accessed on 6 February 2020).

John, A. A. 2018. 'India Has Been Consistently Unsafe for Women But They Are Also Speaking Out'. *Thewire.in*, 13 July. Available at https://thewire.in/women/reuters-expert-survey-india-women-safety (accessed on 6 February 2020).

Juul, J. 2008. 'The Magic Circle and the Puzzle Piece'. In *Conference Proceedings of the Philosophy of Computer Games, 2008 Potsdam*. Germany: Potsdam University Press.

____. 2011. *Half-real: Video Games Between Real Rules and Fictional Worlds*. Boston: MIT Press.

Lehman, C., and K. Roberts. 2013. *Falling in Love with Close Reading: Lessons for Analyzing Texts and Life*. Portsmouth, NH: Heinemann.

Lister, M., S. Giddings, J. Dovey, I. Grant and K. Kelly. 2008. *New Media: A Critical Introduction*. London and New York: Routledge.

Livingstone, S. 1998. 'Mediated Childhoods: A Comparative Approach to Young People's Changing Media Environment in Europe'. *European Journal of Communication* 13(4): 435–56.

Livingstone, S. M. (ed.). 2005. *Audiences and Publics: When Cultural Engagement Matters for the Public Sphere*, Vol. 2. Bristol, UK: Intellect Books.

Mohanty, D. 2016. 'The Loneliness of Long Distance Runner—Budhia Singh'. *The Indian Express*, 24 April. Available at https://indianexpress.com/article/sports/sport-others/the-loneliness-of-a-long-distance-runner-2767531/ (accessed on 6 February 2020).

Mumbai Mirror. 2008. 'Father Killed Aarushi'. 24 May. Available at https://mumbaimirror.indiatimes.com/news/india/Father-killed-Aarushi/articleshow/15813786.cms (accessed on 6 February 2020).

Murray, J. H. 2006. 'Toward a Cultural Theory of Gaming: Digital Games and the Co-evolution of Media, Mind, and Culture'. *Popular Communication* 4(3): 185–202.

____. 2007. 'Games as Joint Attentional Scenes'. In *Worlds in Play: International Perspectives on Digital Games Research*, eds Suzanne de Castell and Jennifer Jenson, 11–20. New York: Peter Lang.

____. 2017. *Hamlet on the Holodeck: The Future of Narrative in Cyberspace*. Boston: MIT Press.

Ola. 2019. 'What Do Women and Girls Want from Urban Mobility Systems?' Ola Institute, March. Available at https://olawebcdn.com/ola-institute/ola_women_and_mobility.pdf (accessed on 6 February 2020).

Phelps, M., and B. Cazeneuve. 2012. *Beneath the Surface: My Story*. New York: Skyhorse Publishing, Inc.

Poster, M. 2001. 'Cyberdemocracy: The Internet and the Public Sphere'. In *Reading Digital Culture*, ed. David Trend, 259–71. Malden, MA: Blackwell.

Postman, N. 1985. *The Disappearance of Childhood*. New York: Vintage Books.

Rediff. 2006. 'Budhia Runs Into Record Books'. Available at https://www.rediff.com/sports/2006/may/02budhia.htm (accessed on 6 February 2020).

Salen, K., and E. Zimmerman. 2004. *Rules of Play: Game Design Fundamentals*. Cambridge/London: MIT Press.

Sen, A. 2015. *Aarushi*. London: Penguin.

Sen, K. 2018. 'Mesut Ozil Shows His Love for India—Tweets in Hindi, Wants to Meet Ranveer Singh'. Sportwallah.com. Available at https://www.sportswallah.com/football/features/mesut-ozil-shows-his-love-for-india-tweets-in-hindi-wants-to-meet-ranveer-singh/ (accessed on 6 February 2020).

Wood, Aylish. 2012. 'Recursive Space: Play and Creating Space'. *Games and Culture* 7(1): 87–105.

5

REFLECTIONS AND REPRESENTATIONS
Reading about Children in Indian News

Mehak Siddiqui

Children represent the future of our world. And in a country as diverse and complex as India, they come from a wide range of socio-economic conditions, spanning the secure and well-sustained to the hungry and the homeless. According to the 2011 Census, India is home to 17 per cent of the world's children and has the world's largest child population. Despite this, a majority of the country's children experience neglect and their rights are ignored. Of the 430 million children in India, an estimated 55 per cent (236.5 million) experience violations of their rights (Kumar n.d.).

The ways in which we conceptualise childhood and treat children in terms of laws and policies to protect and benefit them, derive from our collective view of them. This perception is shaped by, among other social and cultural factors, the information that we have about children, and a primary source of such information is the news. McCombs and Shaw (1972) developed the agenda-setting theory that describes how the media attempts to influence viewers by emphasising certain issues through allocating a greater proportion of the newshole to them or by placing them more prominently in the news, while rendering other issues less important by devoting less space and attention to them. This framework continues to be relevant and it can therefore be said that the press serves as a gatekeeper of the messages that the public receives about the status of children in the country, often setting the agenda in terms of what is important and filtering those that are considered trivial. The messages that make it through ultimately define public opinion and awareness about child-related issues.

Therefore, it is interesting to consider the following questions. How does the Indian news media cover children and child policy issues? How are children represented in the news? How are they co-opted or framed within certain narratives or ideologies? These questions seem to have largely escaped the focus of media research in India, which leans more towards studying the effects or impact of news and other media *on* children. Perhaps this is indicative of the overarching view of children as passive recipients or consumers of media messages rather than as active participants within a democratic system. In fact, children are generally not perceived as citizens, or even citizens-in-the-making (Buckingham [2000], as cited in Alon-Tirosh and Lemish 2014: 109), a view that largely dominates even globally despite recent work establishing children as an important 'public' and an emerging part of the citizenry. For instance, Nolas (2015) describes how an intersectional approach is needed to improve young people's lives and opines that they should be among the key voices in the dialogue between different knowledge communities.

In this regard, the purpose of this chapter is to study and describe the Indian news media coverage of children and child-related topics. On the whole, it offers a glimpse of the tapestry that the news weaves about the youngest denizens of India by looking at three events that dominated the news sphere in the six-month period from December 2019 to May 2020. These are, in order of chronology, the coronavirus pandemic, the introduction of the controversial Citizenship Amendment Act that sparked nationwide protests, and the issues in Jammu and Kashmir post the abjuration of articles 370 and 35A.

All of these events can reveal, to an extent, how news covers children during times of crisis, which might, in turn, point to how they are generally seen within our society. At this point, it may be pertinent to recall Livingstone and Third's (2017) description of the child as an ambiguous discursive figure that often mirrors and projects adult aspirations and anxieties. Further, Al-Ghazzi (2019) notes how children are mythologised and often framed within factors such as race and class and archetypes of innocence and victimhood. Therefore, the child can be conceptualised in a manner that goes beyond the basic definition as an individual under the age of 18 years.

Finally, the UNICEF (n.d.) guidelines for journalists reporting on children provide a useful backdrop against which we can understand the reporting of events under review. These broadly include:

1. Avoiding descriptions that further stigmatise children or expose them to negative reprisals such as abuse or discrimination
2. Providing accurate contexts for stories or images of children
3. Protecting the identity of children who are victims of sexual offences, living with HIV/AIDS, perpetrators of abuse, or charged or convicted of crime
4. Protecting the identity of children who are or have been combatants, asylum seekers, refugees or otherwise displaced, if they are at potential risk of harm or retribution
5. Protecting children against harm and stigmatisation after their identities have already been used in reportage
6. Confirming the accuracy of what a child has to say, either with an adult, or other children and preferably with both
7. Opting to report on the general situation for children rather than on an individual child when there is a potential risk involved, no matter how newsworthy the story

While it is beyond the scope of this essay to analyse how journalists in India implement these guidelines, it is useful to keep them in mind while sampling some of the reportage.

Coronavirus and Child-Related Issues

As of 25 April 2020, according to the Worldometer website (n.d.), the novel coronavirus had infected over 20,000 people and claimed over 800 lives in India. A look at the media coverage of the pandemic up to that date reveals the extreme disparities that the country is known for. On one hand, there is a multitude of reports about urban, school-going children's responses to the pandemic, such as children in Kolkata making fashionable face masks (Loiwal 2020) and some in Tripura creating graffiti about social distancing (Deb 2020). *India Today* (2020a) reported on a Varanasi school's 'karona' awareness campaign for students while multiple news websites ran feature articles about how parents were keeping their children occupied at home through the nationwide lockdown (Fazili 2020; Kuriakose 2020; Ojha 2020).

On the other hand, even a cursory review of the reportage on the plight of less privileged children during the lockdown reveals that they are not extended the same treatment. A nationwide lockdown was put in place from 25 March 2020 and resulted in thousands of migrant workers from big cities attempting to travel back to their hometowns and villages. In the absence of public transport, they embarked on their journeys by foot and the resultant crisis revealed 'the government's apathy toward the workers who power the country's growth' (Chatterjee 2020). Ghose (2020) further elaborates how migrant workers, with their contributions as masons, artisans, drivers, delivery men, etc., are the hands that keep cities moving, growing and thriving. Yet they are treated without empathy, as a generalised mass of faceless and unwelcome guests.

Not surprisingly, the children of these workers have not received much representation in the news; barring the 12-year-old girl who died while walking from the village where she worked in Telangana to her home in Chhattisgarh (Verma 2020). While this sparked a child labour probe (Nagaraj 2020), it also reiterated how we as a nation have generally accepted child labour as an inconvenient but unavoidable reality of the extreme dualities we inhabit.

While international media, including the BBC (Pandey 2020) and Al Jazeera (Yadav 2020), have covered the plight of destitute Indian children during the lockdown, the mainstream Indian news outlets seem to have largely ignored the issue. Moreover, even when children's issues have made it to the news, their voices have still been missing from the story. For instance, a *Mint* report (Sharma 2020) on the impact of the lockdown on midday meals has no quotes from the children who benefit from this programme. While this absence of children's voices on issues impacting them may be due to ethical issues of consent or privacy, there is an apparent inconsistency in the application of such journalistic principles when it comes to poor children versus urban middle-class children.

Another major story in April 2020 involving children amid the pandemic in India was that of state governments deploying buses to fetch students studying in Kota,[1] an initiative that has been widely covered and lauded (*The Week* 2020; *Outlook India* 2020; *India Today* 2020c; *The Times of India* 2020b). This reportage can be contrasted to the parallel coverage of Muslim students in madrasas. On 10 April 2020, *India Today* claimed to have conducted an investigation that implicated madrasa students as flouting the lockdown and social distancing regulations (*India Today* 2020b).

The independent news website *Newslaundry* (Tewari 2020) countered this investigation by revealing how the children, originally from Bihar, were unable to go back home because of the lockdown. A report in the *National Herald* (Quraishi 2020) further detailed how these madrasa students became a target of communal politics as they are extremely poor and often have no families. Moreover, they stand out with their attire of traditional kurta-pyjamas and skull caps, fitting into a stereotypical image which dominant right-wing narratives continue to vilify.

The coronavirus lockdown also brought forth the pressing issues of child abuse and exploitation. *The Hindu* (2020) reported, 'Childline India helpline received more than 92,000 SOS calls asking for protection from abuse and violence in 11 days.' Further, several news media houses, including *The Times of India* (Pandit 2020), ABP News (2020) and News18 (2020) ran stories about an India Child Protection Fund (ICPF) report highlighting an increase in the demand for child pornography during the lockdown.

At the same time, reportage of the pandemic has also included the kind of children's stories that are perhaps most popular, those that highlight achievements. For instance, a group of teenagers from Delhi invented a robot to help deliver food and medicines to Covid-19 patients to reduce their contact with medical workers (Sirur 2020). Another teen from Maharashtra created a wrist band with a buzzer that could help prevent people from shaking hands with others or touching their face to reduce the risk of getting the virus (Parmar 2020).

Overall, the Covid-19 crisis has shone a spotlight on the disparities as well as the deep chasms in our social fabric when it comes to protecting child rights. It is indicative of our larger systemic biases about children. While we privilege the voices and celebrate the achievements of some, we tend to either be apathetic or turn a blind eye towards those from disadvantaged backgrounds.

Children in Protests against the Citizenship Amendment Act

Since December 2019, India witnessed several protests against the controversial Citizenship Amendment Act (CAA). Of these, the site that gained most media coverage was Delhi's Shaheen Bagh with its women and children protestors. A report in The Quint noted:

> We have seen the National Commission For Protection of Child Rights (NCPCR) issuing an advisory against the 'misuse' of children in the anti-CAA protests, and comments on social media from across a spectrum have also expressed unease with what they call 'indoctrination' of children (Mishra 2020).

This points to the discomfort that many people feel with the involvement of children in political matters. So while we as a society may encourage school-going children to take part in 'model' parliaments and 'Model United Nations' conferences, it becomes a cause for concern when they step out to participate in the real-life political systems they inhabit. Alon-Tirosh and Lemish (2014) find an interesting dialectic regarding the genre of news. It is at once a source of information essential to protect, inform and help citizens dialogue about important issues in the country and the world as it is inappropriate, possibly even dangerous, for children (Gunter et al. [2000] and Seiter and Pincus [2004] as cited in Alon-Tirosh and Lemish 2014: 108).

Alon-Tirosh and Lemish (2014: 108) write, 'Children are assumed not to have the necessary cognitive tools to handle such contents: they are not mature enough emotionally, they have not developed critical thinking skills, and they lack the necessary knowledge to absorb the information.'

Despite this, there are instances when children in India are politicised to push certain agendas. For instance, the Bharatiya Janata Party (BJP) launched a nationwide 'Support CAA' campaign in schools. Interestingly, news reports about the implementation of this campaign either do not feature the opinions of the students at all (*The Times of India* 2020a; *The Indian Express* 2020) or include quotes from only those who are apparently supportive of the CAA but none from those who may be opposed to it (Banerji 2020; Dhupkar 2020).

On the other hand, children belonging to classes IV to VI at the Shaheen School in Bidar, Karnataka, were repeatedly interrogated by the police after they participated in a play critical of the CAA. Out of five news reports that I read about this incident (Bhatt 2020; The Wire 2020a; Shreyas 2020; Pinto 2020; The Logical Indian 2020), only one (Shreyas 2020) included a quote from one of the children, a six-year-old whose mother was arrested. Interestingly, photos and videos that emerged from this incident feature children in headscarves and skull caps, once again portraying children within a stereotypical image that has received a fair amount of bad press in recent years. It is not surprising then that an *India Today* headline (Pinto 2020) rather sensationally implicated the children as participating in a 'seditious school play'. The Wire (2020a) had the sensitivity to enclose the word 'seditious' within quotation marks in their headline, implying that such a description of the play is open to debate.

Shortly after this incident, on 13 February 2020, the news website Scroll published an article describing how children protesting the CAA were allegedly detained and brutalised by Uttar Pradesh police in several areas including Bijnor, Muzaffarnagar and Firozabad (Suresh and Ali 2020). This story seems to be missing from most of the mainstream news websites. There is a mention of it over a month earlier in HuffPost India (Sethi 2019). However, only a singular report in The Wire (2020b) gives voice to the teenagers who were victims of this alleged police brutality. Later, on 4 March 2020, the *Mumbai Mirror* (2020) picked up the story but only included the information already conveyed in The Wire's report.

As the protests continued to gain momentum, the consequent roadblocks in Delhi sparked a series of events that resulted in communal riots between 23 February 2020 and 1 March 2020 in the city's north-eastern areas. One of the haunting images that emerged from the media coverage of this carnage was that of a child grieving at an uncle's funeral. This brings to mind how traumatic photographs involving children often emerge from coverage of crises around the world, whether it is the 1972 image of a naked girl running down a road in Vietnam after suffering a napalm attack, or a 1993 photo of a starving Sudanese child being preyed upon by a vulture (Boukanoun 2016). More recently, news media has photographed children's suffering in wars or armed conflicts in Syria, Iraq and elsewhere (Lewis 2016), and many such images continue to be reused in misleading contexts (Kaur 2020; Sidharth 2018).

As Al-Ghazzi (2019) notes, children are often represented as witnesses of conflict, particularly in today's networked media environment wherein the news converges with social media content and reaction. In such a scenario, voice is celebrated, but not heard (Couldry [2010], as cited in Al-Ghazzi 2019: 3226), and the image is widely circulated but ultimately not seen (Della Ratta [2018], as cited in Al-Ghazzi 2019: 3226).

In the aftermath of the Delhi riots, several news reports focused on children's experiences of the violence, from witness accounts (Sengupta 2020) to stories of their individual suffering (Shali 2020); from their response to grief (Shakil 2020) to the trauma they had suffered (Shrangi 2020). All four reports referenced evoke empathy and emotion by including quotes from children impacted by the riots and detailing the lasting effects the violence will leave on their lives. Perhaps these narratives appeared in the news because they took place in the capital city and imprinted onto our collective consciousness by simultaneously appearing on social media platforms such as

the psychiatric ward of a Srinagar hospital almost doubled between 2016 and 2019, from around 17,000 to 30,000 (Wallen 2019). While there are several news reports available online about Kashmiri children's psychological health, it is difficult to find any words from the children themselves in these stories. They are primarily represented through images such as in reports by *The Hindu* (Ashiq 2019) and *India Today* (Roshangar 2018). All in all, it seems that children of Kashmir sometimes find a voice in stories about school and education but rarely in those about larger geopolitical or social issues that impact them.

Conclusion

Even a cursory review of news in India will reveal a general repeated pattern of children being consistently underrepresented. Moreover, as is the case with the portrayal of adults, certain social categories of children are seen (and heard) less than others. Media reflects the power and privilege hierarchies of society and the perceived value of different population groups inherent within these structures.

However, news media thrives on sensationalist stories, particularly in today's ever competitive media sphere, and children often get co-opted within this. As the lines between news and propaganda blur into each other, young denizens are susceptible to being used as pawns to promote political agendas. News media, while sometimes condemning this practice, often ends up catalysing it. This may be due to the changing role of emotion in journalism and how images and voices of children can be used to advocate specific political stances (Al-Ghazzi 2019).

This essay uses a limited sample of news stories related to just three events over the specified period of time from December 2019 to May 2020. Nevertheless, it gives us a glimpse into the possibilities for a more in-depth and thorough study and nuanced analysis about the representations of children in the Indian media. For instance, it would be pertinent to examine gender and caste representations of young people in the news as well as representations related to violence and crime. Moreover, it would be valuable to analyse how this coverage fits within the purview of the law as well as the UNICEF guidelines for journalists reporting on children, mentioned in the introduction of this essay.

A decade and a half ago, Joseph (2005) wrote:

> The media today reflect little active awareness of the fact that they have an important role to play in enabling children to learn about and make sense of the highly complex world they live in, which they cannot but be conscious about, bombarded as they are by random information from a variety of sources, including multiple forms of media. There is not much space or time in the media for children to express their thoughts, articulate their doubts, fears, hopes and aspirations, and offer their ideas on current affairs.

In 2022, more than fifteen years later, there has been some progress with a few news reports giving children a chance to voice their experiences and thoughts, but even this varies profoundly depending on the kind of story it is or the kind of children that it involves. Certain children are portrayed as cute, innocent or endearing, while others seem to be regarded with contempt and boxed into stereotypical portrayals of their class and religion. For instance, it can be argued that news has helped propagate an image of madrasa children as mistrustful or 'terrorists in the making', or of Kashmiri youth as flighty and aggressive.

Finally, I would like to close with a personal anecdote. At the end of a panel discussion about fake news at the Jaipur Literary Festival in January 2020, I witnessed a group of exuberant teenagers ask the journalist Faye D'Souza what they can do about their parents being gullible to false or hateful narratives propagated by media. This, along with enthusiastic young adult participation in varied sessions with other prominent journalists at the fest, reiterated to me that children are indeed keyed into news and interested in what happens in their country and the world. It should be a priority of the press and the polity then to create opportunities and safe spaces for young people to communicate their ideas, opinions and experiences in authentic ways.

Note

1. The city of Kota in Rajasthan is known for its coaching institutes that have made it a hub for students from across the country preparing for competitive exams needed to seek admission in leading engineering and medical programmes in the country.

References

ABP News. 2020. 'Sharp Rise in Demand for Child Pornography in India Ever Since Covid-19 Lockdown Imposed: Report'. 14 April. Available at https://news.abplive.com/news/india/coronavirus-lockdown-rise-in-demand-for-child-pornography-in-india-says-report-1197519 (accessed on 19 April 2020).

Al-Ghazzi, O. 2019. 'An Archetypal Digital Witness: The Child Figure and the Media Conflict over Syria'. *International Journal of Communication* 13: 3225–43.

Alon-Tirosh, M., and D. Lemish. 2014. '"If I Was Making the News": What Do Children Want from News?' *Participations: Journal of Audience & Reception Studies* 11(1): 108–29.

Anand, H. 2019. 'Article 370: Chandigarh, Panchkula Schools Ask Pupils to Write "Thank You" Letter to PM Modi'. *The Times of India*, 19 August. Available at https://timesofindia.indiatimes.com/city/chandigarh/tricity-schools-make-kids-write-letter-to-thank-pm-modi-for-stripping-special-status-of-kashmir/articleshow/70734413.cms (accessed on 25 April 2020).

Ashiq, P. 2019. 'J&K Children to Get Psychological First Aid'. *The Hindu*, 30 August. Available at https://www.thehindu.com/news/national/other-states/jk-children-to-get-psychological-first-aid/article29302100.ece (accessed on 19 April 2020).

Banerji, A. 2020. 'Punjab RSS Schools Garner Students' Support for CAA'. *The Tribune*, 20 January. Available at https://www.tribuneindia.com/news/punjab/punjab-rss-schools-garner-students%E2%80%99-support-for-caa-29083 (accessed on 10 April 2020).

Bhatt, P. 2020. 'Cops Turn Up at Bidar School for Fourth Time, Question Kids over Anti-CAA Play'. *The News Minute*, 3 February. Available at https://www.thenewsminute.com/article/cops-turn-bidar-school-fourth-time-question-kids-over-anti-caa-play-117405 (accessed on 25 April 2020).

Boukanoun, A. 2016. 'The Iconic Images of Children Suffering in War'. Euronews, 22 August. Available at https://www.euronews.com/2016/08/22/the-iconic-images-of-children-suffering-in-war (accessed on 30 April 2020).

Chakravarty, I. 2021. 'Killing the Story: How the Kashmiri Press Was Silenced After the Region Lost Autonomy'. Reuters Institute, 24 August. Available at https://reutersinstitute.politics.ox.ac.uk/killing-story-how-kashmiri-press-was-silenced-after-region-lost-autonomy (accessed on 30 September 2022).

Chatterjee, P. 2020. 'The Pandemic Exposes India's Apathy Toward Migrant Workers'. *The Atlantic*, 12 April. Available at https://www.theatlantic.com/ideas/archive/2020/04/the-pandemic-exposes-indias-two-worlds/609838/ (accessed on 15 April 2020).

Deb, D. 2020. 'Schools Shut, Children in Tripura City Take to Graffiti on Social Distancing'. *The Indian Express*, 21 April. Available at https://indianexpress.com/article/north-east-india/tripura/coronavirus-lockdown-schools-shut-children-in-tripura-city-take-to-graffiti-on-social-distancing-6372760/ (accessed on 24 April 2020).

Dhupkar, A. 2020. 'CAAtching Them Young'. *Mumbai Mirror*, 11 January. Available at https://mumbaimirror.indiatimes.com/mumbai/cover-story/caatching-them-young/articleshow/73196351.cms (accessed on 10 April 2020).

Drèze, J., K. Krishnan, M. Mollah and V. Bhai. 2019. 'Kashmir Caged: A Fact-Finding Report'. Indian Cultural Forum, 14 August. Available at https://archive.indianculturalforum.in/2019/08/14/kashmir-caged-a-fact-finding-report/ (accessed on 24 April 2020).

Ehsan, M., and A. Hussain. 2020. 'How School Kids in Kashmir Are Coping with Curbs After Article 370 Decision'. *Hindustan Times*, 28 June. Available at https://www.hindustantimes.com/india-news/how-j-k-school-kids-are-coping-with-curbs/story-pspbVxaqgX2EpCruXru3yM.html (accessed on 20 May 2020).

Fazili, S. 2020. 'Coronavirus Pandemic: How Indian Parents Are Keeping Their Children Busy as Schools Shut'. News18, 17 March. Available at https://www.news18.com/news/buzz/coronavirus-pandemic-how-indian-parents-are-keeping-their-children-busy-as-schools-shut-2539223.html (accessed on 10 April 2020).

Gaikwad, R. 2019. 'DAV Schools Tell Students to Pen Fawning Letters to PM'. *Mumbai Mirror*, 31 August. Available at https://mumbaimirror.indiatimes.com/mumbai/other/dav-schools-tell-students-to-pen-fawning-letters-to-pm/articleshow/70918091.cms (accessed on 25 April 2020).

Ghose, S. 2020. 'Tale of Two Indias—Corona Reality Check: Treat the Poor as Equal Citizens, Not a Faceless Horde'. *The Times of India*, 23 April. Available at https://timesofindia.indiatimes.com/blogs/bloody-mary/tale-of-two-indias-corona-reality-check-treat-the-poor-as-equal-citizens-not-a-faceless-horde/ (accessed on 24 April 2020).

Gulab, R. 2020. 'Imagine the PMO Bullying School Children to Write Letters of Support on CAA'. *National Herald*, 17 January. Available at https://www.nationalheraldindia.com/blog/imagine-the-pmo-bullying-school-children-to-write-letters-of-support-on-caa (accessed on 20 May 2020).

India Today. 2020a. 'Coronavirus: Varanasi School Comes Up with 'KaroNa' List to Spread Awareness Among Students'. 8 March. Available at https://www.indiatoday.in/trending-news/story/coronavirus-varanasi-school-comes-up-with-karo-na-list-to-spread-awareness-among-students-1653674-2020-03-08 (accessed on 15 April 2020).

———. 2020b. 'Children Not Following Any Social Distancing Norms in Delhi's Madrasa, Reveals India Today'. 10 April. Available at https://www.indiatoday.in/coronavirus-outbreak/video/children-not-following-any-social-distancing-norms-in-delhi-s-madrasa-reveals-india-today-1665683-2020-04-10 (accessed on 18 September 2022).

———. 2020c. 'Over 6,000 Students of Kota Coaching Institutes Make Homeward Journey to UP in Buses'. 18 April. Available at https://www.indiatoday.in/india/story/3000-students-from-kota-enroute-home-up-govt-buses-1668486-2020-04-18 (accessed on 24 April 2020).

Joseph, A. 2005. 'Where Have All the Children Gone?' *India Together*, 8 August. Available at http://www.indiatogether.org/children-op-ed (accessed on 11 April 2020).

Kaur, A. 2020. 'Fact Check: Image of Injured Syrian Child Passed Off as Victim of Delhi Violence'. *India Today*, 3 March. Available at https://www.indiatoday.in/fact-check/story/fact-check-image-injured-syrian-child-passed-off-as-victim-delhi-violence-1652107-2020-03-03 (accessed on 30 April 2020).

Kumar, A. (n.d.). 'Children and the Media'. Indian Media Studies. Available at https://www.indianmediastudies.com/children-and-the-media/ (accessed on 10 April 2020).

Kuriakose, S. 2020. 'School from Home'. *India Today*, 28 April. Available at https://www.indiatoday.in/mail-today/story/school-from-home-1671973-2020-04-28 (accessed on 30 April 2020).

Lewis, H. 2016. 'How Newsrooms Handle Graphic Images of Violence'. Nieman Reports, 5 January. Available at https://niemanreports.org/articles/how-newsrooms-handle-graphic-images-of-violence/ (accessed on 24 April 2020).

Livingstone, S., and A. Third. 2017. 'Children and Young People's Rights in the Digital Age: An Emerging Agenda'. *New Media and Society* 19(5): 657–70.

Loiwal, M. 2020. 'Coronavirus Outbreak: Kolkata Kids Make Boring Face Masks Fashionable with Glitter, Crystal Stones'. *India Today*, 13 April. Available at https://www.indiatoday.in/trending-news/story/coronavirus-outbreak-kolkata-kids-make-boring-face-masks-fashionable-with-glitter-crystal-stones-1666392-2020-04-13 (accessed on 15 April 2020).

Majid, Z. 2020. 'Jammu and Kashmir Students Unable to Attend Online Classes due to Slow Internet Speed'. *Deccan Herald*, 1 April. Available at https://www.deccanherald.com/national/north-and-central/jammu-and-kashmir-students-unable-to-attend-online-classes-due-to-slow-internet-speed-819947.html (accessed on 20 May 2020).

Maqbool, M. 2019. 'Children of Kashmir: Away from Schools, Disconnected from Friends'. The Wire, 1 October. Available at https://thewire.in/rights/children-of-kashmir-away-from-schools-disconnected-from-friends (accessed on 20 May 2020).

———. 2020. 'In Kashmir, Why Students Are Children of a Lesser God'. *The Telegraph*, 6 April. Available at https://www.telegraphindia.com/india/coronavirus-restrictions-on-high-speed-mobile-internet-services-in-jammu-and-kashmir/cid/1762615 (accessed on 24 April 2020).

McCombs, M., and D. Shaw. 1972. 'The Agenda-Setting Function of Mass Media'. *The Public Opinion Quarterly* 36(2): 176–87.

Mir, T. 2020. 'India is Using the Pandemic to Intensify Its Crackdown in Kashmir'. *The Washington Post*, 30 April. Available at https://www.washingtonpost.com/opinions/2020/04/30/india-is-using-pandemic-intensify-its-crackdown-kashmir/ (accessed on 30 April 2020).

Mishra, S. 2020. 'Children of Protests: Resistance Will Make Them Inclusive Citizens'. The Quint, 18 January. Available at https://www.thequint.com/voices/opinion/children-at-caa-protests-being-shaped-by-resistance-or-used-for-gain (accessed on 8 April 2020).

Mumbai Mirror. 2020. 'Report: Uttar Pradesh Police Violated Norms of National and International Laws'. 4 March. Available at https://mumbaimirror.indiatimes.com/mumbai/other/report-uttar-pradesh-police-violated-norms-of-national-and-international-laws/articleshow/74482783.cms (accessed on 24 April 2020).

Nagaraj, A. 2020. 'Death of 12-Year-Old Indian Farm Worker Spurs Child Labour Probe'. Reuters, 21 April. Available at https://www.reuters.com/article/us-health-coronavirus-india-workers-trfn/death-of-12-year-old-indian-farm-worker-spurs-child-labour-probe-idUSKCN2231OQ (accessed on 24 April 2020).

News18. 2020. 'Demand for Child Pornography in India Spiked Since Coronavirus Lockdown: ICPF'. 13 April. Available at https://www.news18.com/news/india/demand-for-child-pornography-in-india-spiked-since-coronavirus-lockdown-icpf-2576017.html (accessed on 15 April 2020).

Nolas, S. 2015. 'Children's Participation, Childhood Publics and Social Change: A Review'. *Children and Society* 29(2): 157–67.

Ojha, M. K. 2020. 'Parents Engage Children in Creative Pursuits'. *The Telegraph*, 19 April. Available at https://www.telegraphindia.com/states/north-east/coronavirus-lockdown-parents-engage-children-in-creative-pursuits-in-assam/cid/1766321 (accessed on 24 April 2020).

Outlook India. 2020. 'Lockdown: 3,000 Kota Students Leave For UP in Govt Buses; 7,000 Wait for Their Turn'. 18 April. Available at https://www.outlookindia.com/website/story/india-news-lockdown-3000-kota-students-leave-for-up-in-govt-buses-7000-wait-for-their-turn/351005 (accessed on 24 April 2020).

Pandey, G. 2020. 'Coronavirus: The Children Struggling to Survive India's Lockdown'. BBC News, 11 April. Available at https://www.bbc.com/news/world-asia-india-52210888 (accessed on 12 April 2020).

Pandit, A. 2020. 'ICPF Report Warns of Sharp Rise in Demand for Online Child Pornography During Lockdown'. *The Times of India*, 14 April. Available at https://timesofindia.indiatimes.com/india/icpf-report-warns-of-sharp-rise-in-demand-for-online-child-pornography-during-lockdown/articleshow/75127399.cms (accessed on 24 April 2020).

Parmar, R. 2020. 'Maharashtra Teen Invents Wristband from Scrap to Keep Coronavirus At Bay; Proposal Sent to PM Modi, ICMR'. *Hindustan Times*, 25 April. Available at https://www.hindustantimes.com/india-news/maharashtra-teen-invents-wristband-from-scrap-to-keep-coronavirus-at-bay-proposal-sent-to-pm-modi-icmr/story-wHSRBbHMVZI8McZNSWVioL.html (accessed on 30 April 2020).

Pinto, N. 2020. 'Seditious School Play: Police Question 60 Students, Ask If School Spreading False Info on CAA, NRC'. *India Today*, 2 February. Available at https://www.indiatoday.in/india/story/seditious-school-play-police-question-60-students-bidar-karnataka-1642512-2020-02-02 (accessed on 24 April 2020).

Quraishi, H. 2020. 'Madrasa Children an Easy Target of the Communal Virus in Times of Corona'. *National Herald*, 16 April. Available at https://www.nationalheraldindia.com/opinion/madrasa-children-an-easy-target-of-the-communal-virus-in-times-of-corona (accessed on 20 April 2020).

Roshangar, R. 2018. 'Children Caught in Conflict: Kashmir's Untold Story'. *India Today*, 4 September. Available at https://www.indiatoday.in/india/story/children-caught-in-conflict-kashmir-s-untold-story-1331194-2018-09-04 (accessed on 19 April 2020).

Sengupta, A. 2020. '"She Only Says One Word—Home": How Delhi Riots Have Left Children with Scarred Minds and an Uncertain Future'. News18, 13 March. Available at https://www.news18.com/news/india/she-only-says-one-word-home-how-the-delhi-riots-have-left-children-with-scarred-minds-and-a-scary-future-2535421.html (accessed on 12 April 2020).

Sethi, A. 2019. 'CAA: UP Police Tortured Children Swept Up In Citizenship Law Protests'. HuffPost India, 24 December. Available at https://www.huffingtonpost.in/entry/caa-uttar-pradesh-police-tortured-children_in_5e0207b5e4b05b08babab722 (accessed on 25 April 2020).

Shakil, S. 2020. '"Papa Ke Paas Le Chalo": The Numbing Angst of Kids Who Lost Their Fathers in Delhi Riots'. *The New Indian Express*, 1 March. Available at https://www.newindianexpress.com/thesundaystandard/2020/mar/01/papa-ke-paas-le-chalo-the-numbing-angst-of-kids-who-lost-their-fathers-in-delhi-riots-2110675.html (accessed on 12 April 2020).

Shali, P. 2020. 'Delhi Riots: 8-Year-Old Girl Attacked with Acid, Mother Wonders If Her Child Will Fully Recover'. *India Today*, 6 March.

Available at https://www.indiatoday.in/india/story/delhi-riots-violence-northeast-shiv-vihar-gokulpur-acid-girl-trauma-1653190-2020-03-06 (accessed on 12 April 2020).

Sharma, N. C. 2020. 'Corona Impact: Free Lunch Scheme for School Children Goes Off the Menu'. *Mint*, 1 April. Available at https://www.livemint.com/news/india/corona-impact-free-lunch-scheme-for-school-children-goes-off-the-menu-11585682505885.html (accessed on 11 April 2020).

Shrangi, V. 2020. 'North-East Delhi Riot-Hit Children Get Help to Overcome Trauma'. *Hindustan Times*, 5 March. Available at https://www.hindustantimes.com/delhi-news/north-east-delhi-riot-hit-children-get-help-to-overcome-trauma/story-xtocMJagHfWvHBkJJoEZ0N.html (accessed on 12 April 2020).

Shreyas, H. S. 2020. 'Bidar Cops Interrogate 85 School Kids 5 Times over 9 Days for "Anti-CAA Play"'. *The Times of India*, 6 February. Available at https://timesofindia.indiatimes.com/india/bidar-cops-interrogate-85-school-kids-5-times-over-9-days-for-anti-caa-play/articleshow/73977593.cms (accessed on 24 April 2020).

Sidharth, A. 2018. 'Amidst Human Tragedy, Fake Pictures of Syrian Conflict Flood Social Media'. ALT News, 9 March. Available at https://www.altnews.in/amidst-human-tragedy-fake-pictures-of-syrian-conflict-flood-social-media/ (accessed on 30 April 2020).

Sirur, S. 2020. 'Delhi Teens Invent Robot to Help Medical Workers & Covid-19 Patients Reduce Contact'. *The Print*, 5 April. Available at https://theprint.in/tech/delhi-teens-invent-robot-to-help-medical-workers-covid-19-patients-reduce-contact/395736/ (accessed on 10 April 2020).

Suresh, N., and S. Ali. 2020. 'UP Police Detained 41 Children During CAA Protests, Some Were Tortured, Says Citizens' Report'. Scroll, 13 February. Available at https://scroll.in/article/952964/up-police-detained-41-children-during-caa-protests-some-were-tortured-says-citizens-report (accessed on 25 April 2020).

Tewari, C. 2020. 'Anatomy of an "Investigation": How India Today's Madrasa Sting Misled Its Viewers'. *Newslaundry*, 15 April. Available at https://www.newslaundry.com/2020/04/15/anatomy-of-an-investigation-how-india-todays-madrasa-sting-misled-its-viewers (accessed on 19 April 2020).

The Hindu. 2020. 'Coronavirus Lockdown | Govt. Helpline Receives 92,000 Calls on Child Abuse and Violence in 11 Days'. 8 April. Available at https://www.thehindu.com/news/national/coronavirus-lockdown-govt-helpline-receives-92000-calls-on-child-abuse-and-violence-in-11-days/article31287468.ece (accessed on 24 April 2020).

The Indian Express. 2020. 'Rajkot: School Gets Students to Form "CAA" Human Chain'. 2020. 11 January. Available at https://indianexpress.com/article/cities/rajkot/rajkot-school-gets-students-to-form-citizenship-amendment-act-caa-human-chain6210558/ (accessed on 10 April 2020).

The Logical Indian. 2020. 'Police Interrogate Bidar School Students for Fifth Time After Arresting Headmistress, Parent for Anti-CAA Play'. 4 February. Available at https://thelogicalindian.com/exclusive/bidar-school-students-19597 (accessed on 24 April 2020).

The Times of India. 2020a. 'Gujarat: Schools Enlisted in BJP's CAA Drive, Write Postcards to PM'. 3 January. Available at https://timesofindia.indiatimes.com/city/ahmedabad/gujarat-schools-enlisted-in-bjps-caa-drive-write-postcards-to-pm/articleshow/73080497.cms (accessed on 10 April 2020).

———. 2020b. 'UP Government Sends 250 Buses to Rajasthan's Kota to Bring 7500 Students Back Home'. 17 April. Available at https://timesofindia.indiatimes.com/india/up-government-sends-250-buses-to-rajasthans-kota-to-bring-7500-students-back-home/articleshow/75205145.cms (accessed on 24 April 2020).

The Week. 2020. 'BSP Welcomes UP Govt's Decision to Bring Back Students from Kota, Seeks Help for Stranded Labourers'. 18 April. Available at https://www.theweek.in/wire-updates/national/2020/04/18/des15-up-students-mayawati.amp.html (accessed on 24 April 2020).

The Wire. 2020a. 'Bidar Police Question School Children for Fourth Time on "Seditious" Play on CAA'. 4 February. Available at https://thewire.in/rights/bidar-karnataka-school-play-caa-sedition-police (accessed on 24 April 2020).

———. 2020b. 'UP Police Brutalised Minors During Anti-CAA Protests Crackdown: Fact-Finding Team'. 14 February. Available at https://thewire.in/rights/up-police-minors-protests (accessed on 25 April 2020).

UNICEF. (n.d.). 'Principles and Guidelines for Media Reporting on Children'. Available at https://www.unicef.org/eca/media/ethical-guidelines (accessed on 15 April 2020).

Verma, G. 2020. '12-Year-Old Walks 100 km, Dies Just Short of Bijapur Home'. *The Indian Express*, 21 April. Available at https://indianexpress.com/article/india/12-yr-old-walks-100-km-dies-just-short-of-bijapur-home-6371779/lite/?__twitter_impression=true (accessed on 24 April 2020).

Wallen, J. 2019. 'Kashmir: How Conflict and Stigma Are Creating a Mental Health Crisis'. *The Telegraph*, 16 May. Available at https://www.telegraph.co.uk/global-health/climate-and-people/kashmir-conflict-stigma-creating-mental-heath-crisis/ (accessed on 26 April 2020).

Worldometer. (n.d.). 'India: Coronavirus Cases'. Available at https://www.worldometers.info/coronavirus/country/india/ (accessed on 20 May 2020).

Yadav, A. 2020. 'India: Hunger and Uncertainty Under Delhi's Coronavirus Lockdown'. Al Jazeera, 19 April. Available at https://www.aljazeera.com/news/2020/04/india-hunger-uncertainty-delhi-coronavirus-lockdown-200418095253032.html (accessed on 24 April 2020).

PART III

INTERACTIONS

6

TO BE OR NOT TO BE...WITH TECHNOLOGY

Kamala Mukunda

I work in a semi-residential school outside Bengaluru, India. Our senior school students, who are 15–18 years of age, stay on campus from Monday through Friday, returning home on the weekends. The school policy is that students must not bring their smartphones to campus. Whenever they need to make or receive a call, they use a teacher's phone or the one in the office. These are young people who (with very few exceptions) own individual smartphones, and use them freely on weekends and holidays. On Monday morning, they leave their devices behind and step into the school bus for a five-day, Internet-free school week. What reasons do we adults have for this policy, and how does our thinking fit into current analyses regarding smartphones in school? In this essay I explore these questions, touching upon some of the wider debates surrounding smartphones in schools. I will also share the thoughts and feelings of students, alumni and teachers regarding the 'ban', quoting extensively from focus group conversations and email interviews with 35–40 individuals.

Ours is not an unusual policy. In several schools across the world, students are disallowed the use of their personal phones for significant periods of time. Age makes a difference, with most bans extending till age 12 or 15 years at the oldest. At one end, the French government in September 2018 banned students 15 years old and below from bringing their smartphones to school (Rubin and Peltier 2018). The UK government (as covered in *The Guardian* 2018) responded to this by saying that while they would not follow suit, they strongly recommend that schools themselves institute smartphone bans. Several schools in Canada and the US have put such bans in place. Here in India, the Central Board of Secondary Education (CBSE) sent out a circular recommending that schools restrict student use of mobile phones during the day, because these can be 'a serious cause of distraction, lack of concentration, anxiety, fear and sometimes even misuse' (2009: 1). Several prominent Indian city schools require students to hand over their phones when they arrive at school in the morning, and return them in the evening (students need their phones for the commute home or to coaching class). The wave of bans has not spared college campuses worldwide, and this in itself is a curious phenomenon. After all, mobile phones are a normal part of daily life for adults, and 18 years is the age of majority in most countries. All this is in contrast to the general excitement that prevailed when such devices first became available not so long ago, and some campuses encouraged use of Internet-connected devices in classes, even going to the extent of subsidising or outright supplying them. Numerous articles in popular and peer-reviewed publications have been written pointing out how the new technologies can revolutionise classroom learning (see Roschelle et al. 2000; Zhu et al. 2011).

The alternative to bans at the state or school level has been to give that authority to individuals: students, teachers, parents. Even those who agree that there is a problem with smartphones in classrooms might prefer that the responsibility for safe use lie with teachers rather than any higher authority. Some 'friendly' and creative strategies include giving control to the teacher to turn off and on the Internet connectivity of students' smartphones (using services like Xerofone); and a so-called 'Stoplight' policy whereby teachers use red and green stickers to indicate to students whether their phones can be on in particular classes or not. Many teachers ask students to put their phones in a box near the door. In all these situations, students are typically permitted to use their phones during breaks have internalised the reasons for it. I will present an explanation of what we believe are the benefits of senior students being away from their phones for long periods of time, and an analysis of how our curriculum supports this decision in meaningful ways. I believe that within such a curriculum, and with the space for dialogue and mutual understanding, we can go beyond merely banning to learning how to relate with digital devices in healthy ways.

Both in research literature, and in most popular debates, the most obvious concerns regarding students holding on to their phones while in the classroom have to do with learning and achievement losses. Several studies have shown that significant though small test performance gains do indeed occur when students are not permitted to use smartphones in class. These gains are the most for low-achieving students, as Beland and Murphy (2015) found when they calculated the exam-score impact of mobile phone bans in a large number of schools in England. They advise: 'Given heterogeneous results, banning mobile phones could be a low-cost way for schools to reduce educational inequality' (ibid.: 17–18).' Other research has shown that learning is disrupted when students are distracted by apps, notifications or other possibilities on their phones, while supposedly listening to a lecture or discussion (see Sana et al. 2013). And in one much-quoted study published in 2017, the mere presence of a student's smartphone in the pocket or in the room, even though switched to 'silent', reduced working memory and performance on an intelligence test (Ward et al. 2017).

In what appears like a direct contradiction, some scholars note that smartphones can enhance learning within the classroom (Graham 2017). Typically, the benefits of technology in the classroom are the result of a creative, deliberate interweaving of digital experiences with the curriculum (see Ruthven et al. [2004], who describe six such projects in good detail). The teachers in Ruthven et al.'s study were unusually committed to making the Internet-related projects work for better student learning, and this points to an important generalisation: unless teachers and students are ready for a continual, high level of creative engagement with digital technology in the classroom, learning will not improve. Ultimately, the quality of learning that a computer or a phone can make possible depends on the teacher's ingenuity. In the case of a computer in the classroom, the worst that can happen is that it is used unimaginatively, or remains unused in a corner of the classroom. In the case of smartphones in the classroom, however, the 'worst' that can happen is that screens are regularly turned to shopping, chatting and gaming sites. True, most schools that take the BYOD approach have rules and norms in place that are intended to help students use their devices responsibly (Pavan 2014). But without a conscious, nurturing environment that actively engages students' minds emotionally and cognitively, there is bound to be some degree of breaking of the rules.

We have looked so far only at the potential harm or benefit of a smartphone to academic learning in the classroom. Now this kind of learning is only one part of an education defined more broadly. The traditional, rather narrow, purpose of education is to train young people in the knowledge and skills necessary to find a career and fit into society. But there is also a long tradition of alternative, progressive streams of education, both in India and abroad. In these philosophies, education is conceived of as something beyond academic learning alone. How might such a school view the issue of students using smartphones? The Steiner schools tend to have a strong philosophy against technology use in schools, and the Waldorf school in Silicon Valley in California, for example, has hit the news several times for the fact that several of the industry's employees send their children there (Richtel 2011; Waldorf School 2019). The belief in these schools is that digital devices discourage imagination, physical activity and social interaction, all of which are tremendously important for growing up intelligently.

Our School's Philosophy

Our school also has a broader educational intent, and we do share some of the above reasons for our smartphone ban. But there is more to it, as I will attempt to clarify. Our educational philosophy stems from a collective interest among the teachers in the work of the late philosopher-educator J. Krishnamurti. Krishnamurti founded several schools in India and two abroad, and spoke and wrote extensively on a vision of education as a way to fundamentally regenerate society. Social transformation, he said, begins with individuals who see the danger (and ultimate meaninglessness) of self-centred thought and action, bound by tradition, conformity and fear. He repeatedly pointed out that the suffering and destruction of the world is a reflection of conflict and divisiveness within the individual. To deeply understand oneself, therefore, is essential to changing the world.

For example, can we become aware of the mind's obsessive, habitual patterns of thinking and feeling? We can see that these lead to a dulling of the senses; we feel the difference in the quality of the mind when our senses are alive, taking in the world without the constant chatter of interpretation, comparison, judgement. Krishnamurti believed that alertness and sensitivity are qualities of the mind that schools can nurture in children, as well as in adults. We can together learn what it is to watch the movement of thought and feeling in the mind, be aware of it in the same silent way as we look at a landscape.

> ...it seems to me that the very essence of freedom lies in understanding the whole mechanism of habit, both conscious and unconscious. It is not a question of ending habit, but of seeing totally the structure of habit. You have to observe how habits are formed and how, by denying or resisting one habit, another habit is created. What matters is to be totally conscious of habit; for then, as you will see for yourself there is no longer the formation of habit. To resist habit, to fight it, to deny it, only gives continuity to habit... A mind that is attentive from moment to moment—attentive to what it is saying, attentive to the movement of its hands, of its thoughts, of its feelings—will discover that the formation of further habits has come to an end (Krishnamurti 1995: 164).

Krishnamurti did not lay down clear prescriptions or specific recommendations for teachers and school administrators to follow. He was also very insistent that he not be made an authority of any kind on matters of education or, indeed, how to live one's daily life.

Therefore, our decisions regarding curricula, practices and norms at school can only arise from a personal interest in the questions that he raised about learning. Since each adult at school inevitably makes his or her own interpretation and has a subjective understanding of Krishnamurti's questions, it is only through continuous dialogue among the teachers that a common understanding can evolve.

Krishnamurti died in 1986, so there was no way he could have had anything to say about smartphones in school. But he did explore, in great depth, the nature of the mind and phenomena such as thought, desire, attention, boredom and restlessness. A little quiet observation reveals that the mind is constantly chattering with thoughts and feelings, and there is very little ability to remain quietly unoccupied in the present. The mind is always reaching for distraction, if not from the outside, then from internal fantasies, repetitive memories and future imaginings. Personal devices have tapped precisely into the human psyche's Achilles' heel—with detrimental results. Krishnamurti has suggested that the tendency of the mind to move away from the here and now has both personal and global consequences. Interestingly, modern psychological theory suggests that psychological well-being is increased when we are mentally present to the tasks we are engaged in (Killingsworth and Gilbert 2010; Twenge 2017). If a school is interested in the well-being of its students and teachers, surely it will carefully consider its approach to smartphone use.

Life in a semi-residential school community such as ours rests on the quality of attention that each of us can bring to the present moment. Whether we are cleaning plates, playing games or just being with and listening to each other, attending to our surroundings is crucial to creating a culture of care in school. We are interested in a sense of order that comes from within, instead of imposing external discipline with its rewards and punishments. Simple awareness of one's motivations and actions, without condemnation or justification, can bring about this order. We are exploring what it means to 'be present' to one's surroundings, not as a tiresome task, but as an effortless state of attention. Finally, nurturing our relationship with the natural world is a large part of our curriculum. Here too, we have seen that attention to natural surroundings—the blue of the sky, the neem tree flowering, the tiny ferns under the rocks—is a large part of our intimate affection for plant and animal life. We teachers are very aware of the attentional costs of phones on ourselves. We have not placed a school-wide ban on the adults, but as individuals we are watchful about our use and restrict it to certain times of the day.

Given all this, our greatest concern with smartphones is not that attention will be compromised in class, but that the quality of attention in daily life will be seriously depleted. Attention to the moment (often called mindfulness) is central to our curriculum, not only because it smoothes the way through a school day, but also because we see 'simple awareness' to be the key to personal and therefore social transformation. Everything else we do to address life's challenges, whether it be planning, rational thinking or problem solving, rests on our ability to be attentive in the moment.

One could rightly argue, of course, that there is nothing new about the human inability to remain mindfully in the present—the roots of this probably go very far back in evolutionary time. Krishnamurti has pointed out that thought itself does the job of taking us away from the present very well. Whenever it finds itself without anything to 'do', the mind goes off into imagination, rumination and planning—this is easily observable. The personal smartphone has become a sort of substitute for internal preoccupation. And it is merely the latest in a long line of external preoccupations—such as television, radio, even books—that help us escape into other worlds. A more media-centric approach to the role of digital technology in our lives might celebrate the opportunities for immersion and absorption that various media offer. It may even be seen as a neat 'solution' to the problems of restlessness, boredom and loneliness. Either way, there is nothing particularly pernicious about the personal smartphone.

Or is there? Actually, if one were to design an object that closely fuels and feeds off human vulnerabilities, it would look remarkably like a smartphone loaded with apps. Psychologist Dan Levitin (2015) is one of the growing number of scientists who are concerned about the effects of a smartphone culture on the brain. He describes the harmful effects of several related features such as multitasking, frequent checking and notifications. When our brain is constantly switching between activities, there are metabolic costs. Repeated decision-making and adjustment to new tasks depletes our capacity for impulse control, and creates a constant, low-level stress which maintains a level of corticosteroids in the brain that is physically and mentally unhealthy. Meanwhile, centres in the brain that respond to anticipated rewards and seek novelty (both evolutionarily adaptive behaviours) are kept in a state of constant activation. Messages and updates are always available, and each time one is accessed, the brain registers the pleasure. Notifications and 'likes' trigger the dopamine circuits, making the brain expect rewards always just around the corner. Eventually, it falls into what Levitin calls a 'dopamine addiction feedback loop'. He writes, 'Make no mistake: email-, Facebook- and Twitter-checking constitute a neural addiction.'

This last point has been picked up by several voices in society, and some media and mental health centres even explicitly use the term 'internet addiction' (Rao 2018). Now the very word 'addiction' raises spectres of drugs and alcohol, and no school would encourage students to experiment with either of these, on or off the school premises. It is also well-documented that adolescent brains, whose motivational and impulse-control circuits are still developing and very sensitive to external stimulation, are more susceptible to addictive inputs than either younger children or adults (Crews et al. 2007; Chambers et al. 2003). We have to exercise caution in any conclusions we draw, however. The literature has studied alcohol and drug use, not smartphones—although this will be an important area for future research. Further, the most recent versions of mental health manuals used by thousands of psychiatrists and psychologists worldwide—the fifth edition of the *Diagnostic and Statistical Manual of Mental Disorders* (American Psychiatric Association 2013) and the ICD-11(World Health Organization 2018)—do not list Internet addiction as a syndrome (although the ICD does include the condition gaming disorder). There is as yet no consensus among psychologists and psychiatrists on the question of whether spending too much time on your phone can be considered a clinical obsession (see Ryding and Kaye 2018).

If we believe that obsessive use of smartphones does not amount to a clinical addiction, might we be less concerned about allowing students to bring and use them in school? It would certainly not be the first time we at school have seen students obsessively engaged with something or other, from paper planes to Rubik's cubes. Most discussions of the issue compare phones with other sources of learning in students' lives such as textbooks and teachers' lectures, which completely misses an important point: we might learn more by comparing them with other toys or games that young people engage with. At our school, for example, we notice that students repeatedly go through phases of intense involvement with some toy or game, and unless we actively intervene, in a few weeks the craze has passed. Soon enough, another one emerges—wooden tops, hopscotch, cricket cards, football, fidget-spinners—the list goes on. Almost everything on this list involves a fair amount of informal, spontaneous social interaction, and often across age groups. There is a great deal of innocuous fun involved, even though we adults sometimes wonder if there is something unhealthy about the period of obsessive engagement. Very importantly, each activity seems to have its own limited life, dying out as mysteriously as it arose.

But smartphones are a very different kind of toy. Here, the obsessive engagement is likely to be solitary and, from all indications, may never die out. And there is nothing accidental about this fact. Large numbers of professionals are being paid handsome salaries to figure out exactly how to keep us increasingly attached to our smartphones. These professionals have access to more data about each and every Internet user than we can even imagine, as well as a very good understanding of human psychology, both adult and child. Two people have written and spoken a great deal about this fact: Tristan Harris, the founder of the Center for Humane Technology, and James Steyer, the founder of Common Sense Media. Both Harris (2019) and Steyer (Common Sense Media 2016) are advocates of the well-being of adults and children in this age of the personal, Internet-connected device. Harris believes that the industry can be made accountable for the widespread impact of inventions on all users, and particularly young people. This impact is felt primarily in the way attention is being manipulated by programmers whose sole aim is to keep our eyes glued to their screens (as opposed to rival screens). Quite possibly, nobody set out to draw young people away from the outdoors or face-to-face interactions; it is in competing with each other for the users' attention that this runaway situation has emerged.

Other scholars have also expressed concern regarding the psychological impact of hours of smartphone use by young people, citing rising rates of depression and even suicide among teenagers coinciding with the increase in the percentage of teenagers owning such a device (Twenge 2017). There is always a counter-voice, however, and Twenge's conclusions in particular have potential problems, such as mistaking correlation for causation. A large body of researchers—for example, Sonia Livingstone (2008) and danah boyd (2014)—conducts ethnographic studies into the lives of digitally connected teenagers, revealing a complex and often intelligent engagement with the media. For teenagers, 'hanging out' has always been more fun in public spaces than either at home or school under adult supervision. In recent years, however, safe public spaces are increasingly unavailable, and technology has provided a way to meet up with friends in 'networked publics'—a term used to describe the interconnecting presence on several social media platforms. From this point of view, technology per se is not a problem. Of course, it is not all light and happy—there is distress too. But boyd (2014: 212) cautions adults not to get into an unnecessary state of panic about this: 'Not all youth are doing all right, just as not all adults are. Technology makes the struggles youth face visible, but it neither creates nor prevents harmful things from happening even if it can be a tool for both.'

The substantial and rigorous body of work of these scholars casts the time that young people spend on their smartphones as perfectly normal, sometimes even desirable. This gives me pause as a teacher: am I doing the right thing by separating my students from their smartphones for long periods of time? It is indeed true that 15- to 18-year-olds' preoccupation with social status, identity, reputation and peer popularity is seen as normal for this age group. The problem with seeing things as 'normal', however, is that their inevitability can never be questioned. At our school, we see that emotional knots emanate from a strong sense of a self separate from other selves, and this is something that does not really go away with age. Adults also struggle with social status and identity; we, too, worry about what others think of us, and these have become deeply habitual patterns of thought. These insecurities fuel our actions down paths that are harmful to us and to the world around us. Can our education question the inevitability of all this, and can we explore the possibility of living without the conflict that such insecurity brings?

One could, of course, argue that smartphones are an inevitable part of our students' lives, and that our educational questions about identity, self and insecurity can well be examined without banning them in school. Our view is different, as I will attempt to explain here. In principle, protection is a necessary aspect of caring for the young. The idea of creating a controlled environment in the interests of a child's safety and security is acceptable to almost anyone: differences appear only in our ideas about what age is old enough for certain controls to be relaxed. At our school, the adults manage aspects of the environment—course material, food in the kitchen, time tables, curriculum. We do this in much the same way that parents give thought to selecting what their children read, eat and do in their leisure time. Livingstone (2008) herself acknowledges that the risks of going online for teenagers call for certain public policy measures, such as improved site design, Internet literacy and parental guidance. And as we have seen, Tristan Harris speaks eloquently of the possibility of a more ethical industry (Bosker 2016). As a teacher and an adult more directly responsible for my students' well-being, however, I cannot wait for public policy or industry to wake up. So it makes no sense to me to put a smartphone in my student's hand and say, 'Use it sensibly.'

While we teachers see ourselves as rational decision-makers, senior students in particular might experience a controlled school environment as a taking-away of their autonomy. Understanding this very real possibility, we have made sure that we are in constant communication with our senior students about school norms and practices. We have many forums in which adults and young people sit together in conversation, sharing their worries and frustrations, listening to each other and acknowledging feelings. Even so, students sometimes report feelings of rebellion and resentment. I was, therefore, very interested to know what our 15- to 18-year-olds think and feel about the smartphone ban in their own school lives.

The idea also came to me from reading two well-known surveys of students' impressions of the digital gap between school and life, both conducted some years ago. In 2002, the Pew Internet and American Life Project published a report of over 300 students' feelings about the increasing sense of disconnect they were feeling between their own digital-rich lives on the one hand, and what they experienced at school which had outdated policies about the Internet, on the other (Levin and Arafeh 2002). Many were quoted as feeling frustrated about not being able to access the Internet while at school, but the reasons given were all to do with schoolwork and homework. Students who were accustomed to using the Internet as their virtual library, tutor as well as study group expressed their dissatisfaction with their schools' Internet policies and inabilities to provide them with what, to them, had become an essential part of their learning lives. One high-school boy is quoted as saying: 'It is my education. I get all my information off the Internet. I don't even look at books anymore' (ibid.: 4). A few years later, a similar research project was conducted in the UK (Selwyn 2006). In this report, while students did express dissatisfaction with the lack of Internet access in schools, they appeared to be more philosophically accepting of the situation. As Selwyn explains, students in his survey tended to see Internet restriction as just another thing that schools control, like what students wear or the language they use.

Method and Findings

I arranged for focus group discussions with two small groups of six to seven senior students each—nearly all of whom own a personal smartphone—together with a neutral adult. I provided the adult with a few suggested questions (given in italics below). The sessions were transcribed, and I have selected the following responses that were representative of the overall spirit of the discussion.

How do you feel about not having your phone in school?

> It's actually quite nice that we don't have it here, 'cause we end up talking to each other a lot.
> I used to miss it, but now I don't miss it so much…most of it was unnecessary chat anyway.
> It's not unbearable, I don't think about it that much, and it's fun being here.
> Mostly on my list of hangouts it's people from school! So it's kind of pointless.
> Monday mornings I miss it maybe a little bit.

What do you believe to be the reason behind the school's norm?

> It's a distraction, from the outside world.
> It's like a space, you just get into this tiny little square…
> It's a bit annoying when people are on their phones all the time, here we are used to conversation, chatting, dialogue, even taking a walk.
> We have a lot of informal time here, to catch up, chat, hang out, be outdoors, play sports…
> Also there's no need for it, it's not like it's a skill, it's not like something you have to learn in any way…unless you're going to be using, like, a programme.

What would school be like if you did have your phones with you?

> It would be quite destructive I guess, people would use it a lot, it would defeat the purpose of such a place.
> We would talk to each other less, I feel we would lose the informal interactions.
> We would start sending each other videos and stuff…it would become a large part of our culture.
> In hindsight I feel this is so much better. Because on the weekends I get so distracted by my phone. Even if one message comes, you go to see it, you spend half an hour or something! So even though I kind of miss it I feel it's so much better here.
> We seem happy without it, but if we had it in school we would use it, we wouldn't then say, oh we're happy without it!

So why are we so drawn to it then, if we prefer time without it?

> It's the fact that if at that moment you want to, you will pick it up and use it. If it was in school and we were told not to use it, it would be so much harder than not having it at all.
> Endless entertainment, you feel it will satisfy you but it never does...

It was not surprising to me that the students stated no resentment at the no-smartphone policy at school, but the level of conviction and agreement with the spirit behind the policy was unexpected. I did not expect, for example, that they would say they prefer the policy to stay in place. Thus, I was curious to see if alumni of the school would have a different perspective on the matter. I was also interested to see if they would articulate a more sophisticated analysis. I reached out to recent alumni of the school who are now in college, and who were willing to consider the technology issue thoughtfully, receiving responses from 15 of them. They use their smartphones fairly extensively now, while still remembering what it was like not to have one for long stretches of time. I asked them how they see the school policy in hindsight, and how they would describe their own lives as having changed significantly now that their phones are almost always with them. These responses were sent in by email, and samples are therefore reproduced word-for-word below. As you will see, they all acknowledge the importance of having a smartphone at this point in their lives, and for very good reasons. However, looking back they feel two things: a sense of being 'free' in some indefinable way, and a feeling of gratitude that they went through such a time.

> I have recently been very appreciative of having constant internet access. Firstly most of the academic work we do in college requires us to look up on the internet for specific papers. Other than that, due to internet access I feel I can do a wide variety of things. I use internet in my phone for doing exercise, for reading news, for watching movies, for keeping accounts and even for meditation! I feel it can be very helpful :)
>
> When I think about school, I never remember feeling the lack of not having access to internet. Most of our work did not require us to use the internet. Also we had structured time slots to do

exercise, there was quiet time, we had movie sessions. We were also constantly around friends and teachers and on weekends we went home. In college, people are more independent and I feel isolated at times, so I feel the need to keep in touch with others through WhatsApp or other social media.

What has been worrying me a bit is that, at times when I have to wait for a bus or wait for somebody, I feel lost and agitated if I don't have my phone and I have to just wait and sit quietly thinking to myself. This is because if there is nothing else to do, I am so used to doing something on the phone. I don't remember feeling like this when I was in school.

[My college] functions on the assumption that you have a phone, that you are accessible at all hours of the day, and on all days of every week. Now I am very much a part of the system but it has always been difficult to shake off mild irritation at being expected to be 'on' and 'available' all the time.

I don't think phones should be allowed in school. I'm really happy they were not. Though in a different way from [college], life at [our school] also needs everyone in the community to be present most of the time. Not every minute, but you need to be paying attention. In the context of school, I feel they would be counterproductive.

One of the few times that not having access to the internet and my phone has bothered me is when old friends complain that I don't keep in touch with them. And I agree that it is hard to stay in touch and somehow constantly texting a person has become equivalent to being the best of friends with them. So perhaps, I may have lost a few old friends since I didn't chat with them on some social platform often.

However, reflecting on my life as of now, sometimes I feel the relationship with the internet in those three years was better than what I have right now. Out of school, I have access to the internet all the time and this has resulted in a funny change of behaviour. Now, some days it gets to a point where if I don't see any new notifications from my friends, it results in all kinds of weird emotions like 'oh I don't have any friends'. Lack of notifications brings out a different kind of loneliness which I hadn't experienced before. My insecurity about relationships with people increases

> through texting, and is becoming linked to how often we text each other.
>
> My time at [school], where i was able to have a gadget or internet free environment helped me a lot. And i realised that only after i came to the 'outside world'. Although i use the technology now i don't feel the continuous urge to keep checking social networking sites or chat messages. i am easily able to forget and disconnect them and in fact using them too many times is a hindrance!!
>
> During senior school, we all had a well planned time table and even in the free time, we got to engage in different activities. Being disconnected with the virtual world helped us to explore ourselves, understand, be curious and question oneself. Being aware, attentive and conscious of oneself has made me a better person.
>
> In the senior school not having access to many kinds of media was not really on our minds as there were classes and other things to keep us occupied. It wasn't something that I felt I needed and wasn't bored by the lack of it either. Having access in the weekends didn't lead to binging either. Any spare time we had on our hands in school we would spend on activities or sometimes just sitting about idly in the rooms and talking, often with some food to accompany it. I think being away from media during the senior school has prevented a strong dependence on digital media being built. Though I do use it to a fair extent, its absence hasn't made me feel restless or anything—well not most of the time at least.
>
> While I liked being aware of current affairs, I equally enjoyed being unreachable and offline. It was a relief going to school and not having to constantly be in touch with the world digitally. Thus, I recognised that my week in school was more wholesome.

These alumni were, of course, a self-selected sample of those who took the trouble to reply to my queries. As with all such biased samples, it is possible that those who feel differently did not respond. Finally, I spoke with a few colleagues at school to better understand our reasons for discomfort with senior students carrying their phones to school. The questions I raised with them were more searching, and I took the role of a 'devil's advocate'. Inevitably, our senior students will leave school at 18 years and enter a world where they can use their phones almost whenever they want. Do we believe that at that age they will become more digitally literate, responsible users, and if so, why not earlier? Or should they learn digital literacy and responsible use while still under our care—and how can this happen if we disallow them the use of phones during their school week? I also shared the gist of research that puts a more positive spin on media use among youth, and that, for example, we should not be quick to assume the concomitant decline of face-to-face interactions. Should any of this cause us to rethink our smartphone policy?

Responses to these questions revealed several clear lines of thinking, which I summarise here. Eighteen-year-olds aside, perhaps no age is 'mature enough' to easily self-regulate their use of a smartphone. Therefore, at least as long as they are in school, we can and should provide an environment that is rich in 'real' social and natural experiences for our students. Smartphones would interfere fundamentally with our curriculum, which is centred around nurturing affectionate relationships among children and adults. In fact, if we adults are mindful of our own tendencies towards obsessive use of smartphones, this is an invaluable learning in the community. Similarly, our curriculum emphasises an intimate relationship with the natural world. Ample time and space are given for students to play outdoors, go for walks, climb trees and rocks, and engage with a diversity of plants, fungi, insects, reptiles, birds and mammals. Creating such an environment is our responsibility, as it all but removes the need for personal gadgets in school. There is a clear value in such environments for young people whose brains are still developing and therefore vulnerable to the continuous dopamine-triggers of a smartphone.

My colleagues also expressed that it is our responsibility to educate young people to meet various challenges through life, not only to prepare for a 'successful' career. In our experience, 15- to 18-year-olds are capable of reflective learning about states of the mind such as restlessness and boredom. It is also possible through gentle questioning to investigate the strong urge for identity formation. So what is the point of a device, however powerful, that merely offers new tools to construct identity? Through quiet observation and open dialogue, we can together learn how to be aware of subtle movements in ourselves that make us vulnerable to emotional ill-being. Such awareness is perhaps the best way to prepare for a future life of digital immersion.

Discussion

To summarise, I have described in this essay the reasons why most schools might wish to curtail their students' use of smartphones while in school, and most of these have to do with academic learning and performance. Concerns regarding the addictive nature of smartphone use were also touched upon. The essay went on to share a third and, to me and my colleagues at school, even more compelling concern that has to do with the nature of the human psyche. Movements of restlessness, preoccupation and mindfulness are subtle and often overlooked as being of any importance to personal and social well-being, yet they are central to our school's work, and they are the reason for our no-smartphone policy. Interestingly, scientific psychology has increasingly turned its attention to these subtle psychological movements, and several fascinating lines of research have emerged: see Tang et al. (2015) for the neuroscience of mindfulness, and Zenner et al. (2014) for a review of mindfulness interventions in schools. It is very likely that in the years to come, human beings' relationship with their personal media devices will be critically examined through these lenses. Whatever we learn from the research will surely help us to create thoughtful and nurturing environments for the well-being of our children.

References

American Psychiatric Association. 2013. *Diagnostic and Statistical Manual of Mental Disorders*, 5th edn. Arlington, VA: American Psychiatric Publishing.

Beland, L., and R. Murphy. 2015. 'Ill Communication: Technology, Distraction and Student Performance'. Centre for Economic Performance (CEP) Discussion Paper No. 1350, May. The London School of Economics and Political Science.

Bosker, B. 2016. 'The Binge Breaker'. *The Atlantic Monthly*, November. Available at https://www.theatlantic.com/magazine/archive/2016/11/the-binge-breaker/501122/ (accessed on 25 September 2022).

boyd, d. 2014. *It's Complicated: The Social Lives of Networked Teens*. New Haven and London: Yale University Press.

Central Board of Secondary Education (CBSE). 2009. *Restriction in the Use of Mobile Phones in Schools*. Delhi: CBSE. Available at http://cbse.nic.in/circulars/cir2009.htm (accessed on 24 January 2020).

Chambers, R. A., J. R. Taylor and M. N. Potenza. 2003. 'Developmental Neurocircuitry of Motivation in Adolescence: A Critical Period of Addiction Vulnerability'. *American Journal of Psychiatry* 160: 1041–52.

Common Sense Media. 2016. 'New Report Finds Teens Feel Addicted to Their Phones, Causing Tension at Home'. Available at https://www.commonsensemedia.org/press-releases/new-report-finds-teens-feel-addicted-to-their-phones-causing-tension-at-home#:~:text=%2D%2D%20A%20new%20report%20issued,that%20their%20kids%20are%20addicted (accessed on 25 September 2022).

Crews, F., J. He and C. Hodge. 2007. 'Adolescent Cortical Development: A Critical Period of Vulnerability for Addiction'. *Pharmacology, Biochemistry and Behavior* 86: 189–99.

Graham, E. 2017. 'Using Smartphones in the Classroom'. National Education Association. Available at https://www.nea.org/professional-excellence/student-engagement/tools-tips/using-smartphones-classroom#:~:text=Use%20smartphones%20to%20stay%20organized%20and%20assess%20learning&text=Not%20only%20does%20it%20help,the%20homework%2C%E2%80%9D%20he%20says (accessed on 25 September 2022).

Gregory, A., D. Cornell, X. Fan, P. Sheras, T. Shih and F. Huang. 2010. 'Authoritative School Discipline: High School Practices Associated with Lower Student Bullying and Victimization'. *Journal of Educational Psychology* 102: 483–96.

Harris, T. 2019. 'About Tristan Harris'. Available at https://www.tristanharris.com (accessed on 24 January 2020).

Kagzi, V. 2017. 'Are Schools and Institutes Adapting "Bring Your Own Device (BYOD)" to Enhance the Education System in India?' Available at https://www.franchiseindia.com/education/Are-Schools-and-Institutes-Adapting-Bring-Your-Own-Device-BYOD--to-Enhance-the-Education-System-in-India.9227 (accessed on 24 January 2020).

Killingsworth, M. A., and D. T. Gilbert. 2010. 'A Wandering Mind is An Unhappy Mind'. *Science* 330(6006): 932.

Krishnamurti, J. 1995. *The Book of Life*. San Francisco: Harper.

Levin, D., and S. Arafeh. 2002. 'The Digital Disconnect: The Widening Gap between Internet-Savvy Students and Their Schools'. Pew Internet & American Life Project. Available at https://www.pewresearch.org/internet/2002/08/14/the-digital-disconnect-the-widening-gap-between-internet-savvy-students-and-their-schools/ (accessed on 20 September 2022).

Levitin, D. J. 2015. 'Why the Modern World is Bad for Your Brain'. *The Guardian (Neuroscience)*, 18 January. Available at https://www.theguardian.com/science/2015/jan/18/modern-world-bad-for-brain-daniel-j-levitin-organized-mind-information-overload (accessed on 25 September 2022).

Livingstone, S. 2008. 'Taking Risky Opportunities in Youthful Content Creation: Teenagers' Use of Social Networking Sites for Intimacy, Privacy, and Self-expression'. *New Media and Society* 10(3): 393–411.

National Centre for Educational Research and Training (NCERT). 2005. 'National Curriculum Framework'. New Delhi: NCERT.

Pavan, M. V. 2014. 'Now, Schools Have Mobile Policies'. *The Times of India*, 14 October. Available at https://timesofindia.indiatimes.com/city/bengaluru/Now-schools-have-mobile-policies/articleshow/44806596.cms (accessed on 24 January 2020).

Rao, S. 2018. 'Gaming Addiction: 6 Children Seek Help at Nimhans Clinic Every Week'. *The Times of India*, 21 June. Available at https://timesofindia.indiatimes.com/city/bengaluru/gaming-addiction-6-children-seek-help-at-nimhans-clinic-every-week/articleshow/64676694.cms (accessed on 24 January 2020).

Richtel, M. 2011. 'A Silicon Valley School That Doesn't Compute'. *The New York Times*. Available at https://www.nytimes.com/2011/10/23/technology/at-waldorf-school-in-silicon-valley-technology-can-wait.html (accessed on 24 January 2020).

Roschelle, J. M., R. D. Pea, C. M. Hoadley, D. N. Gordin and B. M. Means. 2000. 'Changing How and What Children Learn in School with Computer-based Technologies'. *Children and Computer Technology* 10(2): 76–101.

Rubin, A., and E. Peltier. 2018. 'France Bans Smartphones in Schools Through 9th Grade. Will It Help Students?' *The New York Times*. Available at https://www.nytimes.com/2018/09/20/world/europe/france-smartphones-schools.html (accessed on 24 January 2020).

Ruthven, K., S. Hennessy and R. Deaney. 2004. 'Incorporating Internet Resources into Classroom Practice: Pedagogical Perspectives and Strategies of Secondary-School Subject Teachers'. *Computers and Education* 44(1): 1–34.

Ryding, F. C., and L. K. Kaye. 2018. '"Internet Addiction": A Conceptual Minefield'. *International Journal of Mental Health and Addiction* 16(1): 225–32.

Sana, F., T. Weston and N. J. Cepeda. 2013. 'Laptop Multitasking Hinders Classroom Learning for Both Users and Nearby Peers'. *Computers and Education* 62: 24–31.

Selwyn, N. 2006. 'Exploring the "Digital Disconnect" between Net-Savvy Students and Their Schools'. *Learning, Media and Technology* 31(1): 5–17.

Tang, Y., B. Holzel and M. Posner. 2015. 'The Neuroscience of Mindfulness Meditation'. *Nature Reviews Neuroscience* 16: 213–225.

Thapa, A., J. Cohen, S. Guffey and A. Higgins-D'Alessandro. 2013. 'A Review of School Climate Research'. *Review of Educational Research* 83(3): 357–85.

The Guardian. 2018. 'The Guardian View on Mobile Phones: Schools Are Better Without Them'. 22 June. Available at https://www.theguardian.com/commentisfree/2018/jun/22/the-guardian-view-on-mobile-phones-schools-are-better-without-them (accessed on 24 January 2020).

Twenge, J. 2017. 'Have Smartphones Destroyed a Generation?' *The Atlantic*, September. Available at https://www.theatlantic.com/magazine/archive/2017/09/has-the-smartphone-destroyed-a-generation/534198/ (accessed on 25 September 2022).

United Nations Children's Fund. 2017. *The State of the World's Children 2017: Children in a Digital World*. Available at https://www.unicef.org/reports/state-worlds-children-2017 (accessed on 25 September 2022).

Waldorf School. 2019. 'Media & Technology Philosophy—Waldorf School of the Peninsula'. Available at https://waldorfpeninsula.org/curriculum/media-technology-philosophy/ (accessed on 24 January 2020).

Ward, A. F., K. Duke, A. Gneezy and M. W. Bos. 2017. 'Brain Drain: The Mere Presence of One's Own Smartphone Reduces Available Cognitive Capacity'. *Journal of the Association for Consumer Research* 2(2): 140–54.

World Health Organization. 2018. *International Classification of Diseases for Mortality and Morbidity Statistics*, 11th Revision. Available at https://icd.who.int/browse11/l-m/en#/http%3a%2f%2fid.who.int%2ficd%2fentity%2f338347362 (accessed on 25 September 2022).

Zenner, C., S. Herrnleben-Kurz and H. Walach. 2014. 'Mindfulness-based Interventions in Schools—A Systematic Review and Meta-Analysis'. *Frontiers in Psychology* 5. Available at https://doi.org/10.3389/fpsyg.2014.00603 (accessed on 25 September 2022).

Zhu, E., M. Kaplan, R. C. Dershimer and I. Bergom. 2011. 'Use of Laptops in the Classroom: Research and Best Practices'. Occasional Paper No. 30, Center for Research on Learning and Teaching, University of Michigan.

7

EVERYDAY USE OF DIGITAL TECHNOLOGIES BY ADOLESCENT GIRLS

Anita Sareen Parihar

With advances in technology, many aspects of human experience have undergone a shift with information becoming central to both personal and professional life. Our understanding of time and space, of boundaries between private and public spheres, the centre and the margins has blurred. A growing number of people across the world have the opportunity to access information and entertainment through mass media, the Internet and the mobile phone. Teenagers are in the middle of this global change of communication and media (Carlsson 2006).

Today, information and communication technologies (ICT) are an undeniable part of our daily life. With growing opportunities for dialogue through digital virtual spaces, organisations, institutions and small groups are finding ways to connect in unlimited ways in space and time. Here, access is the enabler. 'Properly designed, a Knowledge Society—with its starting point in the declaration of the Human Rights and the principle of Freedom of Expression—has great potential to support more democratic and just societies' (ibid.: 11).

In India, along with a conventional mass media society, a socially inclined media society has also grown. Youngsters the world over, and a notably significant number in India, are already part of this new, socio-centric media world. To some extent, there is a generation gap in the access to and use of these new media. Youngsters are adept at navigating new media technologies that often go beyond the understanding and abilities of older adults (Carlsson 2006).

Recently, more concern has been expressed about the negative aspects of the information revolution. Parents, academicians as well as decision-makers are anxiously voicing concerns, particularly in relation to films displaying violence, overt sexuality, derogatory advertisements, typical and disrespectful images of young people, women and those at the margins, hate speech as well as computer games. Some of this content is being disseminated widely over satellite/cable television, the Internet and smartphones (ibid.).

While there are heightened concerns around the 'dangers' to children associated with new media, one may find that safety precautions are the same anywhere, be it at school, college, work or home, outside or on the Internet. Only with the Internet and other new media, the sender and receiver of messages may be 'invisible' to each other. Hence the crucial need to speak of 'content that is detrimental and derogatory in media' (ibid.: 12).

Concerned individuals, groups, institutions and organisations have for long advocated limiting the spread of harmful media content to youth. In many communities, protecting the young is seen as a civic responsibility. The youth are likely to be open-minded, accommodating, and so, easy to target. If we are able to educate the youth to be more alert and discerning about derogatory and damaging media content, raise public awareness of the digital media amongst teenagers, parents, other adults as well as decision-makers in their milieu, then, perhaps, we are doing what is needed in terms of protecting our younger generation (ibid.).

This chapter explores how adolescent school girls (13–14 years) studying in an urban private (convent) school in Mumbai perceive and use digital technologies as part of their daily routines. The study combined a media literacy approach with a largely qualitative inquiry into social media practices of adolescent girls in a school that largely caters to the middle class.

The middle class in India, as elsewhere, does not comprise one monolithic group. It may include a suburban dweller, even a small-time farmer, a rickshaw driver, a tailor, a trader, a vegetable vendor, a school or college teacher and, by extension, a convent school–going student, a college student. The main criteria comprising the Indian middle classes were that they acquired prestige not through social status but through education, wealth and power (Misra, as cited in Chanana [1964]: 685).

In an attempt to provide a more complete understanding of the various facets of the middle class, Maryam Aslany of King's College London uses a composite indicator based on multiple economic and social characteristics, including income, skills and credentials, social networks, housing and lifestyles. She borrows from ideologies of three major theorists of class: Karl Marx, Max Weber and Pierre Bourdieu. Using this framework and data from the Indian Human Development Survey (2011–12) at the all-India level, Aslany profiles India's population into different class groups. For instance, she captures the 'lifestyle' aspect of the middle class using data on household consumption, patterns and purchasing power. Likewise, the 'housing' aspect of class is defined using data on house ownership and sanitation facilities. Based on all this, she finds that 28 per cent of India's population is middle class, of which 14 per cent is lower middle class and about 3 per cent is upper middle class. She finds that while there is significant diversity in the types of jobs among the middle class, a large proportion of the middle class is of salaried employees. And, most importantly, contrary to the popular assumption that the middle class is an urban phenomenon, a considerable segment of the Indian middle class resides in the rural areas (Kwatra 2019; Aslany 2019). According to the Ministry of Education, the percentage of 18- to 24-year-olds in India enrolling in university has shot up by 63 per cent in the past four years (Seshasayee n.d.). The opening of India's economy in 1991 has resulted in career opportunities in the private sector, both at home and abroad, unimaginable a few decades ago. Today, India's middle class is more optimistic, more confident and globalised. The rise of India's middle class also heralds a rise in consumption, especially in urban areas, including emerging middle-tier and smaller cities.

The major questions in this study include: specific purposes for which the girls use digital media (particularly, mobile phones), awareness of change (if any) in their behaviour and habits, their perception of relevance of the device and of the use of social media platforms, and other consequences of using digital technologies. The broader study on which this chapter is based included an action research component aimed at raising the level of awareness to enable the participants to use digital media discerningly. The study involved pupils of Class VIII of St. Anthony Girls' High School (SAGHS), Chembur, Mumbai. Founded in 1952, SAGHS is a Christian minority government-aided school that offers education from nursery to Class X. It is run by the Sisters of St. Joseph of Chambery under the Roman Catholic Church and is affiliated to the Archdiocese Board of Education. Recognised by the Maharashtra State Board of Education, it prepares Class X students for the state board's school secondary certificate (SSC) examination (St. Anthony Girls' High School n.d.).

This chapter proceeds as follows: I begin with a review of literature to offer an overview of the socio-cultural context of India where, perhaps like elsewhere, media is seen as a bridge between the home and the world. While catering to promote cultural uniformity, media also ensures that diversity of cultures prevail (Dasgupta et al. 2012). The discussion also draws upon ideas from Amartya Sen's book, *The Idea of Justice* (2009) where he emphasises that an autonomous, ethical and responsible media can stimulate public reasoning. It further includes a relevant reference made by former president of India, Dr A. P. J. Abdul Kalam, to the effect that media are influenced by concerns of business and market (Sen 2009: 5–6).

The literature on 'Being Digital' is relevant for understanding the reason today's teenagers take to navigating digital media easily through time, space and place. The mobile phone that provides an amalgamation of services from communication via calling and messaging to a variety of other applications has become ubiquitous. Studies conducted by the Pew Research Center as well as the Teenage Adolescent Girls (TAG) survey conducted by Naandi Foundation in different ways point to the impact of digital technologies on adolescents. The review draws significantly on Ulla Carlsson's (2006) documentation of growing evidence that new media/ digital technologies, including the mobile phone, are being used in intimidation, harassment as well as malicious peer-to-peer communication. Keeping in mind the challenges faced by parents in terms of getting access to the new (digital) forms of content and contact, guidelines should be determined by sharing responsibilities equally among decision-makers, parents and children, taking into account the children's opportunities and exposure to digital media.

The 'Research Methodology' section recounts how, in the capacity of researcher as well as an associate of SAGHS, I endeavoured to understand and document the perception and usage of digital technologies by 13- and 14-year-old students of Class VIII using a mixed method approach for data collection and analysis, which comprised personally administering a questionnaire to 100 students followed by two focus group discussions of 12 and 20 students respectively, of which one was a video screening succeeded by written and oral feedback. The findings from the questionnaire are presented collectively in Table 7.1 and accompanied by a narrative summary. The survey analysis proceeds by highlighting specific comments from the respondents on the pros and cons of using mobile phones in their daily lives, along with a more nuanced depiction of the two focus group findings with regard to the perceptions, practices, fears and ideas about cyber bullying through first-hand feedback and their implications with further recommendations.

Changing Media Context: The Case of India

The economic liberalisation policies of India in the early 1990s paved the way for a change in the social and cultural scenario. In spite of encountering challenges in the three decades of its trajectory, it has finally asserted its emerging position globally. India is a melting pot of diversity, recognising each culture's uniqueness and maintaining each one while supporting the need to negotiate between the differences within the country and outside. Media has effectively bridged the varied regions of the outside world with the home and likewise the home with the world, enabling connectivity, communication and better understanding among people. Rantanen's definition supports this media-constructed connectivity: 'Media is about connecting strangers to one another, whether or not they have expressed their willingness. In this sense, when the "neighbourhood" is the world, refusing to hear or see the neighbour is not an option' (Rantanen, as cited in Dasgupta et al. 2012: 125). 'The Indian media is the in-between agent that has the dual potential of ruthlessly perpetrating homogenisation of regional cultures as well as securing the longevity of heterogeneity of cultures from the urban to the tribal sectors' (ibid.).

In his book *The Idea of Justice*, Nobel Prize–winning economist Amartya Sen has specifically identified the role of 'an unrestrained and healthy media' that can generate a 'direct contribution' of free speech as well as play an 'informational role', a 'protective function', and contribute to the 'formation of values', all of which can facilitate and enhance the quality of life of the people, both the advantaged and the disadvantaged classes (2009: 335–36). Sen emphasises that the freedom of the media can prompt people to respond and reason. The media also has to be responsible, and not lean on any ideology or person or be controlled. The free media has to be more responsible in terms of ethics. As is often seen, media can jeopardise ethics and national interests for the sake of a riveting news story garnering public attention. Media is characterised by local, national, global connectivity which may challenge national interests (Dasgupta et al. 2012: 2).

From the 1990s, private television channels in India have multiplied in number to compete with each other for breaking news and even making news. NDTV is a dominant presence followed by CNN-IBN, Times Now, Star News and Zee TV, along with regional channels that involve local cultures and customs with enthusiastic coverage. In his book *India 2020: A Vision for the New Millennium*, Kalam states clearly that media is guided by concerns of business and market, so the content is focused more on the negative and sensational than the positive and matter-of-fact. Kalam comments that though media play a vital role in forming public opinion, it works under its own limitations. It has to make a profit like any other business (Kalam and Rajan 2002). The media gives information, news and opinions of standing, and deconstructs issues of societal relevance while catering to its audience. Its objective is to create attention-gathering headlines, and to seek engaging, riveting and thrilling stories, events and occurrences (Dasgupta et al. 2012: 5–6).

Being Digital

'Digital' is, in simple terms, zeroes and ones, the code that runs computers in the creation, transmission and reception of information for human meaning-making in various activities—whether in day-to-day communication, recreation, entertainment or work. It is also called 'New Media' (Nayar 2012: 2). Common examples of new media include websites such as online newspapers, blogs or wikis; video games; digital arts; mobile communications and social media. New media has transformed production and consumption of cinema, print and television, as well as communication storage and transmission, and forms of leisure. As the primary conveyer of digital media, the Internet has become a pivotal part of the overall media landscape in India, and the growing availability of these media on portable platforms—like the mobile—has only increased their productivity and use. A more detailed discussion of the broader implications of digital media forms and devices on everyday life is beyond the scope of this chapter, but suffice to say that young people have been among the most enthusiastic users of various forms of digital technology. In this chapter, I shall look at one sub-group of users, adolescent girls, and their everyday use and understanding of one digital device, the mobile phone.

Digital Media and Adolescent Girls in India

Adolescence is a stage when youngsters' physical growth is being manifested, when they are finding their way, trying to understand themselves amidst feeling pressured either to conform in a particular way or to rebel against the norm. According to the World Health

Organization (WHO), adolescents are between the ages of 10 and 19 years (World Health Organization n.d.). India has the largest adolescent population in the world, 253 million, and every fifth person is between 10 and 19 years old (United Nations Children's Fund n.d.).

The term 'dependence' was introduced by WHO (in 1964) to replace the terms 'addiction' and 'habituation' (Eddy et al. 1965: 722). Dependence refers to both physical and psychological elements (Eddy et al. 1965). One can be dependent on medicines, drugs, alcohol or other substances. Another kind of dependence could be related to one's habits or behaviours. One could be dependent on eating sweets or even surfing the Internet on one's mobile every now and then.

Smartphones

The growing increase in use of mobile phones/smartphones is of grave concern as regards its effects on mental and emotional health, particularly among Indian adolescents. Mobile connectivity has become so easy that youth in India are frequently using smartphones. This overuse has become more serious since adolescents can use a number of applications on their smartphones even without Internet connection. Perpetual use of smartphones by adolescents is posing a health disorder, challenging the global fraternity to deliberate on it (Davey and Davey 2014).

In 2000, the smartphone was built to allow access to the Internet on a mobile phone. The smartphones today are technologically advanced enough to allow adolescents to surf, chat, entertain themselves at any given time or place. They perpetually keep the mobile in their hands (ibid.).

Indian teenagers constitute a substantial consumer base for the smartphone industry in India. Smartphone users in the age group of 16–18 years has increased from 5 per cent in 2012 to 22 per cent in 2013. In 2013, there were around 51 million smartphone users in urban India and the rate of increase from 2012 was 90 per cent (Nerurkar 2013).

Malicious Communication

'There is increasing evidence that internet-based and mobile communication technologies are being used in practices of bullying, harassment and other forms of malicious peer-to-peer communication' (Carlsson 2006: 12). Research points towards easy availability along with very personal and often anonymous conditions in which these new technologies are being used, underlining the point that online intimidation or coercion may cause new kinds of problems for users as well as accentuate old ones. 'In some ways, it seems, online and offline communication work differently, but in key ways also, they work together. Thus, offline bullying or harassment can exist that continues or extends online, rather than remaining entirely distinct' (ibid.). Collectively, deciding on rules between the decision-makers, parents and children will ease the challenges faced by parents in accessing new digital content.

The Pew Research Center in the US conducted a study on teens and their social media usage in 2018. It revealed interesting results, notably in relation to use of Facebook which was once the most popular social networking site. It has now been overtaken by YouTube, Instagram and Snapchat. It also revealed the increasing connection between teens and technology. Around 95 per cent teens have a smartphone or at least access to one. In fact, 45 per cent of teens said that they are online. The survey also questioned teens on their perceived impact of social media on teenage users. The results were mixed. Some teens described that effect as mostly positive (31 per cent) or mostly negative (24 per cent). But the largest share (45 per cent) said that effect has been neither positive nor negative. Teens stressed connectivity and communication as important positive impacts created by social media but 27 per cent of those surveyed said that social media has led to more bullying and the overall spread of rumours. Meanwhile, 17 per cent of the respondents felt these platforms harm relationships and result in less meaningful human interactions. Similar numbers thought social media distorts reality and gives teens an unrealistic view of other people's lives (15 per cent), or that teens spend too much time on them (Anderson and Jiang 2018).

In India, the picture of teen mobile phone use is yet to emerge tangibly. About 80 million teenage girls in India represent future citizens of the country to be given equal status as per the Indian constitution. We are at the juncture of humanity when the role of girls and young women needs to be taken into cognisance. We are also aware that educating them, maintaining their health and helping them become independent young adults creates a chain reaction which would benefit the society and economy. A survey to find out the status of teenage girls—as regards their aspirations, safety, education, computer literacy, skills in English, mastering of New Age Skills (NAS)—called the Teenage Girls Report (TAG) by Project Nanhi Kali version 2.0, jointly managed by Naandi Foundation and KC Mahindra Education Trust, was conducted by directly conversing with 74,000 teenagers in all the states of India. Outcomes of the survey of teenage girls between 13 years and 19 years indicated:

- 80.6 per cent are currently studying
- 95.8 per cent are unmarried
- 70 per cent wish to pursue higher studies
- 74.3 per cent wish to work after their studies and have a specific career in mind
- In rural as well as urban India, 73.3 per cent want to marry only after they are 21 years old, by which time they would be earning a living (Nanhi Kali 2018).

We live in a rapidly changing world. The set of skills that ensures a life of basic dignity and efficiency today is different from the set of skills that would have been needed 20 years ago. The set of skills that we consider necessary today is encapsulated in Nanhi Kali as NAS (Nanhi Kali 2018). In the TAG survey, teenage girls were asked if they had the NAS. Amongst the 13- to 15-year-old girls, 66.4 per cent said 'yes' to a maximum of five NAS, the most common being the following:

- Ability to make and receive calls on a mobile phone
- Fill forms in English or a local language
- Search for information on the Internet; send and receive emails

- Use social media
- Write a document in English on a computer (Nanhi Kali 2018).

About 33.6 per cent said 'yes' to anything between six and ten NAS, of which the most common were:

- Withdraw money from ATM/bank/post office
- Ask a male stranger for direction/help
- Travel alone for longer than four hours
- Live alone
- Go to a police station to file a complaint (ibid.).

A descriptive study to assess the level of Internet addiction (IA) among adolescents—a case study of high schools in Mangalore—revealed that majority (70.5 per cent) of the adolescents were normal users, 23 per cent had a mild addiction, 6 per cent had a moderate addiction and 0.5 per cent had a severe addiction. The majority (73 per cent) of surveyed participants had a mild impact, 16.5 per cent had a moderate impact and 10.5 per cent had no impact of IA on their lives. Some of their demographic variables like age, class and occupation of fathers have significant associations with both IA and impact of IA (Kayastha et al. 2018).

Dealing with Dependence through Shared Regulations

> Some decades ago, the protection of minors was often discussed in terms of government regulation and prohibitions. In today's complex society in an era of successive deregulation and globalisation, the management of governments have changed. We are living in time of many stakeholders, within public as well as private sectors including the civil society, and on all levels: local, national, regional and international. Governance today is dependent on collaboration and partnership. Against this background, in terms of safeguarding the youth from detrimental media content, the focus has shifted from legislation towards a focus on the responsibilities of the parents and other adults (Carlsson 2006: 13).

The discourse in India may be said to be at a fairly incipient stage and involving a narrow range of elite actors. There is little empirical evidence on how young people are using such media across the heterogeneity of socio-cultural contexts in India.

In the present study, in my capacity as a researcher, as well as on the basis of my two-decade association with SAGHS, the objective has been to understand and document the perception and usage of digital technologies by 13- and 14-year-old students of Class VIII of the school.

Research Methodology

The study began in 2018 and was undertaken for a duration of three years, culminating in 2020. A mixed methods approach was used to collect necessary data: a face-to-face interview with a questionnaire and two focus group discussions of which one was a video screening followed by written and oral feedback. The age group of 13–14 years was chosen based on the permission given by the SAGHS principal to address this group. Further, the adolescents chosen for this study by virtue of their age and nature were judged to be impressionable, less critical and more vulnerable. By participating in the study they could simultaneously share and sharpen their awareness, while analysing their perceptions of managing digital technologies more effectively in their daily routines. In this study I undertook a reflective process into my own pedagogical practices and Ulla Carlsson's (2006) framework on media governance. Through this method, I offered support to adolescent school girls in orienting them to cope with digital technologies that form an integral part of their daily routines. Both quantitative and qualitative techniques were used for analysing the collated data. The questionnaire comprised close-ended questions and one open-ended question (on perception of relevance of the mobile phone). Four divisions of girls from Class VIII, together comprising 100 students, were given the questionnaire in two sessions in the school's multi-purpose hall. All of them were told the purpose of the research before they responded to the questionnaire. For the first focus group discussion, 12 students were present. The focus group discussion was aimed at primarily understanding their digital routines and their perceptions in a more open and conversational setting. The group was not very talkative except for a few who shared their routine of attending school from 7 am to 1 pm followed by lunch and tuition till 5 pm, and returning home by the evening. I encouraged them to write down their personal thoughts on our discussion if they were comfortable with it. Some wrote their opinions which are presented in a later section. For the second focus group discussion, a screening of *Cyber Bully* (2011), a television film of 87 minutes, was followed by oral and written feedback, with the participation of another 20 students. The reason for doing the second focus group discussion was to evoke amongst the adolescent convent girls a response to any personal thoughts or experience related to the topic of the film.

Findings from the Questionnaire

Analysis of data of 100 respondents for the questionnaire on 'Usage of digital technologies by adolescents in their daily routines' revealed an increasing dependence on digital technologies among this group of adolescents as shown in Table 7.1.

Table 7.1 Usage of Digital Technologies by Adolescent Girls in Their Daily Routines

Adolescent Girls and Digital Technologies	**Per Cent**
Access	
Have access to smartphone	60
Have Internet at home	57
Have newspaper access at home	60
Have television at home	83
Surf at cyber café	07

(Contd)

Table 7.1 (Contd)

Adolescent Girls and Digital Technologies	Per Cent
Uses	
Read news, watch TV, listen to radio for entertainment	57
Surf Internet at home for information	84
Use the Internet for class assignments	92
Use Internet to download music	51
Use Internet to collect information about celebrities, film stars	38
Practices	
Watch TV daily	40
Read newspaper daily	37
Listen to radio daily	23
Use the Internet everyday	38
Use social networking sites daily	66
Attitudes and Changes	
Ranked Internet as a major source of information	70
Felt Internet had brought a change in their lives	84
Felt Internet had brought a change in their language	51
Felt Internet had brought a change in their behaviour	28
Felt Internet had brought a change in their dressing style	32
Felt Internet had brought a change in their attitude	14
Believed Internet to be reliable	71
Addicted to the Internet	50
Would feel frustrated if they did not use the Internet	21
Felt Internet has created a feeling of connectedness in the world	77
Felt social networking has become a part of their daily life	66
Safety	
Afraid to post personal details or photos online	40
Admitted to being cyber bullied	11
Worried about online child safety	58
Felt personal information on social media can be misused	70

Source: Author.

Routines and Perceptions of Adolescent Girls Using Digital Technologies

The routines of the respondents clearly indicate increasing use of digital technologies in their daily lives for the purposes of education, information and entertainment. The respondents have also perceived changes in their language, behaviour and personality; distraction in their study time; and reduction in time spent reading books and cultivating social relations as a result of using the Internet. This particular group of girls appears to understand the importance of using the mobile in so far as it is required and not an end in itself.

Access

Of the participants in this study, 57 per cent had access to the Internet at home, 60 per cent to the smartphone as well as newspaper, 83 per cent had television at home and only 7 per cent frequented the cyber café.

Uses

Ninety-two per cent respondents used the Internet for class assignments while 84 per cent surfed the Internet at home for information; 57 per cent read the newspaper, watched television and also listened to the radio. Fifty-one per cent used the Internet to download music and 38 per cent used it to collect information about celebrities and film stars.

Practices

For 66 per cent of the respondents, social networking was part of their daily routine; 38 per cent used the Internet every day, 40 per cent watched TV daily, 37 per cent read the newspaper every day and 23 per cent listened to the radio daily.

Attitudes and Changes

Seventy per cent of the respondents considered Internet as a major source of information, 84 per cent believed it to have brought a change in their lives, 51 per cent felt it brought a change in their language, 32 per cent felt it had brought about a change in their dressing style while 28 per cent believed Internet had brought about a change in their behaviour. Seventy-one per cent respondents believed the Internet to be reliable; 50 per cent admitted that they were addicted to it; 21 per cent felt frustrated when not using the Internet. Seventy-seven per cent of the respondents felt the Internet has created a feeling of connectedness in the world and 66 per cent felt social networking had become a part of their daily lives.

Safety

Forty per cent of the respondents were afraid to post personal details or photos online, 11 per cent admitted to being bullied online, 58 per cent were worried about online child safety and 70 per cent felt personal information on social media could be misused.

The Pros and Cons of the Mobile as Perceived by Adolescents

One particular respondent felt that the Internet 'has made them lazy', but it also 'has helped in completing their assignments easily'. Several felt that the mobile was useful but should not be misused and that it was as important to them as newspapers and books. Some voiced that 'if Internet was not there they could still live but it would be hard to get information'. Students liked the mobile because it afforded them Internet connectivity, convenience and easy communication with their parents, relatives abroad as well as their friends. They enjoyed the mobile for its games, apps and entertainment. They felt that while it was useful for searching information, it was harmful for the neck and eyes. A few used their mothers' phones when required. Some were content with not having a personal mobile as they thought it to be a distraction. One of them said, 'Post standard tenth (SSC)/ completion of school, it would be all right to have one's own mobile.'

Two of the teenagers said that they first went through all the apps like Musical.ly and Gaana.com, and they posted photos on Instagram and songs on Gaana. They practised skits at home, possibly to post on such platforms. They thought a lot about their singing, acting and dancing. Some said they 'wanted to become the biggest models in the world, inspired by the hobbies and lifestyles of other social media personalities'.

Focus Group Discussion 1: Perceptions, Practices and Fears

The first focus group discussion included 12 girls who had responded to the questionnaire. Some of their written opinions have been reproduced here verbatim:

> Today's world we are away from the older devices like radio, newspapers but more close to social media like Facebook, Internet, Instagram, etc.
>
> In today's generation as there are harmful means that can affect a person to a bad phase...such people with mental illness, OCD can seek help...when guided well.
>
> The school should create a healthy atmosphere where we get to interact with teachers and students and learn how to live and work in a team and develop good relations with each other because 24/7 in the house we use net and don't interact with people it's only [online chat]. Nowadays people don't talk face to face if they meet each other but same people chat with each other every day.
>
> We understood about how to use Internet, also to use it in the right ways. We also understood how to be interactive with the social media. We also understood advantages and disadvantages of smartphone and how to use [it] and control ourselves. We also got to know how we can improve ourselves in a good way or manner. We also understand that the school is not encouraging students to be interactive with social media. We also understand that we should not put our personal information on social media without privacy because it can be misused.

Media is useful for education, information, business, sports, etc. But nowadays media is not used for this purpose. Media is a way for helping and getting all the information on the tip of our fingers. The time that should be used outdoors is now used for mobile phones. Social awareness of keeping ourselves safe from crime is available in TV [programmes] like Saavdhan India. Now when we are involved in world full of social life, we are not aware of reality because we only read and understand what we have seen or read. So to understand the right information we need to check the whole history. Checking what is right and blindly not following what we have received as a message helps us to be proven as right users of media. Today we make use of radio, television, mobile phones and Internet to get awareness about recent news and entertainment. Life can be much more with the help of right way of using mobile phones. We can learn many things from social media like YouTube which we did with the help of books.

Mobile phones and technology have a huge impact on children, through social media and net. It can be an advantage and a useful commodity to the society for the betterment of the society and it helps to make people aware of things happening. Or it can be a disadvantage that brings changes and distance between our close friends and family. Awareness should be spread of safeguarding yourself on social sites. School's decision of avoiding usage of net is a good and nice decision. We should learn how to react to offensive messages that we receive on social media. Using social media is useful to some extent. We should understand that social media isn't the reality. Have control over yourself to surf the net.

I believe that we should have control over how we use mobile phones and Internet.

I believe that the idea of not having Internet in school hours is very beneficial for us as we interact with our friends a lot. I believe that I am not addicted to the net but it has become part of my life.

I do not use Internet very frequently. I only use it for knowledge and reading books. I don't own a phone by my own choice, because I feel that people change by its overuse. Phone is a blessing in limit but a curse if extended.

I started the focus group discussion by orienting as well as running through some questions from the questionnaire as to which medium of entertainment was most used by them, to which television was the unanimous answer. Further, on asking if they surf the Internet at home, several of them nodded in agreement. Eight of the respondents had access to mobile and Internet on an average of two to three hours per day. Most watched television daily. To my question on how many had a Facebook account, four girls raised their hands; when asked if they posted their photos online, two of them affirmed while the other two said they hesitated to put their photos on social networking sites. When I prodded why they hesitated, they said they feared that such posting might be misunderstood. When I asked the two girls who regularly posted online about how they safeguarded themselves, they replied that they selected the privacy settings so that the pictures were shared only within a group close to them. To my question if they could recall any instance of cyber bullying, there was no overt response though I sensed their curiosity and interest. I then shared a personal experience with cyber bullying which they all listened to attentively. I also described how I had dealt with it, with the help of my husband, trying to make the point that it was important to share such an experience with family members who could offer support. Fake news, especially on social networking sites, was another area discussed and cautioned about by tracing the source on Google of the particular news before assuming the truth and sharing it further. Because of the ease of access and use of social media, ethics and self-regulation are more important. Towards the end of the session, one student came up and talked about her friend being cyber bullied and how she would now be able to help her by sharing her learning from the focus group discussion.

Focus Group Discussion 2: Ideas about Cyber Bullying

The second focus group discussion followed the screening of an 87-minute film, *Cyber Bully* (2011). The film's story is about a teenage girl who falls prey to online bullying, and how it traumatises her. She is a 17-year-old school student, attractive, but shy and self-conscious. Her mother gifts her a computer for her birthday and she is thrilled by the idea of going online, getting her freedom. She soon becomes a victim to bullying and is apprehensive to face her friends at school as well as her best friend. The girl's mother pursues the matter, exonerating her daughter from this serious predicament by taking the school authorities to task (IMDb 2011). Below are selected verbatim responses from the students after the screening of the film.

> Sometimes we try to change our character to match others even though it does not suit us. There are always some friends who are jealous and always look for a situation to comment on bad things or to put your name down and this mostly happens through social media. Even though people talk bad things or try to bully you we know we are not that type of person. At such times we can always ask someone like our mothers to help us as she is the one who will never think something bad for us. Getting depressed or trying to attempt suicide will never help. I am aware that in today's life cyber bullying exists. Like the others, I am also on social media but to protect myself I don't accept the follow requests of unknown people.
>
> One step I would take from now onwards to protect myself online will be to try to be aware about the pros and cons, online. I have created an account online, however it does not have any detail of me and it has a fake name. I made that account not to harm anyone but to protect myself while using Internet.
>
> Once on Instagram, a boy asked me for my phone number. I ignored the message. Then he asked for my address. That day, I blocked him. Now, I never use any social media app except WhatsApp and YouTube.
>
> The most impactful part was when Taylor tried to commit suicide and then I understood that cyber bullying can go till heights; and I will avoid to go in such a trap by not talking to strangers or texting them and I will avoid posting pictures of myself with my personal details. I will share this film with my friends and I will surely download the child safety act. Once I had posted a picture

on Instagram of my bedroom because we had just painted it pink, so at the time my account was not private, someone posted a comment, "Wow! What bedroom." The moment I read the comment I blocked the person.

There are positive as well as negative effects of online. We should not hold fear. Be alert. Locate the local cyber police station. The film was so encouraging.

Everyone who is a victim of cyber bullying should be fearless and keep yourself safe and have positive uses of the Internet rather [than] being on social media. I think I liked the scene when the actress's best friend came and truthfully said that she was the one who made the fake account to bully her. Once my friend opened her Instagram account and saw there were some requests by some unknown person who was asking her to expose her body. And I warned her to keep herself to limit in using the app.

By this film I get to know that being online is not an issue. It is just that I have to be careful and not share my personal information. I [do not] have to take the issue in a negative way but I can also take it positively and react good.

The part that touched me was that the girl's own friend was the 'cyber bully'. I am very active on Instagram, and now I will mostly reduce it and be more active physically by playing sports and stuff.

If I am cyber bullied, I will speak up. We should follow child safety guidelines. Keep our account 'private'. A boy on Insta started giving comments on my sister's pictures that you look 'hot', 'cute'. I told her to block him but she just ignored, slowly this got more and more and at the end she had to delete her account. Best scene in the film was when the counsellor told the students you should be even and tell/speak out, share with someone we trust. This session has helped me a lot.

Watching this movie has given me a lot of points against [cyber bullying] and now if myself or any of my friends is being a victim of cyber bullying I will surely be able to help them.

I learnt that we must not use abusive words in retaliation in anger, online…

Some of the observations made by all participants included the following (when faced with an objectionable text):

- Print the chat and do not keep to yourself; share—with parents, teachers, those you trust. Do not keep quiet, tell someone who understands.
- Do not spread or share your personal stuff.
- Do not use abusive language in retaliation to the cyber bully.
- Inform the cyber police, locally.
- Do not accept the friend request of a stranger or person you do not know.

Most of the participants in this study reported that they use the Internet for an average of three hours and view television for approximately the same duration daily.

Conclusion and Implications

This study illustrates the increasing connectivity of middle-class adolescents with digital technologies as part of their daily routines for the purposes of education, information and entertainment. While a large number of them have access to the Internet, this group of girls appears to understand the importance of using the mobile phone insofar as it is required and not as an end in itself. They have also perceived the effects of using the Internet on their behaviour and personality as well as many aspects of their daily life and are thus aware that they need to further equip themselves with appropriate guidance and support systems, be it through their school, parents, teachers, cyber experts or even close friends whom they can trust in order to ably manage and be in control of their social media interactions.

We must make the youth more alert and discerning about derogatory and damaging media content, and raise public awareness about media amongst teenagers, their parents and other adults in their milieu. The focused engagement with the children, with a tangible media literacy input (using the film) and interaction (focus group discussions), resulted in a fruitful discussion and increased awareness of the possible harms of social media use. Through such orientation workshops, consciousness-raising discussions, campaigns that are embedded in their curriculum, in their schedule of learning, as well as other events specially organised and undertaken by all the stakeholders, we can support democratic and just societies.

References

Anderson, M., and J. Jiang. 2018. *Teens, Social Media & Technology 2018.* Pew Research Center, 31 May. Available at https://www.pewresearch.org/internet/2018/05/31/teens-social-media-technology-2018/ (accessed on 24 September 2022).

Aslany, M. 2019. 'The Indian Middle Class, Its Size, and Urban–Rural Variations'. *Contemporary South Asia* 27(2): 196–213.

Carlsson, U. 2006. 'Introduction. Media Governance: Harm and Offence in Media Content'. In *Regulation, Awareness, Empowerment: Young People and Harmful Content in the Digital Age*, ed. U. Carlsson, 11–19. Gothenburg: The International Clearinghouse on Children, Youth and Media, Nordic Information Centre for Media Communication and Research (Nordicom), Gothenburg University.

Chanana, K. 1964. 'The Middle Class in India'. *The Economic Weekly,* 11 April, pp. 683–89. Available at https://www.epw.in/system/files/pdf/1964_16/15/the_middle_class_in_india.pdf (accessed on 24 September 2022).

Dasgupta, S., D. Sinha and S. Chakravarti. 2012. *Media, Gender and Popular Culture in India: Tracking Change and Continuity.* New Delhi: Sage Publications.

Davey, S., and A. Davey. 2014. 'Assessment of Smartphone Addiction in Indian Adolescents: A Mixed Method Study by Systematic-review and Meta-analysis Approach'. *International Journal of Preventive Medicine* 5(12): 1500–11.

Eddy, N. B., H. Halbach, H. Isbell and M. H. Seevers. 1965. 'Drug Dependence: Its Significance and Characteristics'. *Bulletin of the World Health Organization* 32(5): 721–33.

IMDb. 2011. *Cyber Bully* (2011 TV Movie). Available at https://www.imdb.com/title/tt1930315/plotsummary (accessed on 31 January 2019).

Kalam, A. P. J., and Y. S. Rajan. 2002. *India 2020: A Vision for the New Millennium*. New Delhi: Penguin.

Kayastha, B., A. Gurung and R. Chawal. 2018. 'A Descriptive Study to Assess the Level of Internet Addiction among Adolescents: A Case Study of High Schools in Mangalore'. *Journal of Child & Adolescent Behaviour* 6(3).

Kwatra, N. 2019. 'The Anatomy of India's Middle Class'. *Mint*, 24 April. Available at https://www.livemint.com/news/india/the-anatomy-of-india-s-middle-class-1556088919798.html (accessed on 24 September 2022).

Nanhi Kali. 2018. TAG Report. Available at https://www.nanhikali.org/pdf/TAG-Report.pdf (accessed on 24 May 2020).

Nayar, P. K. 2012. *Digital Cool: Life in the Age of New Media*. New Delhi: Orient BlackSwan.

Nerurkar, S. 2013. 'Teens Drive Indian Smartphone Sales, Study Finds'. *The Times of India*, 8 September. Available at https://timesofindia.indiatimes.com/business/india-business/teens-drive-indian-smartphone-sales-study-finds/articleshow/22406572.cms (accessed on 24 September 2022).

Sen, A. 2009. *The Idea of Justice*. London: Penguin Books.

Seshasayee, H. (n.d.). 'India's Middle Class'. *Americas Quarterly*. Available at https://www.americasquarterly.org/indias-middle-class (accessed on 22 May 2020).

St. Anthony Girls' High School (SAGHS). (n.d.). 'Aims and Objectives'. Available at https://stanthonygirlshigh.wixsite.com/saghs/aims-and-objectives (accessed on 24 September 2022).

United Nations Children's Fund. (n.d.) 'Adolescent Development and Participation'. Available at https://www.unicef.org/india/what-we-do/adolescent-development-participation (accessed on 22 November 2022).

World Health Organization. (n.d.) 'Adolescent Health'. Available at https://www.who.int/health-topics/adolescent-health#tab=tab_1 (accessed on 22 November 2022).

8

ADOLESCENTS AND SOCIAL MEDIA

Attraction, Addiction, Image Creation and Necessity

Archana Kumari

It is a well-known fact that social media fever has gripped the whole world, including children. Adolescents are so inclined towards social media that they hide their real age and create their accounts on social networking sites (SNSs) like Facebook and Instagram. These children are vulnerable to the uncontrolled, unfiltered flow of messages, yet many of them create their social networking accounts without the knowledge of their parents. Many times, it is the demand of the system too. Class teachers and school administration create WhatsApp groups or Messenger groups making children part of those groups to keep them updated about school events. We cannot have a dual standard: on one hand, we promote the use of certain SNSs and, on the other, we restrain the use of some other sites of their choice. This essay raises the question whether the use of social media by adolescents can be characterised as attraction, addiction, impression or necessity. This study draws on in-depth interviews and focus group discussions with children in the age group of 10 to 17 years of diverse socio-economic backgrounds on the uses of social media and its importance in their lives.

A recent news item reported that India has over 450 million monthly active Internet users, making it second only to China in terms of the number of users. The study, conducted by the Internet and Mobile Association of India (IAMAI and Nielsen 2019) further stated that 385 million of those users were over the age of 12 years, while 66 million users were children between the ages 5 and 11 years who probably accessed the Internet via family-owned devices. These large numbers force us to think about the way the Internet—and social media in particular—are used by our children. As a parent and a researcher, I was interested in gaining a better understanding of the 'use or misuse' and 'attraction or addiction' of social media by children, and this was the entry point for my research on this topic.

Many authors have provided definitions of social media (boyd and Ellison 2007; O'Keeffe et al. 2011; O'Reilly and Battelle 2009) but, for the purposes of this chapter, I will use the following definition: 'Media and online platforms that primarily support cognition (such as the websites of newspapers) are social media (1), those that primarily support communication (such as e-mail) are social media (2), and those that primarily support community building and collaborative work (such as Wikipedia, Facebook) are social media (3)'(Trottier and Fuchs 2015: 5).

While these definitions differ in terms of detail, the common element is that they are all Internet-based or networked media. One of the most important aspects of social networking is the ability to make connections with people who are spatially distant from an individual. By 2009, participation in SNSs was becoming commonplace and a large number of people worldwide had experienced digitally mediated social networking (Mitra n.d.). According to many research scholars, accounts on SNSs are actually a virtual image of an individual on the Internet (Treem et al. 2016; Koit 2011; Panteli 2009). Papacharissi (2012) argues that social media provides the opportunity of overlapping various social spheres and that the presentation of self on social media is abstract, fluid and ever-evolving. Users form their identity on the site but not in relation to their embodied selves, rather through characteristics of their personalities. They present themselves to other users by using their virtual identity on these sites. It is easy for someone to convey one's identity by projecting one's body (as a photograph), but a virtual projection of one's personality is more difficult to manage (Kumari 2015).

However, since Gen Z—young people born between 1995 and 2010—is considered to be digital natives, and has been exposed to the Internet, to social networks and to mobile systems, it is possible to say that it handles social media and its conventions and requirements with more ease. Despite this supposed ease on the part of the young generation, opinions on merits and demerits of social media are varied. Where on one hand there are those like Sauter (2014) who consider SNSs as tools of self-expression for individuals, there are others who argue that it is important to study socio-cultural challenges that surround access to these sites. For instance, Bamezai (2010) raises the concern of cultural intimidation because social media interaction may offer young people 'possibilities and promises' which are not so easily accepted in their own socio-cultural environment, yet which may be difficult to resist. Bamezai's concerns are at once intriguing and troubling, and merit further exploration.

Most SNSs offer visibility by allowing the user to create a profile of themselves with selected personal information like age, interests, occupation, location, and their pictures as well as videos. The attraction of seeing their images on screen is often enough to hook users onto these sites, and the 'likes' and 'comments' may act as validation and social recognition, creating further incentive to continue to share content and information with one's online social network. Other features of these sites—allowing one to add or request 'friends' or 'follow' one another—are also designed to keep users engaged and interactive. Both the 'friend' and 'follow' features not only allow the users to choose friends, acquaintances or celebrities on the site whom they 'like' but also (depending on privacy settings) allow complete strangers to become friends if they like the profiles of these strangers. These social media profiles act as a virtual reflection of the users and may be created with the intent of attracting or impressing other users.

One of the first researchers who theorised this behaviour was Erving Goffman (1959) who explained the notion of impression management. According to this concept, people try to establish a particular desired (usually positive) image of their self, and they purposefully adopt and project those characteristics which they imagine would be appreciated and approved by their social contacts. Goffman also emphasised that the perception of other people towards us influences and determines our social behaviour. This is a useful way to understand young people's behaviour, as adults may not always understand why their children behave in certain ways, particularly in relation to social media. We must understand that children today are experiencing a completely different social context than their parents, where social media interactions are as real for them as interactions in their physical environment, and this could have an impact on their social behaviour.

Discussing the value of social media in the lives of adolescents, Sonia Livingstone (2011: 352) says: 'In undertaking what Giddens (1991) called the "project of the self", children and young people are experiencing the internet as a valued new place for social exploration and self-expression (Holloway & Valentine 2003).' Buehler (2014) sought to compare motives of using Facebook vs. Twitter and found that they were distinct and led to differences in the way adolescents and young people engaged in practices and strategies of self-presentation and impression management. In this race for impression management on social media, the most vulnerable participants may be adolescents. Though they can be considered digital natives and are quite comfortable operating in this virtual world, many seem to be either unaware of the possible harms or unable to resist temptations which might prove to be risks. In this situation, it is imperative to investigate what factors drive them to use social media, which is the underlying logic of this study.

Views and Counter Views on the Impact of Social Media on Children

A Telenor Group report (2014) about Internet in India claimed that nearly 99 per cent of urban children are online and nearly 84 per cent of them between the ages of 6 and 18 years are active social media users. O'Keeffe et al. (2011) referred to a national poll conducted in the US which stated that more than half of the teenagers surveyed tended to surf SNSs at least more than once a day, 22 per cent of whom logged on more than 10 times a day. This is because three-fourths owned mobile phones and used them for SNSs (25 per cent), for texting (54 per cent) and for instant messaging (24 per cent). The Children's Commissioner of UK also presented a similar report (Children's Commissioner 2017) which acknowledged the role of the Internet as a massive force that can be used for good, but also agreed that it was never designed for children which is why it was alarming that one-third of the users of this technology were under 18 years old. Not only are the users young, they are also increasingly spending more time online; with an average increase of two hours plus across different age groups. Teenagers in the UK can spend as many as 20 hours plus in a week online. As Livingstone (2011) suggested, there are two schools of thought which see children and Internet from two completely opposite points of view: one considers children as vulnerable and easy prey to the negative effects of online media and if proper protection is not provided to them, they will face harms; the other considers children competent and efficient enough to understand and manage Internet harms.

However, we should note that the mere use of the Internet or social media need not be considered problematic, rather with the growth of the Internet it is quite natural for youngsters who are growing up in this era to use it extensively as it has become a part of their lives. Historically, any new media technology that has emerged—think radio, television, video games—has been looked upon with suspicion, forgetting that younger generations might embrace the new technologies and even be pioneers of change. In fact, K. Drotner's work, as cited by Livingstone (2011: 352), and Lievrouw and Livingstone (2006) show us how young people can be 'innovators' where they can creatively use new media opportunities to create their own user-generated media content. They can also be 'interactors' and use new media to engage with others as well as 'integrators' of personal and mass communication, blurring the boundaries between the two and becoming 'cultural pioneers' by realising a new form of and content for mediated communication.

Social media has become a very important factor in the development and growth of adolescents of this generation, at least those who live in contexts where there is some access to Internet-enabled digital devices. The pervasiveness of social media may contribute to shaping their opinions, inculcating social behaviour patterns or habits, and developing emotions and feelings. Livingstone (2011: 351) cites, 'Corsaro (1997) observes that through their daily actions, often invisible to adult eyes, children construct their social worlds as real places where real meanings (rather than fantasy or imitation) are generated, and thus they contribute to social structures which have consequences for both children and adults.' Some studies suggest that social media creates networked publics which is a type of imagined community which provides teens an opportunity to be in public (Helsper 2014). Another popular use of social media is the use of platforms like WhatsApp and Facebook by schools to keep students connected and informed of school-related activities, as observed and experienced personally by the author and others in her social circle. Other studies have shown how challenges and constraints of socio-economic and cultural backgrounds of youth can sometimes be overcome with the help of social media. For example, Rangaswamy et al. (2013) show how urban youth from lower socio-economic backgrounds were able to enjoy friendships, romance, dating and games through social media platforms that may not have been available to them in their offline lives. Such use helps to reduce the gap between otherwise marginalised sections of society and more privileged sections by enabling digital literacy and technical skills. Others have observed that social media can be seen as providing access to health information and to interactions with a wider set of peers, which can help young people manage complexities of puberty, particularly those who may be otherwise marginalised by migration, disability or sexuality (*The Lancet* 2018). These may be counted as some positive and productive uses of social media.

Despite the positive aspects of social media noted in the above-mentioned studies, risks involved cannot be overlooked. Some acknowledged risks of social media use include cyber bullying, online harassment, sexting, depression arising from social comparison, privacy concerns, among many others (O'Keeffe et al. 2011). They have also highlighted problems of Internet addiction and concurrent sleep deprivation among children due to excessive use of social media. In addition, the problem of 'social isolation' among 'socially connected' children on social media cannot be overlooked. Children tend to evade real social contact because they are so comfortable in virtual socialisation and less so with facing people physically. This could have significant social and psychological repercussions.

Thus, the potential of social media to mould attitudes, values and behaviours—particularly in vulnerable groups—has both positive and negative consequences (O'Keeffe et al. 2011). In India too, studies have found that excessive YouTube viewing by children has led to cyber bullying and cyber abuse, health issues among children for which a clinic was established in Bengaluru to offer counselling for Internet addiction (Ramesh et al. 2017).

Since social media has spread rapidly with little regulation, self-regulation appears to be one of the ways for users to protect themselves from its possible harms: in the case of adolescents, given what we know about the propensity for risky behaviour, self-regulation may be more of a challenge, even though as a group they may be seen as among the most vulnerable to the potential harms of digital media. As boyd (2015) argues in her book *It's Complicated*, teens have been struggling with issues of 'identity, privacy, addiction, bullying, risk-taking, literacy, inequalities, and being public' even before the digital world, however problems have magnified manifold due to 'persistence, visibility, spreadability, and searchability' of social media. Helsper (2014: 2783), in a review of boyd's book, explains, 'Instead of asking what is new or different, we should look at our concerns and teens' engagement with the digital world as a way to discuss life and its challenges in general.' boyd not only questions the impact of social media on teenagers but also talks about the diversity of teenagers as users and problems that arise due to this diversity. 'No group of teenage users can be homogeneous, and neither can their problems be the same,' notes boyd, (2015: 180), and also argues, 'Rather than assuming that youth have innate technical skills, parents, educators, and policymakers must collectively work to support those who come from different backgrounds and have different experiences.' That is why this study has tried to speak to children of various socio-economic backgrounds.

Let us for now return to the idea of self-regulation. It is not that adolescents are naïve and they do not realise potential harms social media can cause. The problem is that there is a huge mechanism working against their self-resistance. In his book *Irresistible*, Adam Alter (2017) talks at length about 'why we can't stop checking, scrolling, clicking and watching on social sites'. He considers it a type of addiction and cites the example of Greg Hochmuth, one of Instagram's founding engineers, who realised that he was building an engine for addiction. SNSs and video streaming platforms like Instagram, Facebook, Twitter, Netflix and Tinder are bottomless with an endless feed or a loop of videos and episodes that you can keep binge watching or you can keep swiping through in search of better options. While there are benefits of these applications and SNSs, it is also quite a struggle to manage moderate usage. Tristan Harris, a design ethicist, claims self-regulation is impossible not because we lack the power to do it, but because these SNSs are built to break your willpower to self-regulate (cited by Alter 2017: 12). Considering the addictive nature of social media and the design elements that encourage such constant engagement, self-regulation seems difficult even for mature users. Hence, the vulnerability of adolescents cannot be dismissed.

Purpose of the Study

In the backdrop of the trends of adolescents' consumption of social media world over and its potential impact discussed above, there are a few questions which should concern us regardless of our geography. This study explored the following questions:

- What are the social media consumption habits of the selected group of adolescents?
- What is their purpose of using social media and to what extent is it fulfilled?

- What are the experiences of the respondents with social media (positive and negative)?
- How have they tackled them?
- How do they see the overall impact of social media on their lives?

Methodology

Social media has become pervasive across the world, with young people becoming early adopters everywhere irrespective of geography and, to some extent, social class, even though marginalisation moderates its uptake everywhere. Thus, despite the paucity of region-specific research, it is possible to adopt insights gained elsewhere to inform work in India as well. Based on our review of studies done in the West, and our appreciation of the complex nature of the topic, we chose to use a qualitative, interpretive and self-reflexive approach to answer our research questions.

The study draws on a series of interactive in-depth interviews with adolescents, supplemented by focus group discussions and additional dialogue sessions with them. During these interactions, their thoughts, ideas and issues were documented, forming the main evidence base for this study. The participants were chosen through a purposive snowball which was initiated with help from my son who is in Class XI and my daughter who is in Class IX in a school in urban Jammu.

The comparative study was carried out in two districts—urban Jammu and rural Samba—to understand the reasons for using social media in both urban and rural areas. We also tried to understand the possible role of gender in adolescents' engagement with social media.

A total of eight boys and four girls (12) were selected from a rural background (Samba district) and six boys and four girls (10) were selected from an urban background (Jammu district). Thus, a total of 22 children were interviewed using an interview schedule. Although there is no firm rule on a recommended sample size, McCracken (1988: 17) indicates that recruiting eight respondents is generally sufficient for many in-depth interviews.

To begin with, it was a challenge to get access to the children. Since Jammu is a small city with parents who are quite conservative and concerned about change, parents of the selected children (especially mothers) were called for permission to invite them to my home, where the interactions were planned. Permission was given after explaining the purpose of the study and assuring them of safety as well as confidentiality, confirming that their names would not be revealed. Children were picked up from their homes and dropped back by me personally. They came individually or in pairs. This turned out to be a good approach as I found them to be more expressive when they were alone or only in the presence of close friends. Each interaction began with some general conversation to make them feel comfortable after which we began discussing their day-to-day life and how they spend time at home, which then led to their use of social media. Responses were noted and analysed on the basis of recurring themes which emerged when children spoke to me and did not vary across rural and urban groups. Children were encouraged to speak freely and I took care to keep my own ideas and assumptions out of the conversation.

Demographic Details of Rural and Urban Adolescents

It is important to understand the participants' socio-economic backgrounds in order to properly interpret their responses. The identity of individual respondents has been kept confidential; nevertheless, children were quite vocal in expressing their views and feelings. The participant pool was constructed keeping in mind diversity in terms of both gender and social backgrounds. In both urban and rural groups, there were four girls each and six and eight boys respectively, all in the age group of 13–17 years. All participants were students of either Class IX or Class XI.

Social Media Use

In order to understand the consumption habits of these children, they were asked which SNSs they were using and for how long, and specific times at which they use it. Though not all were comfortable in answering these questions on the first meeting, continuing dialogue in groups helped make them feel comfortable and eventually they opened up. Their answers are summarised below under various heads.

Which Are the Most Popular Sites?

The distribution of girls and boys from rural and urban areas on various SNSs is represented in Figure 8.1.

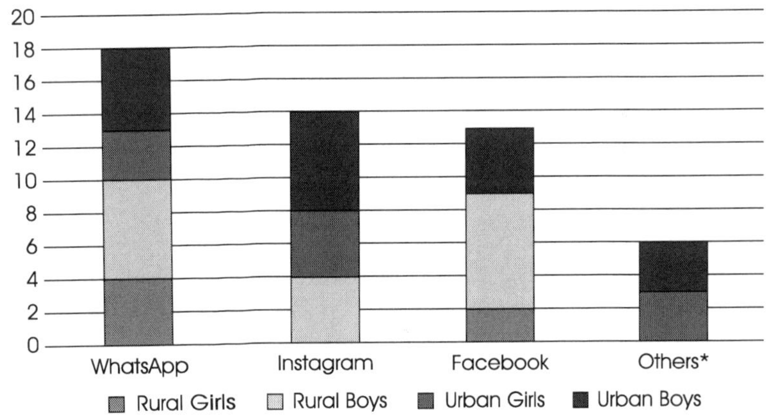

FIGURE 8.1 Distribution of Girls and Boys from Rural and Urban Areas on Various Social Networking Sites

Note: *Others include Twitter, Snapchat and YouTube.
Source: Author.

Figure 8.1 shows that urban adolescents are exploring more social sites than their rural counterparts irrespective of gender, whereas rural girls are limited to mostly two easily available and popular sites, Facebook and WhatsApp. The simple reason cited for this was easy access to these sites for urban adolescents and their greater exposure to social media in comparison to rural adolescents. While Facebook, WhatsApp and Instagram seem to be popular among teenagers of urban and rural Jammu, Twitter was less so, with only one of the urban boys mentioning that he used it.

How Long Have They Been on Social Media?

Based on the responses, it appears that rural adolescents are not very old on social media; most of them had been on these platforms for less than two years, whereas of the 10 urban adolescents, there were 7 who may be described as veterans on these media, having been users for the last four to five years. The reason could be easy access to Internet in urban areas and greater exposure to social media. In comparison to other developed countries, mobile phones became affordable to middle-class Indians much later. With most children accessing social media on mobile phones, it stands to reason that Indian teenagers became active on social media later than those in the West.

When Do They Use Social Media?

In order to understand whether social media distracts these adolescents from studies, they were asked whether they use social media during studies, after studies or both. Their responses show some interesting trends: all the rural adolescents said that they use social media only after studies, whereas most of the urban adolescents said that they use social media all the time, irrespective of their study time. While we may speculate on the sincerity of these responses, in keeping with the spirit of qualitative inquiry, we may assume that the answers reflect what each group sees as the 'desirable' response, without making a judgement about truth or falsity. In fact, this could lead to some interesting ways to unpack the responses relative to the values of each specific group. However, the statement seems correct in case of rural children who were trying to portray themselves as 'good' and 'obedient' children while speaking to the researcher who could sense a feeling that social media was not socially acceptable in the rural setup and children were trying to be acceptable so they were providing desirable answers. In case of urban children, they took pride in being open and blunt irrespective of what others think about their response. This way of expression has also something to do with their reference group, as this group of peers appreciates this bluntness and showing the 'it's okay not being perfect' behaviour. For urban children, it was felt that they were more concerned about their own thoughts with respect to their reference group more than anything else. In other words, we can say that both the groups were trying to give 'desirable' answers according to their respective reference groups.

How Much Time Do They Spend on Social Media?

Most of the adolescents, irrespective of their urban and rural backgrounds, said that they spent at most six to seven hours a day on social media. This is higher than the figures reported among teenagers in the UK which is 20 hours per week (*Statista* 2019), suggesting that this group of Indian respondents is much more active on social media in comparison to the UK children. This group of Indian teens is less active on the Internet than those in the US where teens spend an average of nine hours a day online (Anderson 2018).

Why Do They Use Social Media?

Although the results so far show that most of the adolescents interviewed do not spend more than six hours a day on social media, it still represents a significant chunk of their waking hours; almost one-fourth of a day. This is why it becomes important to understand why these adolescents are using social media. Based on their responses, the various purposes were: to be in touch with friends, engagement, to be updated and to be socially active.

It appears that urban adolescents are quite clear about the purpose of using social sites and they use them for all the given purposes. It is important to note that these were options presented to them, and possibly, if I had given more options they may have opted for them too. However, rural adolescent boys seemed to have not yet explored the wide variety of purposes for using SNSs and they looked a bit confused. Where two of them use it to get in touch with friends, three use it to remain active in the social sphere while one uses it to know the happenings around and one even selected 'engagement'. In comparison, rural girls have more clarity about the purpose of using SNSs and they too, like the urban girls, use it for all purposes.

Children all over the world seem to be on the same ground in terms of articulating why they use social media. Almost all of them used it to remain connected with peers, to create their own social circle and create/maintain their identity in that circle, to gain validation of their virtual existence and to remain aware about each other's lives.

Reason for Opening a Social Media Account

After getting these preliminary details from the respondents, I began to dig deeper into their social media activities, particularly to find out how many of them were using social media with the knowledge of their parents. All of them said that they were using it with the permission of their parents, irrespective of their rural or urban background. I also asked them for the single most important reason they had for opening a social media account. Almost all urban adolescent girls said that one of the most important reasons was to stay connected with friends, except for one who said that she was influenced by friends and got curious. The reasons given by urban young boys were quite diverse, one said he started his social media account to interact with celebrities, to watch 'Do it yourself' programmes and to look at memes, while another said that he wanted to watch travel-related programmes on social media. One boy opened his account as part of an internship on social media campaigns, while another wanted to stay in touch with friends from his previous school. The other two urban boys also said they wanted to keep abreast of happenings around them, so they started their first social media account. Rural adolescents mostly opened their social media accounts just to remain connected with their friends; only one of them said that he opened the account because it was a new trend, while one said that the reason was to know about happenings around him.

PERCEPTIONS AND ATTITUDES

The conversations with these adolescents also drew attention to some of the benefits these young people were deriving from their presence on social media, as well as the ways in which they perceived these advantages. One girl from an urban background said, 'Apart from letting me communicate with friends, it acts as an entertainment source when I am bored and sometimes it has interesting facts and information.'

Another girl saw it offering access to vast knowledge and a way to interact with the world, while yet another found it useful to keep track of celebrity gossip, news and information. One girl said that it is a way to know about new cultures and new people. While urban adolescent girls see a range of interesting benefits from social media, boys mainly find it useful as a means of getting connected to friends and seeing what is happening around them.

Rural adolescent girls saw its benefit in knowing about their surroundings; while boys found it beneficial for knowledge, political news and social activities. Except one, all rural adolescents considered social media as a necessity for them; however, most (9 out of 12) did not consider themselves addicted to it.

In case of urban adolescents, all except one girl and one boy considered social media as a necessity for them. Three of the four girls said they felt they were addicted to it, whereas only one of the six boys considered himself addicted to it. The others felt that they use it in a controlled way. They defined 'addiction' as a necessary thing without which they cannot live. They considered it as essential as 'breathing'.

On asking whether they can live without social media, two out of four urban girls said 'no' while the other two said 'yes, if there are better things to do or better people around'. Out of six boys, four said 'no' because they get their career-related information from social media and it also refreshes their mind. However, one of the boys offered the argument that even before the tech world, children used to survive, so they will eventually learn to live without social media if they had to, while one boy asserted that 'he can live without social media because he is a social person'.

On the other hand, all rural adolescents said that they could live without social media because they were not addicted to it and they could engage themselves in sports and games. All of them, both rural and urban adolescents, said that they consider social media 'misleading and misguiding' for children because for some it drags them away from their real surroundings and studies, while for others it provides objectionable videos and misleading news. In comparison to respondents from a rural background, urban adolescents seemed more mature in dealing with social media and most of them thought that it can be misleading or misguiding for only those who do not understand it or who cannot regulate their own use. One girl said, 'It depends upon how a teen takes up all the social media stuff. Yes, it can be misguiding or misleading for some but not when they are checked upon.'

They were aware that if they reported against an objectionable site, it could be blocked. Two of them talked about trending fake news on social media and apprehensions that young children might be misguided by such information, but most talked about countering such threats by handling social media in a mature fashion and regulating their own use of such sites. The kind of fake news they pointed to had to do mostly with celebrity gossip and lifestyle. However, they did suggest that certain cultural and social trends, such as romance in junior classes, were encouraged on social media. As a result, they said that by Class VIII or IX it was assumed that if you do not have a girlfriend or boyfriend, you are not 'cool' or you are not smart enough.

During focus group discussions, children also said that social media had become an easy platform to approach a girl or a boy. Although the culture of Jammu is still quite conservative, social media provides an easy option for young boys and girls to meet and interact, and even form romantic relationships. None of them, except one urban adolescent girl, admitted that they had encountered any 'bad' sites. She mentioned that she had accidentally encountered such sites but soon found ways to block them. She explained that some adult content started appearing on the site she was surfing and she initially panicked but ultimately found out how to block the site. It is highly likely that children who use social media for six to seven hours a day will encounter pornographic sites, but none of the other participants acknowledged this, possibly for fear of losing access if the information reached their parents or peers.

Nearly all participants advocated restricting some social media sites for children which are not age appropriate or which have objectionable content. One girl stated, 'Yes, few bad social media sites should be restricted because they can influence and manipulate a child and that child could also get caught up into some problem.' There are a few who support the idea of having a special social media site for children to keep them safe and deliver proper content, while others consider it 'lame' in the era of Internet which cannot be regulated or contained.

Even if most of these adolescent boys and girls of both rural and urban areas do not consider all their peers mature and smart enough to use all types of social media, they also do not approve of teachers and parents who try to restrict children from using social media. They think that their parents and teachers do not understand their requirements and try to impose their own ideals and standards on children. They feel that social media fills the gap between them and their parents. Their argument is that restriction would make the teenagers more curious and rebellious. It would be better if instead of restrictions, teachers and parents would just monitor their children. A few of the participants did note that their upbringing helped them, and if others did not have the same kind of upbringing then they may not be able to handle social media as effectively.

What Do Social Media Mean to Adolescents?

All the respondents were asked to briefly define what social media meant to them and describe its overall impact on their lives. Most of the participants from a rural background said that it is attraction, addiction, impression management and also necessity. Three considered it a necessity and only two said that it is no more than an attraction for them, while the others mentioned all these descriptors. On the other hand, urban adolescents gave varied answers. For three of them, it is addiction and necessity, while for two of them it is all of these—attraction, addiction, impression and necessity. Two said it was only attraction, one said it was only a necessity. For one other, it is attraction and impression while for the last one it is attraction, impression and necessity. One girl even said that it is as necessary for their generation as 'breathing'.

While talking about its impact on their lives, most of the urban adolescents praised social media for making it possible to stay connected with their peers and keeping them updated about the happenings in their world. In the words of one of the respondents, who is interested in art, 'It's the best and worst thing [that] ever happened to me. It keeps me distracted from studies but also gives me new ideas for painting.' Another respondent said,

> It has had both positive and negative impact upon me. It lets me communicate with friends, keeps me entertained and allows me to keep track of my favourite celebrities. The only negative impact that it has had on me is that it distracts me. Overall, if one keeps check on right and wrong doings on social media, then actually it is very beneficial.

This fascination with celebrities was also perceptible among rural adolescents, and social media gave them a way to feed this interest. The girls in this group thought that it has both a positive and negative impact on their lives, while the boys believed that the impact is mostly positive, in terms of knowledge and entertainment.

One girl from an elite urban background explained the impact of social media on her life in an interesting manner. She said that she understands its repercussions, but it is the only escape route for teenagers like her from the pressure of society and parents' disregard for their interests. She held the education system responsible for this and portrayed social media as the only way out, so, in her view, it is essential.

From the children's point of view, these arguments seem convincing and leave adults to ponder about the lacunae in our education system as well as inadequacies in proper parental care and social support for our children. However, this cannot be seen as an excuse for the excessive use/misuse of any SNSs, and one that could have a significant negative impact on their lives, an implication that these adolescents seem to be unaware of. All the respondents in this admittedly small study have emphasised the need for controlled and limited use of social media in order to prevent themselves from distraction, but they also said that it is so tempting that it is difficult to control. However, a few of them also presented the other side of the coin by using it constructively: for instance, two of the respondents said that they use social media mostly to watch travel videos and 'Do it yourself' series because they wish to make their careers in these fields. One girl said that she uses social media mainly to look for new ideas that she can apply to her painting. This offers a ray of hope in that it shows that social media can be channelised towards more productive and constructive purposes that these young people have themselves identified, going beyond the stereotype that adolescents use social media only in narcissistic or unproductive ways.

We need to understand that social media is an important part of the everyday lives of today's children for they have grown up with it. The act of clicking selfies before or during a fun trip, taking mobile phone pictures of food before any feast and uploading these on social media, updating their status with their instant thoughts and moods are natural things to do for this generation. However, it does not mean that only social media influences them; rather, they influence social media as well. There are many opportunities to achieve visibility, even become a celebrity, on social media by uploading a stylish picture or a thoughtful quote, although for a limited time. But when young people see their peers achieve popularity or fame or if an idea appears to be gaining traction on social media, they start following it and it starts trending. Often, it is the users who set the trend on social media, but more often than not it is those who use it strategically and purposefully who are able to do this; and this is an understanding that young people seem to acquire through observation and practice.

Conclusion

Before conducting this study and talking to the children, I had assumed that they would express the view that social media is a waste of time and that it has a negative impact on them, but instead I found urban adolescents to be quite vocal in their support of social media. Most of them accepted that they are, to some extent, addicted to it and some of them tried hard to control their excessive use of social media. I had not expected this. They also tried to justify their love for social media by arguing that having been born into a digital world, it is like breathing for them. Some also suggested, quite convincingly, that social media provided a supplementary avenue that allowed them to compensate for a poor education system and parental negligence. However, these are views we may take on board with caution, even if they may be justified to some extent in the Indian context. Some of the adolescents interviewed for this study recommended parental control of the use of social media, but interestingly this view was expressed only by the rural adolescents. Urban adolescents, on the other hand, were completely against any such external control although they recommended self-regulation and self-filtering of content. Rural children appeared a little more hesitant in their handling of social media, possibly because of lower levels of access, greater parental controls or other cultural factors. They seemed to be voicing opinions they had heard from their parents, although this could not be verified. On the contrary, urban adolescents seemed to be speaking for themselves. They were vocal, confident, argumentative, and convincing, to some extent. They exhibited maturity in the way they spoke about handling social media; they seemed to know what they were doing. Some of them put social media to constructive use and almost all of them knew how to protect themselves from its negative effects.

In a nutshell, we may argue that social media is a necessity for today's young people, and their use borders on what we may call addiction. However, the more they use it, the more they understand how to use it rather than being used by it. They learn practices of filtering content, regulating them and using social media purposively rather than aimlessly scrolling through their bottomless feeds. This suggests that we should perhaps place greater trust on this generation and allow them the space to find their own ways of dealing with this digital world, rather than imposing our judgements and fears on them.

References

Alter, A. 2017. *Irresistible*. London: Penguin Random House.

Anderson, J. 2018. 'Even Teens Are Worried They Spend Too Much Time on their Phones'. Available at https://qz.com/1367506/pew-research-teens-worried-they-spend-too-much-time-on-phones/ (accessed on 22 December 2019).

Bamezai, G. 2010. 'Book Review—Children and Youth in the Digital Media Culture: From a Nordic Horizon'. *International Journal of Communication Studies* 4(4): 35–40.

boyd, d. 2015. *It's Complicated: The Social Lives of Networked Teens*. Available at https://yalebooks.yale.edu/book/9780300199000/its-complicated (accessed on 29 January 2019).

boyd, d., and N. Ellison. 2007. 'Social Network Sites: Definition, History, and Scholarship'. *Journal of Computer-Mediated Communication* 13(1): 210–30.

Buehler, E. M. 2014. 'Factors Influencing Adolescent Impression Management on Social Networking Sites'. MA diss., Wake Forest University Graduate School of Arts and Sciences, North Carolina. Available at https://wakespace.lib.wfu.edu/bitstream/handle/10339/39303/Buehler_wfu_0248M_10585.pdf (accessed on 20 December 2019).

Children's Commissioner. 2017. *Growing Up Digital*. January. Available at https://www.childrenscommissioner.gov.uk/wp-content/uploads/2017/06/Growing-Up-Digital-Taskforce-Report-January-2017_0.pdf (accessed on 12 September 2019).

Goffman, E. 1959. *The Presentation of Self in Everyday Life*. New York: Anchor Books.

Helsper, E. J. 2014. 'Book Review: danah boyd, It's Complicated: The Social Lives of Networked Teens'. *International Journal of Communication* 8: 2783–86. Available at https://ijoc.org/index.php/ijoc/article/3274/1252 (accessed on 3 March 2020).

IAMAI and Nielsen. 2019. *India Internet 2019*. Available at https://cms.iamai.in/Content/ResearchPapers/d3654bcc-002f-4fc7-ab39-e1fbeb00005d.pdf (accessed on 30 January 2020).

Koit, N. 2011. 'Virtual Subjectivity on Social Networking Sites: Transforming the Politics of Self-surveillance'. Queen's University. Available at https://pdfs.semanticscholar.org/87a3/882b79e3f164fec3a17146d3477d85bb8953.pdf (accessed on 5 March 2019).

Kumari, A. 2015. 'Evaluating Social Media as a New Tool of Journalism Education'. *South Asia Journal of Multidisciplinary Studies* 1(1). Available at http://journal.edwin.co.in/index.php/sajms/article/view/679 (accessed on 4 January 2020).

Lievrouw, L., and S. Livingstone. 2006. 'Introduction'. In *Handbook of New Media: Social Shaping and Social Consequences*, eds L. Lievrouw and S. Livingstone, 1–14. London: Sage.

Livingstone, S. 2011. 'Internet, Children and Youth'. In *The Handbook of Internet Studies*, eds C. Consalvo and M. Ess, 348–68. Oxford: Blackwell.

Masthi, N. R. Ramesh, Pruthvi S. and Phaneendra Mallekavu. 2017. 'A Comparative Study on Social Media Addiction between Public and Private High School Students of Urban Bengaluru, India'. *ASEAN Journal of Psychiatry* 18(2): 206–15. Available at https://doi.org/10.1016/j.chb.2013.04.002 (accessed on 5 March 2020).

McCracken, G. 1988. *The Long Interview*. Newbury Park, CA: Sage.

Mitra, A. (n.d.). 'Creating a Presence on Social Networks via Narbs'. *Global Media Journal*. Available at http://www.globalmediajournal.com/open-access/creating-a-presence-on-social-networks-via-narbs.pdf (accessed on 21 March 2020).

O'Keeffe, G. S., K. Clarke-Pearson and Council on Communications and Media. 2011. 'The Impact of Social Media on Children, Adolescents, and Families'. *Pediatrics* 127(4): 800–804.

O'Reilly, Tim, and J. Battelle. 2009. 'Web Squared: Web 2.0 Five Years On'. In *Web Squared: Web 2.0 Five Years On: Web 2.0 Summit 2009*, eds Tim O'Reilly and John Battelle, 1–13. San Francisco: O'Reilly Media.

Available at https://conferences.oreilly.com/web2summit/web2009/public/schedule/detail/10194 (accessed on 20 February 2020).

Panteli, N. 2009. 'Virtual Social Networks: A New Dimension for Virtuality Research'. In *Virtual Social Networks*, ed. Niki Panteli, 1–17. London: Palgrave Macmillan UK. Available at https://doi.org/10.1057/9780230250888_1 (accessed on 21 March 2020).

Papacharissi, Z. 2012. 'A Networked Self: Identity Performance and Sociability on Social Network Sites'. In *Frontiers in New Media Research* (1st edn), eds F. L. F. Lee, L. Leung, J. L. Qiu and D. S. C. Chu, 207–21. Routledge. Available at https://zizi.people.uic.edu/Site/Research_files/Ch12.pdf (accessed on 21 February 2020).

Rangaswamy, N., G. Challagulla, M. Young and E. Cutrell. 2013. 'Local Pocket Internet and Global Social Media Bridging the Digital Gap: Facebook and Youth Sub-Stratum in Urban India'. Proceedings of the 12th International Conference on Social Implications of Computers in Developing Regions, Montego Bay, Jamaica, May. Available at https://www.researchgate.net/publication/326735431_Local_Pocket_Internet_and_Global_Social_Media_Bridging_the_Digital_Gap_Facebook_and_Youth_Sub-Stratum_in_Urban_India_Local_Pocket_Internet_and_Global_Social_Media_Bridging_the_Digital_Gap_Facebook_and (accessed on 26 April 2019).

Sauter, T. 2014. '"What's on Your Mind?" Writing on Facebook as a Tool for Self-formation'. *New Media and Society* 16(5): 823–39. Available at http://www2.psych.utoronto.ca/users/tafarodi/psy427/articles/Sauter(2014).pdf (accessed on 14 February 2020).

Statista. 2019. 'Time Spent Consuming Media Per Week Among Children in the United Kingdom (UK) in 2018, by Media'. Available at https://www.statista.com/statistics/397851/hours-of-media-consumption-by-children-by-media-uk/ (accessed on 14 January 2020).

Telenor Group. 2014. 'Safe Internet Sweeps across India'. Available at https://www.telenor.com/safe-internet-sweeps-across-india/ (accessed on 22 December 2019).

The Lancet. 2018. 'Children and Social Media', Editorial. 391(10116): 95.

Treem, J. W., S. L. Dailey, C. S. Pierce and D. Biffl. 2016. 'What We Are Talking About When We Talk About Social Media: A Framework for Study'. *Sociology Compass* 10(9): 768–84. Available at https://doi.org/10.1111/soc4.12404 (accessed on 6 April 2020).

Trottier, D., and C. Fuchs. 2015. 'Theorising Social Media, Politics and the State: An Introduction'. In *Social Media, Politics and the State: Protests, Revolutions, Riots, Crime and Policing in the Age of Facebook, Twitter and YouTube* (1st edn), eds D. Trottier and C. Fuchs, 3–38. Routledge. Available at https://www.routledge.com/Social-Media-Politics-and-the-State-Protests-Revolutions-Riots-Crime/Trottier-Fuchs/p/book/9781138798243 (accessed on 15 April 2020).

PART IV

CONSTRUCTIONS

9

KIDS MAKE ART

Children, Creative Practice and the World

Samina Mishra

Education is the passport to the future, said Malcolm X (Lily 2021), and the approach in educational systems provides a glimpse of how the future is being imagined. Today, the new buzzwords in education are 'design thinking' and 'entrepreneurship' with schools, that can afford to, creating maker spaces that encourage children to work with technology as creators, and not merely remain technology consumers. There is a growing emphasis on innovation fuelled by individual imagination, and so where maker spaces are not possible, this takes other forms; for example, government schools in Delhi introducing an entrepreneurship curriculum Class IX onwards. In the last few decades, a push towards a child-friendly pedagogy has led to a greater amount of creative practice among schoolchildren and a transaction of the curriculum through creative projects. In India, this is generally more visible in the elementary years. While a subject like Art has been available for several decades in high schools affiliated with the Central Board of Secondary Education (CBSE) and Indian School Certificate (ISC), the approach has remained largely traditional and seen within the ambit of the less competitive Humanities. However, today, with the growing popularity of international curricula, there is an increasing emphasis on interdisciplinarity and a more robust approach to the teaching of creative disciplines at the secondary level in the more elite schools. The practice-based approach in educational boards like the International General Certificate of Secondary Education (IGCSE) and International Baccalaureate (IB) emphasises research and the application of learning in individual projects based on student choice. But even the children who are not in this sliver of elite schools are being exposed to the idea of creative practice through the work of non-governmental organisations (NGOs), children's writers, artists and storytellers who come from a belief in creativity, and are responding to the changing arts and media landscape by conducting a variety of workshops that aim not just to transfer skills to children, but also to tap into the potential market for creative goods and services that children represent. This is linked to projection of the changing scenario in the workplace. The jobs of the future, we are told repeatedly, lie in the creative industries (Breckton 2017). Jobs that cannot be quantified and evaluated in a straightforward way, and require interpretation are resistant to automation. These include the arts and design, advertising, publishing and computer programming. According to the Alliance for Useful Evidence at NESTA UK (Nesta 2017: 3), a foundation that aims to meet the challenges of our times through innovations that can 'shift whole systems in a new direction', 87 per cent of jobs that require creative skills, even in the traditional non-creative industries, will also be protected from the onslaught of robotics. This projected scenario of employment has a clear impact on the educational landscape and on the expectations from children who will go on to become this future workforce.

I am a filmmaker, writer and teacher. Much of my work focuses on children and childhood, and I am interested in collaborative work with children that facilitates creative expression. I came to teaching, both formally and in non-formal workshops, from my practice as a filmmaker and writer. I engage with children from different socio-economic backgrounds and learn how they experience the world through the media they produce. My work has taught me that it is critical to include the arts in education if the role of education is to help individuals gain an understanding of the world and a sense of self that can enable them to imagine and work towards a better future. This is an ongoing endeavour of the arts and so, as a teacher of the arts, I also believe that it is important that I continue working as a practitioner in order to bring my learning from the field into the classroom. Thus, my students and I walk similar paths as we struggle to clarify what we want to say and how we want to say it. We are linked by this effort to use creative practice to reflect on the world and to deepen our own understanding of it.

This essay reflects on my work with children and diverse forms of creative practice to understand how children produce media today and what we can learn from that practice about contemporary society. The essay will first examine children's engagement with media today, referring to the work of scholars who have studied media, participatory culture and pedagogy to recognise the changing nature of literacy. It will then go on to present my work with diverse groups of children, in both formal and non-formal spaces, using the language and visual arts to understand how children produce media and what that tells us about contemporary Indian childhood. Finally, the essay will tie up these accounts through the lens of work and global capital, pointing towards the need for the neoliberal economic system to push for creativity in education along with the inherent potential of the creative learner to challenge the system itself. This essay seeks to provide a nuanced understanding of children's creative practice that can enable empathy for young people in an increasingly competitive global scenario.

Children, Media and Participatory Culture

Just as childhood was seen as tabula rasa to be written upon by adults, children's engagement with media was, for long, considered a one-way process with children being the passive recipients of messaging that could either mould them into ideal humans or influence them in negative ways. The old ways of seeing—direct impact theories—have given way to more nuanced understandings of how children engage with media and while there are still those who believe that children, especially the very young, should be left alone and free of modern forms of media, namely television and the Internet, others recognise that such a pure space is difficult, and that what is required is engagement that allows children to negotiate their relationship with the media. The work of scholars like Henry Jenkins on participatory culture emphasises the need to stop thinking of media as a simple, one-way communication in the twenty-first century, and instead see it as a system of interactive processes made up of several actions and activities. 'Consumption becomes production; reading becomes writing; spectator culture becomes participatory culture,' writes Jenkins (2006). Engaging with media is an everyday skill today, and with social media, the line between being a producer and a consumer of media is increasingly blurred. Changes in technology have made phone cameras accessible to more and more people, and thus the creation of media in the form of photographs or short videos shared via social media has turned ordinary citizens into media creators, selecting and curating their own life experiences, interpreting and commenting upon those of others. The idea of telling stories is an organic part of this process with social media portals using precisely this term for the media shared on their sites. I was recently sent a video made on the TikTok app by a 7-year-old girl from a working class family, who had got her younger sister to lip-synch to an exchange between a bargaining customer and a vegetable vendor. The little girl, 4 or 5 years old, had been framed with a basket of tomatoes next to her and the customer was supposedly off-camera. The girl acted out with the appropriate hand gestures in synch with the audio from the app, holding out a tomato when stating the price and raising her hand to the skies as she lip-synched to the punch line of the story, '*Bhagwan se toh dara karo*! (At least fear God!)'—a verbal victory for the vegetable vendor. The child had picked out the audio that resonated with her and put together a little story of everyday life. The scenario was one that she was familiar with and the punch line was one that made her laugh. These and similar examples using apps like TikTok, Dubsmash and Snapchat point clearly to the fact that we need to see children not merely as consumers of media but also as producers.

The changing mediascape has also impacted the way the arts are perceived and practised. There is a greater degree of appreciation for creative work and where, in earlier times, children would have been told to put away the paintbrush and concentrate on 'studies', today parents are often the ones who post their children's artistic endeavours on social media, seeking appreciation and encouragement. This is also tied up with the impulse for self-promotion that marks the contemporary world of work that constantly needs the individual to present herself as a valuable worker. For creative practitioners, this translates to an expectation that the artist is responsible for not just creating the work, but also for its wide dissemination and publicity. Increasingly, the onus is on the individual to present the value of her work rather than on the structures of the creative industries, and social media becomes the tool to do this. The creative arts and media landscapes are thus intertwined and inextricable. In this context, children, especially urban children, begin to learn skills for using media at an early age, outside of formal education. There is an instinctive understanding of visual language among children today. Among teens, this is reflected in the way they use social media platforms like Instagram and Snapchat, combining image and text to create stories from their everyday lives. Apps like TikTok are allowing children to create media in new and playful ways, and play is such a necessary ingredient of creativity. Santosh Desai (2019) comments:

> TikTok is part of a dynamic new force that needs to be harnessed, rather than fought. It is part of a larger mushrooming of creativity that we see among the young all across the country. It represents that the young will find joy in forms of self-expression that do not depend on running other people down.

But even before social media, there was media production by children.

I first began engaging with children and creative practice in the early 2000s with children in working-class neighbourhoods that the NGO Pratham worked in. Pratham's thrust was on reading and the use of stories to build childhood literacy. As an extension, I began to work with the children to help develop their writing skills by focusing on self-expression—stories that came from their lives, their world. We would play with words and syllables, creating rhythm, and talk about what we see and how we see. I remember walking into Haathishala one morning, a *basti* (slum) on the banks of the Yamuna in east Delhi, after a particularly rough storm. People were busy repairing damage to their huts and when the children gathered, I asked them to write single-line sentences about the storm. One boy, probably 9 years old, wrote: *Kal raat toofan mein hamari chat bhaag gayi* (Last night in the storm our roof ran away). I will always remember this sentence for the way in which it captured an entire world from a child's perspective—the reference to the tarpaulin roofs that make up a working-class hut in the city, the storm from which the roof offers little protection and the imagination of a child that sees the falling of the roof in a whimsical way, turning the difficulty of the moment into an almost-magical one by imbuing the roof with agency. So much to learn from this single sentence! And shared as it was in the group, undeniably it was an act of media production.

My work with Pratham was on using stories as a tool for literacy. Pratham, in fact, devised a strategy to enable children to become literate in 30–50 days using simple stories (Freethink 2019). Textual media in the form of stories has always been linked to literacy goals for children with emphasis on questions like: Do they have the requisite skills to communicate? Can they write an application? Will that make them candidates in the future job market? But literacy in the twenty-first century needs a new definition. The New Media Consortium offers one:

> …the set of abilities and skills where aural, visual, and digital literacy overlap. These include the ability to understand the power of images and sounds, to recognise, and use that power, to manipulate, and transform digital media, to distribute them pervasively, and to easily adapt them to new forms (2005: 2).

Jenkins (2006) goes on to clarify that textual literacy remains an important skill in the new participatory culture and that 'new media literacies must be considered a social skill'. Such an approach that emerges from an acknowledgment of participatory culture requires that 'children plan, implement, and evaluate their own learning in social interaction together with educators' (Leinonen and Sintonen 2014: 217). Leinonen and Sintonen refer to William Corsaro's work,

Sociology of Childhood, to point out, 'young children should not only be socialized in the adult world, but they should also be considered active participants who interpret and reproduce the culture of their society' (2014: 219). Learning happens as a process of social interaction, and so it is not merely about content and children, but also about the educator and the transaction of the content. Learning is thus socially constructed and children have to be seen as agents in this process just as much as the educators. And media—both traditional and new—are tools to facilitate a participatory engagement. Leinonen and Sintonen's (2014) study of kindergarten children as active media producers in Finland reflects the need for the adults engaging with children to listen with respect and create a nurturing context that facilitates children's participation. It also points out that educators need to be flexible in using different forms of media.

In contemporary India, while this kind of participatory learning process may still be a distant goal in most formal education spaces, it would be naïve to imagine that this is not taking place. Children are interpreting and reproducing culture all the time. As Jenkins (2006) states, 'Participatory culture is anything but fringe or underground today... The key issue isn't what the media are doing to our children but rather what our children are doing with the media.' Many adults respond in a knee-jerk fashion to young people's use of media and find their expressive engagement—for example, too much time spent on devices or the language used in online interactions—problematic. And yet those same adults also profess the contradictory opinion that media skills are essential for the future job market. What is needed, therefore, is that we listen to children's voices to understand how they see the world and imagine change.

Creative Practice in the Formal Space

I am a teacher of Film in a formal school space. I teach the IB Film programme at a school in suburban Delhi. My students are typically 16–18-year-olds, grappling with the pressures of a highly demanding curriculum that requires that they develop keen research and analytical skills, build an international vision and an ethical approach to being a citizen of the world. The IB curriculum is geared towards developing the creative, interdisciplinary thinker. IB students have to choose one subject from six groups—language and literature, language acquisition, individuals and societies, experimental sciences, mathematics and the arts. While one subject from the first five groups is mandatory, it is not mandatory to choose a subject from Group 6, the arts, under which Film is offered. At the school where I teach, Film class is generally six to eight students, allowing for close individual attention. Many of my students come to Film because they are primarily visual learners, are good with technology and excited about telling their own stories. Since IB is an expensive curriculum, my students are all from affluent backgrounds, but many come from families where cultural capital is of a more limited nature. They may be financially well-off and their parents are, in fact, products of liberalised India and the class that benefited from the new economic policies, but their exposure to culture is mainly within the easily accessible popular realm. So, often Film class is their first exposure to cinema from other spaces and times, and to the idea of art as a reflection of society. Since the learning process requires that students critique each other's work, I always begin the new year by talking about the idea of creativity and where ideas come from, so that students arrive at an understanding of how there are no right or wrong answers and that Film class is a safe space for expression. This is critical for me as the teacher so that students contribute to discussions without being self-conscious—much of the transaction in the classroom depends upon the quality of the discussions. This is of course a long process that continues to evolve through the two years that I teach them, but it is true that from the beginning many issues come up in Film class that foreground the participatory nature of media practice.

One of the early narrative exercises that I do with my students is a short one- to three-minute-long film on the prompt 'Me, Myself'. The parameters are that it should be about an idea that introduces them—a personality trait, a hobby, an experience. This has to be translated into a visual narrative without using any dialogue. They are free to use music, sound effects, archival photographs or video, and text. Over the years, this exercise has yielded a rich array of self-expression among students, although their skill level at this point is still at the beginner's stage. The 'Me, Myself' exercise seems to tap into a font of latent stories waiting for a space where they can unfold.

One year, one of my students responded to the prompt by experimenting freely and created a lovely little film, strong on metaphoric images——shots of her writing, crumpling and throwing the pages into a dustbin, a hand offering her a peeled orange, walking in the night with a friend, and taking the crumpled pages out of the dustbin. These are linked by a series of self-portrait shots—in the first, her face is completely painted black and she is looking serious, and in the last one that comes at the end, the paint has been completely washed off and she is smiling. In reflecting on the process, the student shared that she used the exercise to think about the important things and people in her life and how they could help her to realise her sense of self. For our Film class, it was a very successful exercise because it experimented with creating connotative meanings through images and the narrative created by joining them in a particular order. I shared the film with a Hindi teacher in the school who then devised a lesson around it for her language students. When she first saw the film, the Hindi teacher said to me that she did not realise that 'our kids think so deeply', our kids meaning the students in our school. This points to how being able to choose Film as a subject had allowed this student a possibility for expression that she may not have had otherwise, and the resulting appreciation for the film must definitely have contributed to her self-confidence and the process of self-actualisation.

There are other examples of such self-expression in my classroom. Bullying has come up often as an issue—sometimes they weave fictional stories around the idea and sometimes there is a personal account. In the process of responding to one student's idea around bullying, I became privy to the fact that she had a history of cutting as a response to what had been going on in her life, and she wanted to refer to that in her film. This not only made me think about teen lives in a new light, but again, her engagement with media offered her a way to talk about something personal and share it with more openness. While she may still face psychological challenges, she is no longer cutting and in the two years that she has been my student, this young girl has grown in confidence and the ability to articulate as she has gained mastery over film language and film technology. Another student who identifies as gay made a personal film about that, using images of himself with the pride rainbow in public spaces as well as images of the rainbow painted on different parts of his body. The voiceover is a personal text that talks about his difficulties. While he has shared the film only with a select group of viewers, he has talked about how the Film class gave him the space to talk about this—'I found it so easy to convey something that I didn't think I could tell anyone.'

My Film classroom reflects what Leinonen and Sintonen's (2014) study has showed with kindergarten children that the process of media creation can be extremely empowering. Not only are children able to create their own content, but they are also learning to negotiate, make choices and decisions, and communicate with others. Leinonen and Sintonen emphasise the need to include media creation from such an early age because in the future these kindergarten children will need to negotiate a variety of communicative acts and this requires being recognised and being able to receive feedback from a community that they are connected to. We can see this in my Film classroom—my students have done exactly that. They have engaged in communicative acts with their community—other Film students and the teacher—and have taken on feedback through which they have furthered their learning, both academically and in a more holistic sense. This contained space is a microcosm of the larger media landscape in the world outside the classroom. Of course, the privileges of this space—a small class size, access to resources—do influence the kind of media creation that the students engage in and while this may be a small part of how children are engaging with media today, it is important to remember that this is a visually literate generation and, even without formal education, they find ways to use media and share their perspectives on the world they inhabit. But do adults pay enough attention?

I am also a children's author and sometimes visit schools to share my work and conduct storytelling sessions. Again, the elite English-medium schools push for these sorts of interactions, but this trend of inviting children's writers to schools is now growing in India. The trend is a mixed bag. I have been to schools where the emphasis has been on children keeping quiet and being disciplined so that they can listen to the author instead of the author finding a way to both interact and share work. In such sessions, the author must be respected and the question or comment that pops up in a young child's mind at a particular part of the story needs to be held back for the end and not expressed right then and there. But when the end comes, the question has flown away and the child who could have had a conversation that may have led to something positive just sits quietly. Straightaway, the child's engagement with the arts as social practice is being defined in a certain way. While any exposure to the arts is good for children and even listening to a story with 'a finger on your lips' could be of value, what is needed is that children feel free to engage in their own ways and that the author session is not seen as the end of the learning process. The really valuable lesson comes when the teacher is able to follow up afterwards on ideas that come up in such sessions. This is where the intersection of the arts with teacher education becomes critical. There is a kind of instrumentality in using such sessions if teachers are unable to envision how children's engagement with the arts can be a part of the learning process. They become more than a box to be ticked to show that the school has a holistic vision. Devising strategies to use these sessions as well as other practices means finding a balance between turning art into a lesson plan and the freedom and flexibility that allow for real learning.

I remember one such session in which I was invited to a school to share one of my children's books, *Hina in the Old City* (Mishra 2000), on Old Delhi and the story of a girl from a family that did *zardozi* (a kind of hand-embroidery work). The book is non-fiction and has photographs of the space and the girl and her family. The session was an hour-long one with middle-school children and included time for questions, but what is important is that a few weeks later, I received a stack of notes from the school—the teacher had followed up with the class and asked them to write responses to what had been shared, thinking about Old Delhi and their own Delhi. Of course, the responses were varied and not all of them were thoughtful or well-written, but they did express the children's perspective and some of them gave a glimpse of their creativity. One wrote, with a visual expressiveness, 'I used to think that Old Delhi was just a slum area but there are people there who want to touch the sky.' Thus, the session encouraged a participatory engagement with a particular form of media that also became a prompt for the children to create their own.

Creative Practice in the Non-formal Space

I spend a lot of time working with children in neighbourhood libraries, art classes and centres run by NGOs. The first two are mostly for younger children, up to the ages of 10 or 12, brought to these spaces because their parents believe it is important and want them to experience different kinds of art. Mostly, these are children of middle-class and wealthier backgrounds. In the centres run by NGOs, the children are mostly from working-class families, with parents working as domestic help or in factories and offices, living in bastis and studying in government-run schools. Some are enrolled in low-fee private schools because they are English-medium and English is the acknowledged route for social mobility. Both government and private schoolchildren in these neighbourhoods go for tuition classes as a norm. This is seen as beneficial and it is also true that many of these children cannot get homework support from parents and so require additional help. NGOs working in such spaces have been quick to recognise this need and after-school support for children is one of the things they deliver to such communities. The emphasis is naturally on school curricula but they also try to build in more creative activities for the children, given the changing educational environment. In fact, in the summer of 2018, the Aam Aadmi Party (AAP) government organised art workshops for government school children, culminating in an exhibition. The government has gone on to set up hobby hubs inviting practitioners and NGOs to come in as resource people for a variety of arts such as music, dance, theatre and fine arts. This works as a stamp of approval among working-class parents, and so there is a general push towards increasing children's engagement with art and media in the non-formal spaces.

The Reading Caterpillar is a neighbourhood library in Nizamuddin West that attracts a mostly upper middle–class clientele. It is a cheerful child-friendly space that is used for workshops and storytelling sessions. I have been doing different kinds of activities for several years, with children from the ages of 5 years to 12 years. Children have produced poetry, short non-fiction texts, even films. With the older children, I have begun the practice of doing a short reflection in the form of guided questions that I ask them, one of them being what prompted them to take part in the workshop. Their responses throw open a window into the world as they experience it, where even in childhood what is expected of them is adult-like. One 12-year-old who took part in a film workshop wrote, 'I felt proud that I did something like this and used my holidays productively.' Another child wrote, 'I normally watch Netflix and do social media on my gadgets, but I wanted to learn something more productive.' This emphasis on individual productiveness reflects an internalising of an environment that suggests it is up to the individual to make the most of the opportunities on offer. There is an awareness among children that skills like these can be an advantage in school as there is more project-based learning and, quite often, teachers are not equipped to impart specific skills like shooting and editing. Part of this learning is, of course, the exploration that children do by themselves, so developing these skills is seen in that context. But, even this exploration by children needs some kind of mentoring, and if teachers have not been trained in these specific skills, how are they to provide it? While ideas of curriculum and classroom transaction have changed, the question that needs to be asked is, has teacher training also changed commensurately? So many children clearly feel the pressure to be able to perform well and are happy to spend time outside school building the new skills. Not only is this extra for the children, it is also extra work for the parents, most of the time the mother, who has to put in time and effort in taking children to extra classes and chaperoning them. It also throws up the question of access—how many have the possibility of paying for these extra classes? Children from wealthier backgrounds are able to, but many middle-class children in less elite English medium schools, where the environment continues to be highly competitive, find it difficult to include such extra classes in their everyday life.

In working-class spaces, NGOs are drawing in artists and media practitioners to work with children in response to this changing context. A few years ago, I did a workshop for an after-school centre run by a foundation in a working-class basti. The centre runs a programme that focuses on academic and twenty-first-century life skills for girls in the age group 10–14 years. The centre is close to their homes and the girls come and go on their own, negotiating the neighbourhood without adult supervision. My brief was to engage the girls in creative work that would promote self-reflection. For one of the exercises, I asked them to take a photograph of a space in their neighbourhood that was important to them and talk about why they had chosen it. One of the girls took a photograph of a street in perspective and said that she had selected it because it was the way to the centre, a space she liked coming to and that represented possibility in her life. When, as a continuation of the exercise, I asked them to think of a metaphor for the space they had selected, this girl wrote about *sahi rasta* (the right way), connecting it to *sachchai aur insaniyat* (truth and humanity). In another exercise, I asked them to think of a metaphor for girls and use the device of repetition to create a short poem. One girl wrote:

A girl is a tree because she provides support
A girl is a tree because she provides shade
A girl is a tree because she can grow to such heights
A girl is a tree because she can provide food for all
A girl is a tree because she is beautiful
Like a tree

The workshop was an opportunity to listen to young voices and see the world through their eyes, sometimes in sync with grown-up eyes and at other times, their own poignant vision of possibilities. In another project that culminated in the form of a book, *My Sweet Home: Childhood Stories from a Corner of the City* (Mishra et al. 2017), I worked with children from Okhla, a neighbourhood that is largely inhabited by Muslims. The Batla House encounter of September 2008 had put the area in spotlight and I was interested in children's voices coming from a space that was increasingly being stereotyped as a 'Muslim ghetto' that had given support to terrorists. The children in this workshop were from very modest middle-class backgrounds and studied in the two Jamia schools, one Urdu-medium with quite a low fee and the other English-medium with a higher fee. The workshop, and later the book, became a way for voices of children from this neighbourhood to be heard and to provoke a discussion on how similar or different they are to children from other neighbourhoods in Delhi. The book is an example of how children's creative practice can become a way of promoting dialogue. *My Sweet Home* has been shared at children's literature festivals and schools and often these interactions culminate in an exercise where letters are written to the children in *My Sweet Home*, talking about similarity and difference. One child wrote to a boy in the book, Tabish:

> Dear Tabish,
> I read your story. The story is very good. I also like playing cricket but I play in a field, not on the banks of the river. I liked your story. Your sister was crying when she saw that the bird died... I play cricket with my friends but once my mother asked me to take my cousin along—just like what happened to you.

In another filmmaking workshop, I mentored a group of young women across the ages of 14 years to 23 years from four working-class settlements of Delhi where the Ankur Society for Alternatives in Education has been working for several years and focusing on the right to creativity. We chose to work with lo-tech video, using the mobile phones that the girls had access to. This, of course, comes with many challenges but it opens up the possibility of media producers and content creators emerging from diverse class contexts with varying degrees of cultural capital, allowing for stories to be told and experiences shared from multiple perspectives.

All these are examples of how children are taking on the role of creative practitioners and indicate the possibilities that lie in engaging with them through the arts. In the non-formal space, the possibility for playfulness and experimentation is stronger because the agenda driving these spaces is more fluid and amorphous. Play is critical to creative practice, and while in time-bound classroom or workshop situations, there is need for some kind of structure, to turn the process into a lesson plan is actually counter-productive. In fact, the nebulousness can be an advantage if the mentor/facilitator is able to adapt quickly to what emerges in the course of experimentation. In many cases, the workshops are like bubbles separated from the children's everyday lives, and for many working-class children whose everyday lives often contain adult routines like collecting water, helping with the cooking and taking care of a younger sibling, these bubbles are the spaces where they can savour childhood play. What they create then is valuable because it offers another kind of story, another form of representation. One important role of the arts is to provoke a new imagination of the world, and this is only possible if we accept that art and media are shaped not just by content and form, but also by who is producing them.

Children's Creativity in the Global Marketplace

It is necessary that we examine the issue of children and creative practice from a wide lens that includes the changing idea of work and labour because this emphasis on creativity is linked to the kind of job market that today's children will have to negotiate in the foreseeable future. That creative practice can develop self-confidence and skills is one part of the story; the other is that these will be needed by today's children when they seek work as adults. In contemporary global capitalism, the onus to be gainfully educated and employed is increasingly on the individual. Today's economic paradigm requires what Nina Power (2009) in *One Dimensional Woman* calls the 'feminized worker'—adaptable, flexible, constantly networking, taking on part-time and contractual work. This draws from the idea of women being sensible, pragmatic and good at communication, able to juggle and create their own individual systems when a larger structure ceases to exist. This is what we are experiencing in the world of work today. Under global capitalism, more and more jobs are contracted out to agencies and often work is done piecemeal by faceless individuals at remote distances. What this means is that the workers are denied both employment benefits that accrue from organisational structures as well as the possibilities of forming supportive collectives, in the guise of having the freedom to choose their work hours. This growing precariousness in the job market is one that women are used to, and thus it is argued that labour is becoming feminised.

Today's children, therefore, have to be prepared to become those workers. As good and efficient workers, they will be available 24x7, they will at all times be a brand ambassador for their employer and they will be self-promoting on social media. And so, the separation between the place of work and the private space will continue to shrink till it disappears. The personal, Power says, is no longer just the political but has, in fact, become the economic. In this light, we cannot neglect to see that the recognition of children's creative practice is not about encouraging their ability to participate in cultural transformation, but about their future contribution towards reinforcing an economic paradigm that requires workers who can work efficiently on their own and think out of the box without much support—traits that creative practice encourages and hones.

In her critique of the contemporary workplace, Power contends that the language of feminism has been co-opted by those who would have in the past opposed what feminism stood for. Thus, feminism is a buzzword used for a variety of things—from selling shampoo and vibrators for the purpose of enhancing women's self-esteem to invading Afghanistan for the purpose of rescuing 'oppressed' women (Power 2009). Similarly, the language of the arts has been co-opted by those who would have opposed what the arts stood for—less competitiveness, more heterogeneity, the possibility of multiple ways of seeing and being. Creativity and imagination have become buzzwords in the new economy of child-rearing and education. Both formal and non-formal spaces are using the language of progressive pedagogy—child-centred, experiential, self-expression—to create an environment where children can develop into reflective individuals with creative abilities of varying degrees. And just as there can be the possibility of women's self-esteem being enhanced by a good shampoo alongside the fact that feminism is used as a marketing strategy, it is also possible that spaces that focus on nurturing children's creative abilities simultaneously feed into a competitive economic system.

In the adult workplace, there is a call to individual action and a celebration of those who opt to create their own jobs—start-ups that are promoted as going against the grain when the reality is that the grain of employment itself has changed. A similar highlighting of individual initiative and inventiveness can be seen in the way children are encouraged to demonstrate their creativity—as musical prodigies, through self-published books, as founders of start-ups. While many of them may indeed have talent and may go on to choose work in those fields, what is to be noted is that there is a push towards demonstrating that talent at an early age. Thus, while children may well be participating in cultural production, this is still very much in line with the ethos of competition in the global marketplace. Another issue that the lens of work and labour throws up is the notion of the working child. From the child rights perspective, the popular perception is that child labour is exploitative, but the musical prodigy, the self-published child author or the child-founder of a start-up is seen as quite the reverse. This is not surprising because labour that is put into creative work is rarely identified as labour, even in the adult world. Thus, the scenario of children's creative practice is replete with contradictions, and while the neoliberal economic system may encourage creative practice among children to perpetuate itself, the development of the reflective citizen through the process means that the possibility of subversion is always present, precisely because those traits have been put to use by the system.

Conclusion

In December 2018, *The Indian Express* (Chopra 2018) reported that there had been 49 suicides in the Jawahar Navodaya Vidyalayas (JNVs), residential schools for talented rural children. Half of these were by Dalit and tribal children. The Navodaya schools, running classes VI to XII, were started in the mid-1980s and are known for producing the best results in the country's board examinations. Entry is through a competitive test and although they were set up to be child-centred schools with a difference, over the years, they have merged with the mainstream notions of education. Today, they focus on preparing rural children for the highly competitive medicine and engineering entrance exams. Educationist Krishna Kumar writes (2019), 'I recall the case of a child who was passionate about playing the flute. When he was found away from his classes, playing the flute in a nearby forest, the NV administration did not know what to do with such a child. Ultimately, he had to leave.' According to *The Indian Express* report (Chopra 2018), 'The causes of suicides in JNVs are disparate and range from unrequited love, family problems, corporal punishment or humiliation by teachers, academic pressure, depression, and fight between friends. Of these, the first three are cited most often as reasons behind suicides.' Two things are to be noted in this story of the JNVs: one, that there has been awareness for a while now that the approach to education has to be child-centric, diverse and creative; two, over time, the system overwhelms an innovative attempt and forces a stamp of homogeneity on those who pass through it. While the JNV story stands out as unexpected perhaps because of the rural context, the issue of adolescent mental health in urban areas is something that is more commonly known and easily accepted. Reports of self-harm, depression and substance abuse among teens are quite common in our cities.

So many of the young people I interact with display fragile inner resources. Often, they come to creative practice because they have not been able to find a way to express themselves elsewhere. The possibility of differentiation in the school system is limited and opportunities to truly celebrate difference among children peter out once they move into high school. Not only is this a time of greater academic pressure, but it is also when their need to belong is the strongest. Creative practice and the arts in education offer a way to negotiate these challenges, a way to build resilience in young people that will serve them well in life. This is true not just for those who go on to become artists, but also for everyone who will join the workforce and face the challenges of a competitive work environment—knowing what you really want, being able to communicate clearly, collaborating in a team. While these are strengths that global capital is looking for in its workers, it is in these very strengths that the possibilities of reimagining the workplace lie. It is these that lead to empathy, communication and the ability to celebrate differences that are the foundation of forging community and building solidarity. Clearly, children are taking on the role of creative practitioners in a variety of ways. They are finding their own way to some of these strengths. The question is will they be able to hold on to these strengths and create a shift when they grow up? Or will the system force an atomisation on them and co-opt the strengths for itself?

And while we wait, what does the grown-up do? Be an ally. Listen, observe, facilitate.

References

Breckton, J. 2017. 'Jobs of the Future: The Creative Economy' [Video]. Nesta, UK: Universités Canada. Available at https://www.youtube.com/watch?v=7xIMdeEs1_8 (accessed on 15 October 2022).

Chopra, R. 2018. 'Suicides in Navodaya Schools: 49 in 5 Years, Half of Them Dalit and Tribal Students'. *The Indian Express*, 24 December. Available at https://indianexpress.com/article/india/jawahar-navodaya-vidyalayas-suicides-schools-dalit-tribal-jnv-5506564/ (accessed on 5 February 2020).

Desai, S. 2019. 'TikTok: Leave Them Kids Alone'. *The Times of India*, 28 April. Available at https://timesofindia.indiatimes.com/blogs/Citycitybangbang/tiktok-leave-them-kids-alone/?fbclid=IwAR3z-c6kz29CIv0TZjQI6Y5rXBERUjJ0yFItwj7fG35h4Cv2tSqnp2hkznY (accessed on 5 February 2020).

Freethink. 2019. 'How to Teach Kids to Read in as Little as 50 Days' [Video]. YouTube. Available at https://www.youtube.com/watch?v=LEOavri3e0w (accessed on 15 October 2022).

Jenkins, H. 2006. 'Jenkins on Participatory Media Culture and Youth—New Learning Online'. Available at https://newlearningonline.com/literacies/chapter-2/jenkins-on-participatory-media-culture-and-youth (accessed on 5 February 2020).

Kumar, K. 2019. 'Schools without a Difference'. *The Indian Express*, 25 January. Available at https://indianexpress.com/article/opinion/columns/jawahar-navodaya-vidyalayas-schools-suicides-5554220/ (accessed on 5 February 2020).

Leinonen, J., and S. Sintonen. 2014. 'Productive Participation—Children as Active Media Producers in Kindergarten'. *Nordic Journal of Digital Literacy* 9(3): 217—19. Available at https://www.idunn.no/dk/2014/03/productive_participation_-_children_as_active_media_produce (accessed on 15 October 2022).

Lily, Jade. 2021. '"Education Is Our Passport to the Future, for Tomorrow Belongs to the People Who Prepare for it Today"– Malcolm X'. Medium, 27 July. Available at https://medium.com/be-bold/education-is-our-passport-to-the-future-for-tomorrow-belongs-to-the-people-who-prepare-for-it-7c9fd8b58036 (accessed on 15 October 2022).

Mishra, S. 2000. *Hina in the Old City*. Chennai: Tulika Books.

Mishra, S., S. Dastur and The Children of Okhla. 2017. *My Sweet Home: Childhood Stories from a Corner of the City*. Ahmedabad: Mapin Publishing Pvt. Ltd.

Nesta. 2017. *Nesta Strategy 2017–2020*. London: Nesta. Available at https://media.nesta.org.uk/documents/nesta_strategy_2017-2020.pdf (accessed on 22 December 2018).

Power, N. 2009. *One Dimensional Woman*. London: John Hunt Publishing.

The New Media Consortium. 2005. *A Global Imperative: The Report of the 21st Century Literacy Summit*. Austin: The New Media Consortium. Available at https://library.educause.edu/-/media/files/library/2005/10/21stcentliteracy.pdf (accessed on 22 December 2018).

10

REDEFINING THE POLITICAL BY VISUAL NARRATIVES OF SANGWARI KHABARIYA IN CENTRAL INDIA

Vasuki Belavadi

> Unlike trees or their roots, the rhizome connects any point to any other point (Deleuze and Guattari 1987: 19).

I teach electronic media production to postgraduate students. My interests include pedagogy of video production and community media. Back in 2000 when I first got into academia, I noticed that all content on television was produced by adults for children. In fact, children were, and continue to be, just talent on shows meant for them.

How do children view the world? What do they think of the happenings around them? What do they think of the things that adults do? What if they expressed themselves using media? I have been involved with the community radio movement for over a decade now and the fact that men and women without formal literacy could operate radio equipment and tell their stories fascinated me. Examples of video being used as community media in some European countries also caught my attention. Being an audio-visual medium, would it be the apt medium for children to express themselves? These were some questions that kept me thinking and prompted me into taking notes about the issues.

Community media have often been described by different terms: participatory media, alternative media, citizens' media, free media and autonomous media, among others. These terms have been used based on social, political and cultural orientations of the practitioners (Servaes 1999: 259). Many times the terms community media and participatory media are used interchangeably.

Gareth Benest, Director of InsightShare (as cited in Dutta 2015), prefers to see them as two different practices. According to him, community video refers to processes that engage a community/group in the production of video as an end in itself. On the other hand, participatory video uses video as a tool to achieve the desired social change outcomes of the community involved. It sets out to harness video as a means to address issues and circumstances that might benefit from being aired, shared or documented for the future. However, the term community media is a widely accepted term, given its plurality.

Kevin Howley (2005: 2) refers to community media as those that are locally oriented and predicated on a 'profound sense of dissatisfaction with mainstream media form and content, dedicated to the principles of free expression and participatory democracy, and committed to enhancing community relations and promoting community solidarity'. Maslog (cited in Fuller 2007: 3) describes the characteristics of community media as follows:

1. owned and controlled by people in the community;
2. usually smaller and low-cost;
3. provides interactive two-way communication;
4. non-profit and autonomous, therefore, non-commercial;
5. has limited coverage or reach;
6. utilises appropriate, indigenous materials and resources;
7. reflects community needs and interests;
8. its programmes or content support community development.

The immediacy with which community media can capture local issues and initiate dialogue within the community makes it an ideal tool to bring about social change.

PARTICIPATORY VIDEO IN INDIA

Participatory video (PV) first made its appearance in the 1980s when the Self-Employed Women's Association (SEWA) in Gujarat trained its members in making videos on issues concerning them. The organisation believes that communication and transfer of information is critical to the well-being of women.[1] Later, in 1998, the Deccan Development Society (DDS) launched a PV project with rural, unlettered women belonging to the marginalised communities. The Community Media Trust (CMT) of DDS has a team of 20 women who make videos based on longitudinal research that seek to effect policy change in terms of agriculture, climate, genetically modified crops, etc.[2]

Yet another notable initiative is the Video Volunteers, based in Goa. It has a network of reporters across the country that report on issues of the poor such as government schemes, health issues, success stories, local culture and music. The videos are shared online and also screened in the communities they serve. Every film ends with a call to action that is discussed at the screening sessions.[3]

With inputs from my colleagues at the Department of Communication, University of Hyderabad (henceforth, the department), I set up an initiative called Children As Media Producers (CAMP) in 2007. CAMP was set up as a programme of the UNESCO Chair on Community Media at the department. The Chair—the first ever on community media—was instituted by the United Nations Educational, Scientific and Cultural Organization (UNESCO), Paris, in recognition of the work done by faculty of the department in the field of community radio for over a decade.

The basic premise of CAMP is that children must be seen as producers of information and not mere consumers; that community media can play an important role in strengthening cultural rights and, in particular, the rights of linguistic and cultural minorities and indigenous people (including children, in this case) by providing them access to the means of communication. The objectives of CAMP are:

- to identify the latent communication abilities of children;
- to encourage children to participate actively in the mapping of their issues;
- to enable children to enter into a dialogue with various sections of the community in addressing their concerns;
- to build the capacities of children to report, document, disseminate and monitor various issues affecting them, using media technologies so they grow to be informed citizens.

The First Experiment

In 2008, I got an opportunity to work with about 20 children in Sanga Reddy (part of united Andhra Pradesh and now in Telangana). High school boys and girls from traditionally marginalised sections were involved in a PV project with support from United Nations Children's Fund (UNICEF). Of the 20 children, 12 were boys and the remaining were girls. Most of them belonged to the Dalit community, while three of them were from a backward community. A set of six video camera units were housed at the Behavioural Change Communication (BCC) Cell of Medak district. The children at CAMP went through a training process including visual grammar, basics of camera, the significance of various shot sizes and their use in producing a film under our CAMP initiative.

The children made some fascinating videos on issues such as agriculture, local festivals, their schools and absence of healthcare facilities in their villages. Their videos were entered into the 2009 International Film Festival organised by the Children's Film Society of India (CFSI) and hosted by the government of Andhra Pradesh. UNICEF organised a press meet to announce the entries in the presence of a minister of the Andhra Pradesh state government. The minister, who belonged to the same district, took strong objection to the content of the videos and threatened to pull out of the festival if the videos were screened. The chairperson of the jury intervened and convinced CFSI and the minister that children had the fundamental right to express an opinion and that it would be ironic for a festival celebrating children's films to prevent them from being screened. Finally, they were screened in a small theatre. Fortunately, a local channel had come forward to screen all their videos. The children were happy that their videos could be watched by a wider audience.

The children involved in the project were keen on producing videos even after the project period concluded. However, it had to be wound up because we did not receive the required cooperation from the BCC Cell, presumably due to political pressure. The Sanga Reddy project taught me two lessons. One, that the establishment can be rattled by videos produced even by children, if the stories do not suit their narrative. Two, that an institutional anchor was necessary if the project had to be sustained and children were to have continued access to the equipment.

Sangwari Khabariya

Cut to 2012, UNICEF, Chhattisgarh,[4] approached CAMP for a similar project in Surguja district (see Figure 10.1 for location of the district in the state).

This time, I was a bit hesitant but convinced UNICEF that the project be anchored by an NGO that they regularly work with. After about two months of deliberation, UNICEF finally narrowed down on Manav Sansadhan Sanskriti Vikas Parishad (MSSVP) that works in Surguja. Founded in 1994, MSSVP works with indigenous communities, marginalised women and deprived communities, and strives to secure their right to equality, secularisation, social justice and economic empowerment. MSSVP identified 60 children in the age group of 12–16 years with the objective of building capacities of children to report, document and disseminate issues related to health, education, nutrition, water and sanitation through video.

Children (0–18 years) account for about 41 per cent of Chhattisgarh's total population, with 3.6 million of them under the age of 6 years (United Nations Children's Fund [UNICEF] n.d.). As most of these children belong to remote rural areas, they have limited or no access to education and health services, are unaware of hygiene

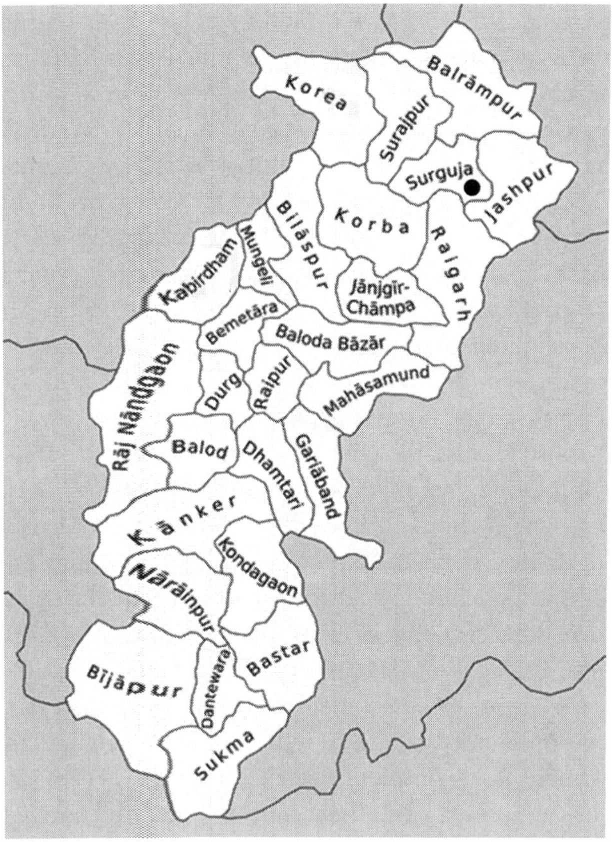

FIGURE 10.1 Map Locating Surguja District in Chhattisgarh State

Source: https://upload.wikimedia.org/wikipedia/commons/3/33/Chhatt%C4%ABsgarhi_ringkonnad.svg (accessed on 16 November 2022).

and sanitation, are ignorant of child rights and are vulnerable to abuse and exploitation in many forms like child labour, trafficking and child marriage.

THE PROCESS

The children selected for the project were initially hesitant to participate as most of them had not been exposed to the world outside of their own village. Of the 60, only four had ever been outside until they came to Surguja for the training. Their exposure to media was limited to watching videos that they would purchase once in a while from the local shops that would 'refill' their media storage chips with some Bhojpuri and Chhattisgarhi songs. Some of them did have access to television. However, even that was limited since frequent power cuts would not allow them to charge the batteries on which most black-and-white television sets operated.

In the early days of the project, we had to visit a number of villages to meet and urge children—mostly school dropouts—and their parents to join the project. The Right to Education (RTE) Act had ensured that their names were enrolled in the school register. However, most schools did not have enough teachers and lacked basic infrastructure. Some of them even had two classes being simultaneously run in the same room. Delays in distribution of government books in the villages often led to waning interest and dropouts. In some schools, teachers admitted that they had to show all eligible children in the village as being on the rolls failing which the supply of material for midday meals would be reduced.

For many students 'the school had very little to offer'. Some of them dropped out because they had to supplement the family income. One of the team members, Dev Kumar Nayak would later go on to say: 'I am glad I dropped out [of] school and joined this team. In my school, weak students would always be left out. Here, everyone gets to have their say and an opportunity to make videos on issues that affect them and the village' (as recorded during a feedback session held in August 2014).

In many cases, parents would refuse to send their children to school beyond the fifth or sixth standard since it made more economic sense for the children to join the parents at work to supplement the family income so that everyone could be fed. Other reasons included the father's addiction to alcohol and other substances, and importantly, the fear that children beyond a certain age would be trafficked (as recorded during a feedback session held in August 2014).

Several parents flatly refused to send their children for training since we were outsiders and they were uncertain of their children's safety. 'Yeh gaon ki ladkiyan kya kar paayengi?' (What will these village girls be able to do?), they would say to avoid sending their girls for training. It was only after repeated visits that they were convinced to participate in the training process.

The children's exposure to the outside world was so limited that many of them had not even seen a train. At the Surguja railway station where we had gone on an outdoor trip, I requested the train driver to stop it for a couple of minutes and he obliged. The children got into the train and had their first experience of sitting in a compartment with the fans on. The children were thrilled and wondered how the train could carry so many people at once to distant places.

The first challenge was to make them comfortable with us and with the process. One way of doing this was to involve them in a street theatre workshop. The training involved asking them to narrate small stories, sing songs and later ask them to identify the three most important things for them in their life. Most of them said that the three most important things for them were getting: (a) a birth certificate, (b) a caste certificate, and (c) an income certificate.[5]

The children then got together and created a story on what could happen if one did not have these certificates. The story was then scripted with a couple of songs woven in. The play was taken to different blocks of the district and performed in villages. The response from audiences gave the children confidence that they would be able to speak with outsiders too, and that their work would be appreciated if they put in the effort. Of the 40 children who joined the initiative, around 10 dropped out soon after the street theatre performances, many of them without a reason.

It was only after six months and a couple of street theatre shows that the concept of PV was introduced to them. The training sessions would be held for about six to seven days almost every month. Soon after the second month, yet another 10 children dropped out citing difficulty in understanding the medium and finally 20 stayed back for the rest of the training process.

These 20 adolescents went through a process of mapping their villages, noting the socio-economic conditions and examining the coverage of mainstream media in detail. Convinced that there was a need for them to reflect on and document 'their own' issues and bring them into the mainstream, the 20 children agreed to participate in the process of understanding the visual language, the video camera, shot sizes and their use in filmmaking.

Peer learning was introduced to help them understand the parts of the camera, the lens and the tripod. I taught one child and she would teach the next one. I would step in only when the peer trainer found it difficult to proceed. Learning from each other was more effective than learning from an 'outsider', I realised.

If understanding the camera, lens and the tripod was difficult enough, the use of video terminology in English, a language completely alien to them, was a major stumbling block in proceeding further with the training. The children decided to create their own vocabulary in the local language, which sounded simplistic but was effective in conversing and engaging with the video equipment. Table 10.1 lists the names they gave to the shot sizes in their language.

TABLE 10.1 Shot Sizes Named by the Children

Shot Size in English	Shot Size in Chhattisgarhi
Extreme close shot	*Ekdum lighe shot*
Close shot	*Lighe shot*
Mid close up	*Chaati shot*
Mid shot	*Aadha shot*
Mid long shot	*Pindri shot*
Long shot	*Door shot*
Extreme long shot	*Ekdum door shot*

Source: Author.

Learning video editing turned out to be yet another challenge. The coordination between movements of the mouse and the cursor on the desktop screen took about a week or so. The user interface of the video editing software had to be explained in terms of *khidkiyan* (windows). Therefore, there was one window that contained all the shots, one that contained all the effects, one window that played the shot, one window in which all editing was done and yet another in which the edited shots played out. Again, they sat together and created a vocabulary for the editing equipment and the software (Table 10.2).

Table 10.2 Vocabulary for Editing Equipment and Software Created by the Children

Part	Their Translation in Chhattisgarhi
Uninterruptible power supply (UPS)	*Battery*
Central processing unit (CPU)	*Computer ka dimaag*
Computer keyboard	*Computer ka kalam*
Mouse	*Chooha*
Monitor	*TV*
Software interface	*Khidkiyan*
Software	*Silaayi machine*

Source: Author.

On being asked why they chose to call the software *silaayi* machine (tailoring machine), they reminded me of the analogy I had used to explain editing. Editing, I had explained to them, was like stitching clothes. We purchase cloth (capture footage). The tailor would then 'design' the shirt/skirt and then go about cutting out all the unwanted portions. He would then bring different pieces together and stitch them on the tailoring machine. Adding frills was akin to adding effects and transitions. While they had begun to shoot decent footage with variety in terms of shot sizes, camera angles and heights, it took almost three months for them to edit their first video.

The challenge of explaining sound balancing and mixing ambient noise and the voiceover (commentary) was tackled next. In spite of demonstrating it with at least two or three examples, it was beyond them to understand why balancing and mixing were important. I then asked them to sit in a circle and asked two of them to come into the centre. I asked them both to speak as loudly as possible and checked with them if the others in the circle could make out what their two friends were saying. When they could not, I asked one of them to speak softly and the other to speak normally. Now, they were able to comprehend what one of them was saying. Balancing and mixing audio would help reinforce the mood of the story while the commentary would provide the viewer with the facts and points that the video would not be able to provide.

By the end of the training, all children were able to edit videos by themselves, although not with professional finesse. However, the edited footage could successfully tell stories from their perspective. Once they were prepared to tell their stories through video, they decided to christen themselves *Sangwari Khabariya* (SK—the friendly neighbourhood reporter). They said that they chose that name as it was apt since they were from the same communities that they were reporting. Further, if the mainstream media reporters were friendly, they would have covered their issues and that has not happened. Thus, in 2016, SK was born.

SK would look out for issues concerning both children and adults in the four blocks they came from. There were very few success stories. Some of the issues that SK reporters have covered during 2014–18 include the poor state of preschools, lack of water and toilet facilities in schools, lack of schools for girls, poor state of health facilities in villages, substance abuse among children, etc. None of the stories that SK produced were covered by the local media.

SK uploads videos on YouTube and arranges screenings in the villages in the evenings (although one must admit that the frequency has reduced). The screenings, done once a week, evoke varied responses from the communities. From 'We know this issue exists' to 'Now we know why the Sarpanch [the elected village head] didn't complete the road', to 'When will we get our borewell?', the videos do evoke responses all the same. Local officials available during the screenings are sometimes made to answer for delays in completing works or questioned why their village is being sidelined regarding development works. Village heads in a couple of villages who had misappropriated amounts set aside for roads have had to lay roads after these videos were screened in the communities. One of the *aanganwadis* (preschool centres) was in a dilapidated condition and hazardous for children and got a new building after the screening of an SK video.

Videos being produced by the children and screened in communities are rattling local officials and making people aware of their rights and privileges. The district administration is, in general, appreciative of the children's videos. However, it does not seem to appreciate those videos that act as an audit of development schemes being implemented in those villages. For example, the district administration did not take a liking to a video that showed none of the toilets constructed as part of the *Swachh Bharat Abhiyan* (Clean India Mission) was usable in a village. In this sense, the videos are quite political and focus on serving the community.

The SK videos have been screened at a couple of festivals and won awards as well. The children explained the impact SK has made in their lives. Rabina Ekka said, 'This training has given me a lot of confidence. I have learnt a new skill. I am positive I will do well.' 'Earlier, nobody knew who we were. We were just illiterate kids. But today we get a lot of respect wherever we go to shoot. I can feel the transformation within me but can't explain it,' voiced Dinesh Kumar Paikra. Dinesh, Dev Kumar and Rabina have taken four more children each under their wings and are training them in PV.

For understanding how SK operates, it becomes imperative to fall back on the four approaches to alternative media as expounded by Bailey et al. (2008). Media, be it mainstream or alternative, do not operate in a vacuum but are embedded in socio-political, economic and cultural settings, and SK is no different. One notices that when the adolescents use the video camera to voice the concerns of their fellow citizens, they are going beyond issues that do not find a place in the mainstream media—they are broadening the definition of the political and questioning hegemonic ideologies.

While emphasising the need to situate alternative/community media in political and democratic theories, Bailey et al. (2008) opine that community media by their participatory nature have broadened the definition of the 'political' itself to include every aspect of the community: the school, the gram panchayat (village administration) and even the agricultural farms. Such a broad definition will, therefore, accommodate struggles of all kinds that relate to human existence.

Differences between community media and participatory media notwithstanding, there is an intersection of sorts in the manner in which SK participates in and members of the community participate through the media in challenging local priorities, nudging policy implementation and providing local perspectives. In that sense, SK can also be described as alternative media. Who represents and who gets represented in these videos and what voices are heard gains significance since the mainstream media tend to promote hegemonic values and prioritise market imperatives. SK videos, on the other hand, present the voices of the poorest, the marginalised and those completely ignored by the mainstream media.

Sustainability

However, like most community-based projects, the biggest challenge for SK is its sustainability. Given the economic conditions of these children, it would be too much to ask them to keep producing stories without any financial rewards. Incidentally, most of the readings that I went through in my initial days of setting up CAMP hardly mentioned sustainability or provided ideas. I tried to explore the possibility of replicating the ideas that came from studying community radio initiatives in neighbouring and other countries. However, the differences in contexts perhaps do not provide for financial sustainability. I am still exploring ways of making such an initiative financially sustainable.

The social sustenance of SK is being addressed by the fact that each reporter from the first batch of trainees has taken under their wings three to five more adolescents and has begun training them in expressing themselves through video. However, to sustain themselves financially, they have had to approach the market and seek assignments. The district collector's office has already engaged them in four such assignments. These children were involved in making a video on birth registrations for UNICEF. The cash inflows are not all that impressive but are just about enough to take care of equipment maintenance.

Alternative media, by definition, are those that reject commercial motives, reject state funding, oppose power structures and limit dissemination of their media products at the local level. If one were to apply these parameters to SK, it would fail the test of being described as alternative media (Bailey et al. 2008). While alternative media are seen to be in an antagonistic relationship with mainstream media, SK seems to be breaking this principle. The group plans to approach regional television channels to broadcast their videos at least once a month. SK is convinced that while screenings are indeed creating a horizontal dialogue in the community, its videos need to reach a wider audience for the state government to sit up and take notice of issues that they reflect on.

Besides not exactly fitting into any of the typologies postulated by media scholars, SK also faces a challenge of coming into its own, independent of funding by an international body. SK will need to find its feet if it has to retain its editorial independence regarding the choice of stories and to expand its repertoire to go beyond stories that are linked to 'child rights'.

To conclude, SK might well fit the description of 'citizens' media' as articulated by Clemencia Rodrigues in 2001. She says citizens' media implies first that a collective is enacting its citizenship by actively intervening in and transforming the established mediascape; second, that these media are contesting social codes, legitimised identities and institutionalised social relations; and third, that these communication practices are empowering the community involved, to the point where these transformations and changes are possible. The videos produced by SK did challenge the modes and methods of storytelling by mainstream media; they did ask the right questions. Did it challenge existing social codes? Certainly, yes. Did it provide an identity to those children? Yes. Did it empower the children and give them confidence? Yes.

Critical media pedagogy certainly helps reinforce critical thinking among children and helps amplify their voices. Projects such as SK do empower and enable children to express themselves through video and also provide them with the confidence to face challenges. However, it also needs to become a movement of sorts for adults to appreciate the children's worldview. In the absence of a well-thought out plan for financial sustainability, such projects unfortunately remain a one-off effort. While several community media projects can claim social sustainability, there is a need to create a model for financial sustainability as well, especially in contexts like ours. I must admit it is a challenge that I am still grappling with.

Notes

1. See 'Video Sewa', available at http://www.videosewa.org/aboutus.htm (accessed on 16 November 2022).
2. See https://www.ddsindia.com/ (accessed on 10 November 2022).
3. See https://www.videovolunteers.org/ (accessed on 10 November 2022).
4. Formed in 2000, Chhattisgarh is among the younger states in the country with a population of 25 million (Census 2021). It was carved out of Madhya Pradesh after an intense struggle for a separate state for over a decade. More than three-fourths of the population live in remote areas of the state (ibid.). Tribal and other marginalised communities constitute about 30 per cent of the population (Ministry of Tribal Affairs n.d.). A large percentage of people in the state live in areas that are not served well by the government and perform poorly on the indicators of development (United Nations Development Programme 2012).
5. Birth certificate, caste certificate and income certificate are crucial for people to be able to access subsidies offered by the government. Subsidies include food grains, health services, etc.

References

Bailey, O., B. Cammaerts and N. Carpentier. 2008. *Understanding Alternative Media*. New York: Open University Press.

Census. 2021. 'Chhattisgarh Population 2021, Sex Ratio, Density, Literacy'. Available at https://censusofindia2021.com/chhattisgarh-population-2021-census-data/#Chhattisgarh_Rural_Population_2021 (accessed on 16 November 2022).

Deleuze, G., and F. Guattari. 1987. *A Thousand Plateaus: Capitalism and Schizophrenia*, tr. Brian Massumi. Minneapolis: The University of Minnesota Press.

Dutta, A. 2015. 'Is Community Video Different from Participatory Video?' Community Communication, 28 May. Available at https://www.comcomm.org/2015/05/is-community-video-different-from.html (accessed on 18 February 2017).

Fuller, L. 2007. *Community Media*. New York: Palgrave Macmillan.

Howley, K. 2005. *Community Media: People, Places, and Communication Technologies*. Cambridge, UK: Cambridge University Press.

Ministry of Tribal Affairs. (n.d.) 'Table 1'. Available at https://tribal.nic.in/downloads/Statistics/Statistics8518.pdf (accessed on 16 November 2022).

Rodrigues, C. 2001. *Fissures in the Mediascape: An International Study of Citizens' Media*. Creskill, NJ: Hampton Press.

Servaes, J. 1999. *Communication for Development: One World, Multiple Cultures*, 1st edn. Cresskill, NJ: Hampton Press.

United Nations Children's Fund (UNICEF). (n.d.) 'Children in Chhattisgarh'. Available at https://www.unicef.org/india/where-we-work/chhattisgarh (accessed on 16 November 2022).

United Nations Development Programme (UNDP). 2012. *The Chhattisgarh State Human Development Report of 2005*. Available at https://www.undp.org/india/publications/chhattisgarh (accessed on 16 November 2022).

PART V

NEGOTIATIONS

11

ROMANCE IN THE TIMES OF FACEBOOK

The Surplus Digital Self and Young Adults in Urban India

Nimmi Rangaswamy

> This self itself does not derive from its possessor, but from the whole scene of his action...The self, then, as a performed character...provides the peg on which something of collaborative manufacture will be hung for a time (Goffman 1959: 252–53).

While the world of academia contemplates 'the fall of Facebook' for young adults (Miller 2013), this essay reaffirms Facebook as 'second life' for youth at the margins of urban Indian society. This chapter dwells on teenagers and young adults, and wonders, as writer Mary M. H. Choi did: if teenagers are 'strange and magical' persons, and 'they seem [to us] a little like soothsayers of a mysterious, social-media-powered hyper-drive future, because this is the realm they're already living in' (2016). This quote is in relation to a recent study of teenagers in the US who are Snapchatting, Instagraming, Facebooking, Yik Yakking and Kiking, all at the same time. Young adults in India, low-resourced and bandwidth-constrained, are equally embedded in magical social media moments, albeit spasmodic and abbreviated. The teen males, my research participants from the slums of Hyderabad and Chennai, 'saw' Facebook coming into their 'mobile pockets' soon after the introduction of the mobile Internet in India, less than a decade ago, which revolutionised access to Internet and began modifying socio-digital experiences. What makes teenagers so special is they are pioneering and annotating digital life on behalf of their communities: creating and persisting with new ecosystems of digital access, use and maintenance. This makes teenagers and young adults occupy one of the sentinel positions letting in and editorialising 'sacred and profane' practices around digital technologies. The questions we as anthropologists will ask are targeted towards breaking down a palimpsest of behavioural etiquettes of young persons, some alluding to deeper meaning-making and some exploring in exhaustive detail the ways and means the digital is made sense of, explored and domesticated. Many a young person in the Indian urban slums is developing an etiquette through trial and error, friending people they do not know; couturing and making over online profiles; encountering, what they call, 'fake' women and dealing with ensuing heartbreaks—all of these practices evolve to architect a 'surplus' digital self. We use the term surplus digital self as an idea to suggest the rich and compelling social media profiles fashioned by teenagers at the margins of digital life. Infusing the spirit of danah boyd's marginalised teenagers who strategically employ the affordances of digital sentience in her book *It's Complicated* (2013), the chapter is an attempt to bring to life the digital selves of young adults in India. Romance is also considered as emerging from and shaped by a networked, interactive human connection wrought on by teenaged actors and their entanglement with digital devices (Cupples and Thompson 2010).

Anthropologists engage in meaning management, handle complex bits of 'thick' data and tease out social patterns of behaviours. Context is everything when tasked with managing an anthropological study of meaning making of human behaviours—the context here is situated at the intersection of Facebook and the urban slum. The central premise of this study is situating 'romance' as an emerging theme rendering Facebook as a 'meaningful' experience in the everyday of marginalised urban youth. Dominating the lived experience of teenage romance is the thirst to connect, interact and friend (Ito et al. 2019; Ganesh 2010; David and Cambre 2016). Heterosexual romance among young adults in India is overwhelmingly restrictive, constrained and defined by the boundaries of sexual behaviour for unmarried youth. Scholarship suggests romantic behaviours of teen and young adults in India are marked and identified by: (a) The platonic 'bhai-behen' ('brother-sister like'), (b) romantic 'true love', and (c) transitory and sexual 'time pass' relationships (Abraham 2002). In addition, romance is also a relationship viewed as occurring between socially equal partners—any transgression of social boundaries is met with serious consequences, including social ostracising, sometimes social and physical death (Lingam et al. 2018). Romance essentially becomes an extremely guarded social behaviour censored by the norms and dictates of a hierarchical, normative and custom-bound Indian society.

Much of established studies of the global North (Ito et al. 2019; boyd and Ellison 2007; boyd 2013) view social media as more expressive than conditional, pervasive than constrained, and private than mediated experience. Youth in the global South, and in India, have digital experiences, though ubiquitous since the arrival of the prepaid packaged mobile Internet, that are nonetheless outcomes of a carefully calibrated and cost-effective usage (Rangaswamy and Cutrell 2012). As mobile technologies become affordable, the youth of India—despite socio-economic limitations, especially in grappling with the English language, 'the language of the State, of the rich, and of the Internet' (Kumar 2014: 1123)—have emerged as rich users of digital media. This unique stream of new and potential Facebook users forms a rapidly expanding group for 'whom the mobile phone is the primary (and sometimes, sole) means of navigating the Internet' (Kumar 2014: 1124). They are youth who have thus far been excluded from the process of globalisation, but the rapid democratisation of new media now allows them to create a transnational identity for themselves for the very first time (Kumar 2014).

We explore these experiences of 'romance', albeit mediated by Facebook, as a component of an evolving 'surplus digital self' in the lives of the youth inhabiting the urban slums in India. Romance, as a theme, feeds off of heterosexual digital liaisons and the appropriation of global imagery in the grooming of an online persona. This chapter will employ a Goffmanesque notion of self and performance of self as dramaturgy to delineate 'romance' as a conceptual tool in the 'presentation of self' on Facebook.

Methodology

The slum communities in urban India are a heterogeneous social segment that are characterised by the type of urban spaces they are attached to (Nijman 2015; Mahabir et al. 2016)—a Dharavi in the heart of Mumbai city is distinctly different from, say, an Urur in coastal south Chennai. Much of our research findings ruminate upon the experiential intersections of slum-dwelling and digital imaginaries and investigate connections between lived social constraints and the more porous boundaries of digital life.

This study followed two qualitative techniques to track and analyse teen behaviours on Facebook: (a) face-to-face in-depth interviews with 31 teenagers and Facebook users in three urban slum communities, two in Hyderabad and one in Chennai; and (b) profiling the same 31 teenagers through an immersive study of Facebook use in 'everyday' of these young adults. The predominant methodology is ethnographic and immersive in the understanding of the social contexts of the youth we profile in the study. Our online ethnography is inspired by 'Second Life' (Boellstorff 2008), adopting participative, observational and formal methods of study. All these teenagers except two are male, between 17 years and 21 years of age, from low economic backgrounds with a family income in the range of Rs 1.4–2 lakhs (US$ 1,700–2,500) per year (a monthly income of Rs 11,000–15,000 or US$ 140–170). They have varied educational backgrounds: some are school-dropouts, some college students and others worked for an average monthly income ranging from Rs 8,000–16,000 or US$ 100–200. An average monthly spend on mobile Internet is around US$ 1–3 per person. A significant portion of our research was 'a day in the life' observations and studying the role of Facebook in it amongst the teenagers who participated in our study. We hung out and observed their lived social contexts, motivations to join Facebook and the social roadways leading them to the social media site. In our interviews we further focused on the meaning-making of their presence on Facebook, their friending patterns, what they post, share, comment, and the myriad ways of tailoring timelines. We requested our participants to show and describe their mobile phones and explain how they accessed and sustained Internet-based activity, especially Facebook behaviours, via applications and client downloads. We also got a good peek of their friend lists on Facebook and gained an understanding of how and why they made friends with these specific people. We built a gallery of images that appeared on their timelines to study aspects of persona-building and the representations they signify. We specifically focused on self-portraits and analysed how photographically modifying one's body wear and physical postures helps to achieve a certain fit of what the teenagers and young adults wanted to see of themselves on Facebook. All research activities mentioned above had full and informed consent of the youth participating in the study (we orally recorded the consent to this study and took signatures on a consent form created specifically for this research). We took the effort to explain the purpose of this research to our participants, the likely implications of representing to and publishing for a global audience the intersections of Facebook use, young adults and urban slums in India (however complex this activity turned out to be notwithstanding). All the subjects in the chapter are referred to pseudonymously.

The author of the chapter spent a year in field interactions with the youth in the Hyderabad and Chennai communities, beginning with contextual studies of the 'everyday' life in an urban slum. Gradually, the study progressed in understanding the making and persistence of community and social networks amongst the subjects of study and extending this understanding to frame online networks they forged on Facebook.

Marginal Youth, Digital Mainstream

Marginality as an interpretative frame is a relationship to several states of being and—in the case of Facebook use by male youth in the urban slums of India—a state of inhabiting marginal social geographies, and teasing out a relationship with a mainstream digital society. Interpreting marginality requires understanding the specifics of the interplay between young persons and social media. Through the availability of uncensored digital products, young adults and teenagers in our study articulated a sense of being 'less marginalised', particularly in their use of digital media. An example is the excesses of digital self-profiling on Facebook, the building of what we call a 'surplus' self, which is a mixed bag of positive and negative experiences encountered by youth at the margins of the digital society. Facebook's forte is its inherent quality of anonymity and lack of 'gating features' that alleviate the influence of various socio-physical stigmas and anxieties preventing the building of offline relationships (McKenna et al. 2002). The urban slum as an 'un-gated' terrain for Facebook activity is a prime focus of this essay.

The introduction of online networks into the lives of young persons is nudging them to 'recalibrate' their social connections in the light of accommodating and exploring new possibilities to forge friending and social relationships into everyday conversations. Of specific interest are the artful strategies to project and perform identities on Facebook, which evolve and magnify over time as users get deeper into the practices of digital identity management. The more interesting parts of these performative practices are the centrality of romantic imaginaries in channelling digital imaginaries of the self. The communities in which our research participants live are constrained by various socio-economic and cultural factors impacting the everyday of Facebook use: limited education, restricted English communication skills and offline personalities constrained by socio-economic barriers. The barriers are also socio-cultural and tied to the lived experiences of youth in the urban slums of India who are economically constrained, socially marginalised and geographically excluded from mainstream citizenship in India (Anjaria 2006; Srivastava 2003; Sambasivan et al. 2009).

Affordances for low-income India on Facebook are driven primarily by the micro prepaid mobile Internet or the 'pocket Internet' and has revolutionised access, affordability and use of the

Internet as an 'everyday' technology. The immense desire to enable and extend one's time on Facebook also points to opportunistic and self-aggrandising engagements in profile creation, in friending patterns, in status updates and photo/video uploads.

Romance emerges as the social theme underlying the power of Facebook to overcome barriers of technology and society. Romance is the dominating emotion overlaying the thirst to connect, friend and chat, and Facebook, as an open-ended medium for social interactions, remains a critical (sometimes the only) channel to navigate and reach across lived worlds of entrenched conventions of sociality. Romance surrounds engagements with Facebook: in profile creation, in friending patterns, in status updates and photo/video uploads. Examples abound in the timelines of our participants' Facebook pages evident in the tailoring of profiles, sometimes 'fake' (and the term 'fake' needs some contextual unravelling we will touch upon later in the chapter), and in the befriending of young women from socially elevated segments, usually a higher socio-economic status. India and its forms of social stratification act as bastions of censorship, particularly in the context of male–female interactions that threaten to subvert the 'bhai–behen' ideal of a platonic relationship (Abraham 2002).

Romance is the medium channelling and staging fantasies, aspirations and play to explore potential possibilities of social mobility. These may range from a rich collage of digitally enhanced photos not only magnifying the social status but also staging a personality makeover for a Facebook user profile to interest, fascinate and eventually friend 'women' of status. As users embed and leave activity imprints on their timelines, their aggrandising digital profiles (and surplus selves as we call them) trigger interesting offline behaviours to forge continuity between the world of Facebook and the world of the urban slum. Uploading photos on Facebook could exemplify multiple instantiations of the bridging of the digital and the social. Some examples are uploading the audio-visual experience of Tollywood (Telugu film industry) fandom through a Facebook page; the romantic relay chat on Facebook messenger between a teenager in a Chennai slum and a London-based 'woman' profile;

pictures of religious heroism sourced from the Internet archive aiding the digital performance of a Sikh teenager in a Hyderabad slum through a Facebook timeline.

At one point in our research process, teenagers and young persons in our study seemed to us as having understood Facebook irresistibly as a communication system allowing 'friending' among persons 'who don't know each other'. In contrast, WhatsApp was perceived as allowing private communication among people who are already allowed 'in the house'. In the opinion of our research subjects, WhatsApp favoured communication between known individuals, as its communication system obstructed connections between unknown users. The long and short, in the eyes of my research subjects, was that WhatsApp enabled privacy to be maintained in a manner that codified social norms in maintaining social hierarchies and exclusivity when it came to communicating patterns with the opposite sex in Indian society. Many of the teens I have spoken to also describe how their use of Facebook, while subverting and irreverently traversing social norms, simultaneously stops short of overturning established social norms. While there are multiple reasons for maintaining more than one Facebook account, 'authentic' accounts to fake profiles where young adults pose as women, the accounts themselves are distinctively described as tools to express and explore romantic relationships and dating possibilities hitherto under strong social taboo. Why 'fake a woman' to do this got interesting replies, one of them being 'it was easy to friend women posing as a woman'. These behaviours seemingly, while maintaining social norms of friending, slyly flirted with and subverted them. How this is done will form the crux of the 'surplus self' narrative in this essay.

Framing the Study

The Internet offers a platform of resources for the active and reflexive shaping of the self, a central feature characterising the era of the web 2.0 and the everyday of the local–global dialectic. Boellstorff (2008) calls this phenomenon the dialectic between technology platforms

making of why youth are on Facebook and how they articulate this need and act it out in their Facebook pages. It is 'Fasbook', for online communities in Trinidad who share social norms internally, such that the use of Facebook can look quite different in two different places. The process by which people convey to others that they are a certain kind of person or possess certain characteristics (Leary 1996) is linked to the belief that those who view one's profile pages the most are members of one's offline social networks (Ellison et al. 2007).

Focused more on relationship building rather than individual need gratification, Facebook is also a mechanism for creating and performing impressions of a particular identity. In our research, much of Facebook involves the customisation of an online space, very much part of an impression management strategy offering a specific public identity for circulation through online networks. Our participants, overwhelmingly young and male, are on Facebook to satiate their needs for fantasy and escape, and to associate with the rich and famous to allow a personal gaze hitherto unavailable in personal or public 'everyday' space. This thirst to associate with people otherwise inaccessible in the 'everyday' of the urban slum life connects to Goffman's 'dramaturgical' everyday self-presentation as role-playing for an 'audience'. Goffman alludes to the socialisation of performance when aspects of a personality are moulded, modified and concealed to fit a specific understanding and expectations of the society in which it is presented.

For Goffman, any social situation with more than two people is a 'dramaturgically' inflected attempt to persuade a version of one's self—an attempt to socially 'sell' oneself, making a social connection with the 'other' self, almost like a 'conversational sales pitch'. The expressions a person 'gives off', the things we say and pose with deliberate intention can be understood as 'elements of our expressiveness', as manipulating a 'personal front'; this also includes playing with personal 'props' like hair, clothing, body language and even one's social-sexual identity. The Goffmanesque universe of dramaturgical sociology is the constant interplay with the creation and grooming of a projected understanding of the 'self'—like actors in a play conveying to an audience a particular impression of themselves in the social context of the theatrical experience. Inhabitation of online spaces presented in terms of persona adoption, masking, anonymity and pseudonimity as strategies of self-projection can be viewed as a process of constant 'dramaturgy', of 'giving-off' (Bullingham and Vasconcelos 2013)—in the Goffman sense of the term—'face', whereby one 'keeps face' and constantly 'grooms' the impression that they likely make on an audience in order to 'live up to' the constructed idea of the self. This 'construction of face' is a dramaturgical device—a face donned by a person interacting online. On Facebook, profiling a self is profiling a persona to confirm, modify or completely change impressions about this self.

'Habitus' as the physical and psychological disposition of any individual structured by society is intercepted regularly through practices of the digital life. The following sections will dwell on the multifaceted 'acts' of our young subjects of study, who take hold of and rewrite their 'habitus' albeit digitally.

The Faceted Digital Self and Diminishing Anxiety of Facebook Use

We explore three ideas connoting and emblematising the 'romantic surplus digital self' through the three themes of heterosexual love, globality and politics. Each of these themes will resonate in the ethnographic stories from the field and the lives of young persons approaching digital platforms as a passage through teenage and young adulthood. The surplus self encapsulates an idea, demonstrating rich digital activity in the midst of resource poverty for the youth in urban slums of India. Through their Facebook activity, young adults forge and perform 'second lives' and the surplus self is connotative of 'Goffmanesque' performativity animating digital activity stretching the boundaries of lived experience. For teenagers in our study, the urban slum becomes a background 'to flee' and a social reference 'to escape' through the tailoring of online selves—an excessive, vigorous and transformative tailoring culminating in the production of the 'surplus self'.

Mudassar (19, male, Hyderabad) has just updated his timeline with a picture. It is of him in fancy ethnic attire connotative of his ethnicity and he has made modern tweaks to the photo, rendering himself beyond the space that embeds him. It is shot from afar, from a height, and he looks like an exotic yet identifiable young man—the grace and confidence with which his picture appears is hypnotising. He is otherwise shy with people who are unfamiliar to his milieu. Mudassar never leaves his suburb, near the Hi-Tech global IT park in the city of Hyderabad. He moves around chatting conspiratorially with his friends at the mobile repair shop he manages, another reminder of how acutely geographically constrained he is. This belies his substantially rich play with Facebook through daily updates, photo uploads, likes, comments and private chats, sometimes with women from outside his country, India. Sometime in 2009, Mudassar discovered Facebook, and small prepaid packets of mobile Internet access and a plethora of client and browsing apps helped him get to the social media site with optimal costs to his data packs. He began inhabiting his timeline with cute baby pictures, pearly shimmering natural sceneries and greetings of the day delivered in the style of cards available in 'Archie' stores. He moved on to romantic pictures of lovers doing sweet nothings in open exotic landscapes, expressing love and other affectionate emotions towards each other. To him and his young group of friends, on the Facebook platform, over-friending is considered 'the best thing to have happened'—the more friending invitations, the more the chances you have to friend women.

Poovarasan (20, college-going, male, Chennai) is the spokesperson for a bunch of youngsters in their late teens/early twenties in Urur Kuppam, a coastal slum in south Chennai. He calls himself 'Flowking' on Facebook, a loose translation of his name from Tamil to English. He comes across as quite reserved, but his friends claim that he has opened up a lot after using Facebook. He heard of Facebook from friends in college and created his profile from his home personal computer with access to the Internet. This was sometime in the year 2011. He has helped his band of boys create their individual Facebook accounts. Flowking has a narrative to offer around Facebook adoption: Facebook is for entertainment (as something to do when they are bored), chatting and making new friends. All of them had entered their complete and true, to the best of their knowledge, details on Facebook, including their profile pictures. But some refrained from giving out their phone numbers more out of unease than controlling privacy. This band of boys having friended each other on Facebook were clear about why they use Facebook. Deena (18, male, Chennai) articulated, 'there is no point becoming Facebook friends with people we already know... adding people we do not know is like a new experience. We can be free and more expressive with them...anyway we are not going to meet these people face to face'. As I probed further, it seemed new experiences were offered by Facebook's format and structuring of friending experiences.

One of the ways in which the boys go about making friends is typing their geographic area/city/college and then adding friends through the 'people you may know' option. Photographs and details that the photos present as visual markers are important in deciding who to add as a friend. Sathish (18, school dropout, Chennai), who is Sathish Always Cool on Facebook, chipped in that the profile picture was a deciding factor: it gave away 'a lot of vibes to someone who is hanging in there to friend someone'. He added that most of his friends wanted to add more girls as friends than boys. Mani (17, school-going, male, Chennai) said the status update is a great feature to be aware of stuff 'on the spot', especially if it is one's birthday—which then makes for a nice conversational poke on Facebook to friend someone. He admitted he knows only 50 out of the 100 friends on his friend list. Flowking, however, is a power user: 'I use Facebook every day for at least half an hour, depending on whether I see my "friends" on chat... I also share new videos, look around for new ones, but I always want to chat'. ViviCena (19, school dropout, male, Chennai) has no Facebook account because he cannot read and write. He engages in proxy use of the site through his friends, glancing at the photos of their 'girl friends', sometimes liking posts. Deena chips in, 'If you use Facebook, shyness will definitely go. Some people get contact numbers of people through Facebook and might be able to chat with people over the phone. I know one boy who never used to speak in class, but once he opened a Facebook account, he started talking to girls well in person also'. He adds that he does not see any change in himself, 'I am still the same... but Flowking has definitely changed after using Facebook and has become less shy'. Deena opined that not all profiles are 'original' on Facebook. He said:

> I know one story where one boy and one girl met on Facebook and decided to meet. They had put up their profile pictures and all that... The two finally met at one place and they didn't like each other at all and became 'very vexed' since the pictures they saw did not match the person in front of them. They stopped using Facebook after that. There are many incidents like that.

Sentamil Selvan (19, college-going, male, Chennai) said that he likes to change his Facebook status and types 'stanzas' and 'slogans' and also news. He 'copy-pastes' most of these and likes the way he appears very 'well-read' on his page. The Urur boys were forging a relationship with Facebook as their anxiety gave way to emboldened use to connect and flirt with girls. Facebook and teenage participation in the margins of urban Indian society continued to remain a male space—young women from Urur faced challenges in the form of costs—they could not find money to buy a phone; even if they managed to borrow a phone, there was not sufficient privacy or independence to get on to Facebook; more importantly, brothers and male cousins exercised a tight control over how, when and where their sisters used Facebook. Deena, in a candid moment during the interview, said, '...we worry that they might just get all those request from...err...boys...we know that, don't we?' Facebook and the mobile Internet by and large remained out of reach of these young teenage girls who could not garner resources to get a phone or a data card. This situation shifts when the girls grow up to become young women and find economic and social independence to manage their own phones and the mobile Internet.

The Surplus Interrupted

The surplus self is explained as a seamful, multifaceted idea—it acquires a variety of expressions in the form of Facebook posts on the Timelines of our teenaged subjects. The surplus self is a response to the evolving use of Facebook: understanding its functionalities—gaining the technical expertise and using it as a social tool for networking and connecting with friends—as well as cataloguing romantic hopes, aspirations and disappointments. The surplus interrupted maps the trajectory of use over time and the gamut of emotional states it produced among our subjects.

The romantic surplus self soon gives way to sadomasochistic love displayed in words and pictures of self-despair, of unrequited intimacy and loss of the romantic presence of love. The pictures represented an externalisation of disappointments among our young adult participants, singed by the lack of response from women—especially women of status they were pursuing to make a 'Facebook friendship'. There was a period in time when Mudassar's pictures on Facebook bemoaned the treachery of women who sense the power they had over lovelorn men like him. Self-admittedly Mudassar had friended a lot of 'fake women' and was 'ploughing what he sowed'—he was banned, albeit temporarily, by Facebook, for sending an extraordinary number of friending requests, and because there were reports to block him from some of the 'women' whom Mudassar had intended to friend. Facebook 'unblocked him after 3 days'. Mudassar recovered and was back with a vengeance, plastering his timeline this time with plenty of frontal close-ups of his face, sometimes in casual attire and sometimes in costume symbolising his religious community affiliations. Self-admittedly, Mudassar was consciously reaffirming his comfort 'ethnic' zone to 'get over' the cross-cultural strides he had had to make to gain digital entry into the alluring world of women of status, in the hope of forging friendship with them.

I asked if over time he ever deleted the pictures. He answered, 'Facebook is my go-to space. I don't have money to buy external storage devices and the timeline is where I keep my photos.' In Mudassar's photo feeds he is mostly alone with hardly any friends featuring in his pictures. He posts multiple images of himself with several backdrops sourced from the Internet or morphed in an automorphing program or Internet service, in this case, PhotoFunia (https://photofunia.com/), where the visual effects/makeovers are highly exaggerated. Mudassar appears on the cover of a national newspaper; on the sides of a coffee terracotta cup; on a billboard cut-out overlooking a highway. He told me one of his youngest friends and Facebook aficionado, Sonu, is also the only one he learns from. Sonu's attitude is reassuring. He is 15 years old, individualistic, self-reliant, with an exclusive sense of photo aesthetics. He is exploring Instagram and Prisma, and he also introduced Mudassar to these platforms.

I cannot help but wonder what it all signifies, and when I ask, he tells me 'I don't know' or that 'it doesn't mean anything'. Actually it means a lot and he slowly articulates: sometimes these projections are for himself, a sort of white space where he can store his photographs that he so lovingly crafts. 'Where else will I save them?' he said. And while he would never outright call them rules, he would recognise guidelines that govern his posting strategy. Facebook is his most public-facing account and probably the only one. He has no other social media account on Twitter, Instagram, WhatsApp, YikYak, Kik or Snapchat. Mudassar felt he did not belong to these sorts of social media and had no friends or community on these platforms. He said, '...you go when there are people you know and others like you over there'. 'Like you' is a giveaway to the discomfort Mudassar felt about the social cues and signals many of the other digital platforms project. Apart from Facebook, there was no social media that made him feel 'at home' or socially comfortable—his friends adored his Facebook activity; they conspired to do similar things like him to friend women; they shared and exchanged friending strategies that brought both delight and sorrow.

Mudassar's young friend Sonu (15, male, Hyderabad) calls Facebook 'Mental' (Rangaswamy and Yamsani 2011; Rangaswamy et al. 2013) which is a ubiquitous word to denote a feeling of headiness from being socially desired, 'a sort of a drugged state', and usually implies 'when you or a friend encounter a mind-blowing activity/performance on FB'. As Mudassar pointed out, 'this usually means an "attractive rich women" has friended you'. One example of 'mental' plays out in the form of and akin to a 'deep like'; a deep like is where you lurk on someone's account, and in the case of the teens in the slums I studied, it is randomly searching for women to friend on Facebook, going way back into their archives (if open), browsing the contents to explore, exhaust and ultimately friend women on Facebook. Ask Deena how many girls he routinely 'deep likes', he's unequivocal; 'too many' he says. His social media liaisons rarely result in actual hook-ups. In fact, he often does not meet these women in real life. Later in an interview, he clarified that he had talked to girls, sometimes with those living in Dubai and once even in London. He said, 'I've never been out of Chennai and she just said she was from London… so I was like "All right—I hit a jackpot"…'. For him, texting and chatting on FB Messenger, sometimes video calls, are the equivalent of hanging out in a trendy mall or multiplex (that is threatening to him in real life) and 'trying to "check out" if lucky, to catch the eye of a young women hanging out like himself over there [sic]'. As much as technology has changed the way we talk, think and do things, some of the critical problems of young adults are as they have always been. For now, Deena will have to keep most of his flirtations digital.

The surplus self is gendered. Facebook appropriation by teenagers in the urban slums of India belonged almost exclusively to young males. The era of the mobile Internet and pay-as-you-go data cards has ushered in new ways of becoming media literate. The mediated, shared and public ways of acquiring media literacy ensured digital participation and composition were predominantly male (Rangaswamy and Cutrell 2012). Internet was operationalised in mobile phone stores; the knack of downloading content happened in street corners; social media etiquette was learnt in groups of teenagers hanging out together in public squares—all of these exclusive male spaces. Facebook acquired an intensely gendered participation, its young adult male users collectively inhabiting social media functionalities and features to feel the sense of heightened anticipation to friend a female, desirably of a higher status as well as the betrayal when women of status do not respond to friending requests; to find an easy alignment with global imagery by decorating Facebook timelines with football and wrestling icons symbolic of male bonding, and visuals of historical valour celebrating war and warriorhood.

'Digital Margins' as Perspective

Class- and gender-based differences in Facebook/social media use illustrates how technologies are adopted and domesticated into social contexts. Some of the practices we see among the youth in ecosystems like urban slums touch upon broader questions of shifts over time as social media use perpetually triggers users towards specific modes of using technologies. What are the internal shifts in user perspectives from engagements with digital media? Does it change interactional elements between Facebook and a specific set of users? How might we position fake profiles, as inherent to the surplus self on Facebook, from the perspective of social marginalisation? We ruminate on these questions below.

1. On the nature of relations among networked spaces: It is interesting to note that digital exclusion can still be a portent reality that bars access to privileged social-digital spaces, and renders these spaces off-limits to youth from specific social geographies by simply making these networked spaces unavailable for interaction. Would the creation of the surplus self be then an instance to overcome social taboos and infiltrating the mainstream? What then are the self-management strategies to deal with negative backlash? (Some examples include friending other fakes, Facebook bans and the prospect of digital excommunication.)

2. Nonetheless, it might be interesting to problematise the hermetic notion of these exclusions (based on class, caste, social geography, gender) and the permeability of digital boundaries to render exclusion, at best, a contested one: How are digitally networked spaces different? Are these spaces porous enough to include a wide variety of influence? What are the kinds of privileges networked

spaces embody by virtue of being digital? Rural India is another kind of marginalised space if viewed from the prism of urban India. Youth in slums are a privileged lot in the face of marginalisation of rural India when we employ a mainstream yardstick to compare Facebook use—marginalised spaces such as urban slums may contain or retain features that characterise aspects of privilege.

3. How is accessibility to the mainstream both limiting and empowering for the margins? Could we make an argument about social barriers being, sometimes/somewhat, opportunistic for the margins to experiment with technology?

As users drive content, the social media landscape is being incrementally representative of a range of forms, production practices, aesthetics and politics. Even a quick examination of content of Facebook profile pictures might muddy notions of what is mainstream and marginal—a plethora of self-profiling practices consumed, uploaded, distributed, commented on from across nations, cultures and population segments that portray a user-generated diversity contributing to discussions about alternative politics of the digital self contradictory to the view of the world as a neat hierarchy of the digital haves and have nots. The opportunity and potential to democratise the digital self may be fuelled by the interplay of socio-cultural, ideological and technological shifts: the question is what, how and when do these shifts take place and what is the role of the 'digital' in these? Some of the questions we have attempted to unpack in this essay are the following: As even the less privileged in developing countries become ambient broadcasters to stay connected, how will these digital broadcasting behaviours seep through to impact other lived spheres of life, lifestyles and opportunities? Will the social dimension of the surplus digital self play out, and if so, how and where? Is it an artifice to draw boundaries between the digital and other dimensions of the social when we discuss impact, outcomes, empowerment and social mobility? We explored the themes of heterosexual friending, globality and political agency through a study of the democratic and romantic affinities young adult males developed through Facebook functionalities—an agency interrupted by offline social hierarchies setting limits to offset digital dividends. However, digital dividends did have consequences in offline contexts of young adults—self-admittedly, the Urur boys gained confidence 'to talk to girls', discuss politics, and speak conversational English.

Socio-economic difference in social media use is explained and illustrated by how technologies are adopted and domesticated into social contexts (Miller 2011). Rather than technology injecting social norms and behaviours into users, this study exemplifies how young persons can knead technologies to subvert social norms—even social norms usually thought of as deeply embedded in social systems where technology is least expected to bring a dramatic, sometimes impactful, change. This essay centres on the use of Facebook as a lingering social experience amidst youth living in the urban slums of India and in the margins of the digital networked society. The essay is also about an interactive and creative group of online users eager to socialise at scale, initiate and actualise the sharing of everyday routines, habits, opinions and sometimes deep-seated desires on the social digital media platform of their choice (Wang 2013). Just as social media is being credited with catalysing a platform for hitherto unheard voices, the jury is still out on whether the rise of social participation can democratise the universe of digital media for a 'surplus' construction of the digital self.

References

Abraham, L. 2002. 'Bhai-behen, True Love, Time Pass: Friendships and Sexual Partnerships among Youth in an Indian Metropolis'. *Culture, Health & Sexuality* 4(3): 337–53.

Anjaria, J. S. 2006. 'Street Hawkers and Public Space in Mumbai'. *Economic & Political Weekly* 41(21): 2140–46.

Bakardjieva, M., and G. Gaden. 2012. 'Web 2.0 Technologies of the Self'. *Philosophy & Technology* 25(3): 399–413.

Blumler, J. G., and E. Katz, eds. 2006. *The Uses of Mass Communications: Current Perspectives on Gratifications Research*. Beverly Hills: Sage Publications.

Boellstorff, T. 2008. *An Anthropologist Explores the Virtually Human: Coming of Age in Second Life*. Princeton: Princeton University Press.

boyd, d. 2013. *It's Complicated: The Social Lives of Networked Teens*. Yale: Yale University Press.

boyd, d., and N. Ellison. 2007. 'Social Network Sites: Definition, History, and Scholarship'. *Journal of Computer-Mediated Communication* 13(1): 210–30.

Bullingham, L., and A. C. Vasconcelos. 2013. '"The Presentation of Self in the Online World": Goffman and the Study of Online Identities'. *Journal of Information Science* 39(1): 101–12.

Burrell, J. 2012. *Invisible Users: Youth in the Internet Cafés of Urban Ghana*. MIT Press.

Chaney, D. 1996. *Lifestyles*. London and New York: Routledge.

Choi, M. 2016. 'Like. Flirt. Ghost: A Journey Into the Social Media Lives of Teens'. Available at https://www.wired.com/2016/08/how-teens-use-social-media/ (accessed on 12 February 2020).

Cupples, J., and L. Thompson. 2010. 'Heterotextuality and Digital Foreplay: Cell Phones and the Culture of Teenage Romance'. *Feminist Media Studies* 10(1): 1–17.

David, G., and C. Cambre. 2016. 'Screened Intimacies: Tinder and the Swipe Logic'. *Social Media+ Society* 2(2): 258–270. Available at https://doi.org/10.1177/2056305116641976 (accessed on 19 October 2022).

Doron, A. 2016. 'Unclean, Unseen: Social Media, Civic Action and Urban Hygiene in India'. *South Asia: Journal of South Asian Studies* 39(4): 715–39.

Ellison, N. B., C. Steinfield and C. Lampe. 2007. 'The Benefits of Facebook "Friends": Social Capital and College Students' Use of Online Social Network Sites'. *Journal of Computer-Mediated Communication* 12(4): 1143–68.

Ganesh, I. M. 2010. '"Mobile Love Videos Make Me Feel Healthy": Rethinking ICTs for Development'. IDS Working Papers, 2010(352), 1–43.

Goffman, E. 1959. *The Presentation of Self in Everyday Life*. New York, NY: Bantam Doubleday Dell Publishing Group.

Houghton, D., A. N. Joinson, N. Caldwell and B. Marder. 2013. 'Tagger's Delight? Disclosure and Liking Behaviour in Facebook: The Effects of Sharing Photographs amongst Multiple Known Social Circles'. Birmingham Business School Discussion Paper Series, No. 2013-03.

Ito, M., S. Baumer, M. Bittanti, d. boyd, R. Cody, B. Herr-Stephenson, H. A. Horst, P. G. Lange, D. Mahendran, K. Z. Martínez, C. J. Pascoe,

D. Perkel, L. Robinson, C. Sims and L. Tripp. 2019. *Hanging Out, Messing Around, and Geeking Out: Kids Living and Learning with New Media*. Cambridge: MIT Press.

Kumar, N. 2014. 'Facebook for Self-Empowerment? A Study of Facebook Adoption in Urban India'. *New Media & Society* 16(7): 1122–37.

Leary, M. R. 1996. *Self-Presentation. Impression Management and Interpersonal Behavior*. Boulder, CO: Westview.

Lingam, L., I. Bhallamudi and N. Rao. 2018. *Adolescent Subcultures and Smartphones: Exploring the Implications for Gender, Sexuality and Rights*. Report prepared for Tata Institute of Social Sciences and UNICEF For Every Child. Available at https://www.academia.edu/36836888/Adolescent_Subcultures_and_Smartphones_Exploring_the_Implications_for_Gender_Sexuality_and_Rights (accessed on 19 October 2022).

Mahabir, R., A. Crooks, A. Croitoru and P. Agouris. 2016. 'The Study of Slums as Social and Physical Constructs: Challenges and Emerging Research Opportunities'. *Regional Studies, Regional Science* 3(1): 399–419.

Martin, L. H., H. Gutman and P. H. Hutton, eds. 1988. *Technologies of the Self: A Seminar with Michel Foucault*. Amherst: University of Massachusetts Press.

McKenna, K. Y., A. S. Green and M. E. Gleason. 2002. 'Relationship Formation on the Internet: What's the Big Attraction?' *Journal of Social Issues* 58(1): 9–31.

McLean, S. A., S. J. Paxton, E. H. Wertheim and J. Masters. 2015. 'Photoshopping the Selfie: Self Photo Editing and Photo Investment are Associated with Body Dissatisfaction in Adolescent Girls'. *International Journal of Eating Disorders* 48(8): 1132–40.

Miller, D. 2010. *Stuff*. Cambridge: Polity Press.

———. 2011. *Tales from Facebook*. Cambridge: Polity Press.

———. 2013. 'What Will We Learn from the Fall of Facebook?' Global Social Media Impact Study, Project Blog. Available at http://blogs.ucl.ac.uk/global-social-media/2013/11/24/what-will-we-learn-from-the-fall-of-facebook/ (accessed on 19 October 2022).

Nijman, J. 2015. 'India's Urban Future: Views from the Slum'. *American Behavioral Scientist* 59(3): 406–23.

Rangaswamy, N., and E. Cutrell. 2012. 'Anthropology, Development and ICTs: Slums, Youth and the Mobile Internet in Urban India'.

In Proceedings of the Fifth International Conference on Information and Communication Technologies and Development, Atlanta, Georgia, 12–15 March (pp. 85–93).

Rangaswamy, N., G. Challugulla, M. Young and E. Cutrell. 2013. 'Local Pocket Internet and Global Social Media. Bridging the Digital Gap: Facebook and Youth Sub-stratum in Urban India'. In International Conference on Social Implications of Computers in Developing Countries, 19–22 May, Jamaica.

Rangaswamy, N., and S. Yamsani. 2011. 'Mental Kartha Hai or Its Blowing my Mind: Evolution of the Mobile Internet in an Indian Slum'. EPIC (Ethnographic Praxis in Industry Conference), Boulder, CO, 18–21 September (pp. 18–21).

Rugnetta, M. 2014. 'Why Do We Hate Selfies?' [Video]. Idea Channel: PBS Digital Studios. Available at https://www.youtube.com/watch?v=2j7SIxMGj5Q&feature=share&list=PLbpi6ZahtOH5VEwH2hdnMyblo8D794JKb&index=1 (accessed on 19 October 2022).

Sambasivan, N., N. Rangaswamy, E. Cutrell and B. Nardi. 2009. 'Ubicomp4D: Infrastructure and Interaction for International Development—The Case of Urban Indian Slums'. In Proceedings of the 11th International Conference on Ubiquitous Computing, Ubicomp 2009, 30 September–3 October, Orlando, Florida (pp. 155–64). Available at https://www.microsoft.com/en-us/research/wp-content/uploads/2016/02/Ubicomp4D_Ubicomp2009.pdf (accessed on 15 October 2022).

Senft, T. M., and N. K. Baym. 2015. 'What Does the Selfie Say? Investigating a Global Phenomenon'. *International Journal of Communication* 9(Feature): 1588–1606.

Srivastava, R. 2003. 'Formal Sector and Urban Poverty'. Available at http://www.infochangeindia.org/urban_india_04.jsp. [Link discontinued]

Turkle, S. 1985. *The Second Self: Computers and the Human Spirit*. New York: Simon and Schuster.

____. 1994. 'Constructions and Reconstructions of Self in Virtual Reality: Playing in the MUDs'. *Mind, Culture, and Activity* 1(3): 158–67.

Wang, T. 2013. 'Talking to Strangers: Chinese Youth and Social Media'. Ph.D. diss. Available at http://static1.1.sqspcdn.com/static/f/451223/24352563/1392053988513/Dissertation_Tricia_Wang_021014.pdf?token=xytwdHalzxGLlrzxr94LrQRv6rU%3D (accessed on 19 October 2022).

12

RELIGIOUS SOCIALISATION OF CHILDREN

Narratives from Villages in Gujarat

Kiran Vinod Bhatia

> You switch on the TV, and they tell you how the Muslims are bad. How all of us kill cows! We feel bad. I do not eat beef. Everyone watches this and then we do not feel like talking with our Hindu classmates. They disrespect us; they think we will steal their cows and kill them. We do not like watching local channels in Gujarati, so we have our own periodicals in Urdu. They are written by scholars in our community and are distributed personally. They are good. They tell us how everyone thinks Islam is bad. We must fight back! (Najma, April 2017).

Najma is a 12-year-old Muslim student enrolled in Class VIII of a municipal primary school in a village in Gujarat. What is evident in this excerpt from an hour-long conversation with her in the drawing room of her house is that she identifies as Muslim and her religious identity is situated within a complex web of her social relations and media engagements. Children like Najma acquire religious identities through a process of socialisation wherein they are trained to regulate and discipline their conduct as religious subjects. It is, however, important to note that in this process, the media play a crucial role in defining how different religious identities are perceived in public life. Media discourse creates interpretive limits on how a particular religious community is situated within the socio-political landscape of the state. Scholars such as Banaji (2018),

Rajagopal (2001) and Bhatia (2018), for instance, have combined a reading of contemporary mediascapes and political rhetoric in Gujarat to suggest that religion has emerged as a political rationality to influence the masses. The meaning of religious identities is slowly changing in the lives of children in Gujarat. Religious identities and practices are not just limited to everyday religious rituals, stories and conversation, but have emerged to acquire a political and public dimension.

From countries in the global North such as the US, Canada and nations in Europe, to developing and diverse societies in areas of global South such as China, Sri Lanka, Pakistan and Myanmar, religion has emerged as a regulatory force disciplining individuals to enact their citizenship based on the modalities of their religious identities. We have witnessed instances of violence and discrimination against particular religious communities, especially the minorities, in several countries. The bombing of churches in Sri Lanka, the persecution of Rohingyas in Myanmar, the shooting at a mosque in the Quebec City of Canada, cases of lynching individuals from minority communities by vigilante mobs in parts of India—these examples and many more indicate how religious identity is being strategically used by individuals, communities and the state to marginalise and persecute minorities in various socio-political contexts across the world. India is no exception.

Since the late twentieth century, individuals in societies across Gujarat, for instance, have faced discrimination and othering because of their religious and caste identities, social class and gender. With a surge in politico-religious ideologies, religion has emerged as a new modality of regulation, dominance and control in contemporary politics and systems of governance in Gujarat (Sud 2012; Yagnik and Sheth 2005). Several policies, including budget allocation and welfare schemes, are planned and implemented to appease religious groups and communities. Such policies and discourses perpetuate animosity among religious communities because individuals internalise the reality that their access to intellectual, economic and administrative resources is influenced by their religious identities. Particularly significant in this regard is the growing intolerance between Hindus and Muslims in Gujarat and arguably across the country—more often experienced in everyday interactions (or the lack of it) and the routine media representations of various religious communities. When children are raised in such a religious and political context and regularly consume media narratives of interreligious conflicts, discrimination and violence, they are at a greater risk of submitting to exclusionary citizenship discourses (Antal 2008). They are encouraged to operate from within the felt contours of their religious identities which often restrict them within binaries such as self–other, good–evil and Hindus–Muslims.

In studies published earlier (Bhatia 2016, 2018; Bhatia and Pathak-Shelat 2017, 2019), we have established that media discourse has the potential to cast children into imaginaries of religion by determining the possibilities in which they can speak, act and behave in relation to the (religious) self and the other. Media reinforces a particular type of 'descriptive and analytical' language (Carrette 2000) which is designed to normalise certain forms of conduct and discipline among individuals who identify as religious subjects. For instance, when Najma engages with media texts where the Muslim community is represented as the religious other, she feels a sense of alienation. As a member of the Muslim community, she interprets this representation in ways which inform her own conduct in relation to both her own community members and her Hindu classmates. As a result, children often adopt an outward-looking approach allowing them to experience the self as opposed to the religious other. I argue that children occupy an ontological space where allegiance to one's community is practised as apathy, felt and enacted, towards the religious other.

What is important here is to acknowledge that media are the discursive fields in the society implicated in socialising children as religious subjects. The theoretical force of this argument rests in examining how media socialises children to enact their religious subjectivities in their lived realities. How do media promote religion as the dominant rationality to regulate the actions and behaviour of children?

The chapter is divided into two parts. In the first segment, I draw a theoretical map to delineate how religion acts as a regulatory force socialising children into adhering to the normalised codes of conduct and discipline within their societies. In doing this, I argue that media act as a crucial capillary of collective life[1] in and through which the dominant rationality of religious socialisation permeates drawing room conversations, peer-based discussions, interpersonal relations and interfaith engagements in villages of Gujarat. The need to understand these patterns of socialisation stems from how we can use it to better inform media literacy and education efforts. In the final segment of this chapter, therefore, I elaborate on some critical media education initiatives and exercises designed to create interfaith dialogues among children from different religious communities through collaborative practices and classroom activities.

To Do or Not to Do? Formation of a Religious Subject

Religious socialisation of children is conceptualised as a process which provides guidelines for analysing how children must conduct themselves: how they should think, speak and behave in relation to both the self and the religious other. It is a project of surveillance wherein children are taught how to account for themselves as members of their religious community and how to articulate their membership in their everyday interactions with the other. This definition draws force from Foucault's theory of governmentality (1997) which offers analytical frameworks to examine how religious guidelines manifest in the form of media texts and discourse to regulate individual bodies. These religious guidelines have two crucial dimensions.

Regimes of Knowledge

Under this dimension, children observe how a religious community is perceived in societies. They rely on various channels of communication, especially media, to examine what it means to be a Hindu/Muslim. They draw from the public discourse, dominant frames of interpretations used in their societies, and interpersonal interactions. Media also provides them with a language to understand which forms of conduct are normal/abnormal, acceptable/ unacceptable and sane/insane. Children learn to participate in the meaning-making process and attribute specific characteristics, behavioural patterns, utterances and social context to religious communities.

Regimes of Practice

Once children learn to articulate their situatedness as religious subjects, they must learn to practice their religious identities. This involves observing how people from their community articulate their identities in the society, especially in their interactions with the religious other and what forms of conduct/practice are legitimised in media. Children learn to perform their religious identities and allegiance in and through various forms of conduct: the peer group they affiliate with, the kind of language they use while referring to the religious other, the public spaces they inhabit/occupy/frequent and, most importantly, the kind of public leaders/discourse they support.

The media is a material site used to define the dominant regimes of knowledge and practice and normalise certain forms of conduct. Media discourses are thus the practices which 'form the objects of which we speak' (Foucault 1972: 49) and how ideas manifest as actions. According to Hall (1994), media representations make a few forms of thoughts and conduct possible by classifying all other forms as unacceptable. As a result, those who choose to conduct themselves differently are identified as deviants and mitigated as threats to the sanctity of the society and/or unity of the religious community (Amin 2010; Lallement 2014). Accordingly, discrimination against the deviant body is enacted through everyday doings—punishing, reprimanding, encouraging, excluding, and so on (Brubaker et al. 2004). The regulatory function of media discourse can thus be conceived as the practice we impose on individuals and the violence we inflict on things we consider unacceptable just so that we may regularise events and actions of individuals (Lemke 2001). Through the process of religious socialisation, therefore, children acquire skills, techniques and competencies required to enunciate their stake in reifying the dominance of religion in their lived realities.

It is important to acknowledge that religious identities operate in conjunction with other forms of social identities populating the life-worlds of children, especially gender, class and caste. Each of these social identities operates to reinforce the influence of religion in the lives of children. For instance, gender norms dictating the conduct of young girls are deeply rooted in religious teachings emerging from their engagements with religious books, teachers/leaders, parents and peers. As a result, when young Muslim girls enact their religious identities by wearing a hijab, they are simultaneously dealing with concepts of modesty defined to discipline female bodies and limit their conduct. Similarly, Hindu children are often trained to uphold caste hierarchies in and through their socialisation as followers of the Hindu religion. Caste references and teachings are drawn from the religious texts and often inform their conduct as religious subjects. As is evident, children's religious identities intersect with their other social identities in ways which reinforce existing power relations in their communities.

In the following section, I submit empirical insights from a two-year-long ethnographic study with children in three villages[2] of Gujarat to examine how children use media to identify with their religious communities, practise their religious identities and reinforce religion as a dominant force of socialisation.

Media and Drawing Room Conversations

Many cultural studies scholars emphasise the need to situate the analysis of children's media cultures within the larger social structures and relations which inform the interpretive frames children use while engaging with media texts (de Certeau 1984; Drotner and Livingstone 2008; Lemish 2015). Our previous work (Bhatia and Pathak-Shelat 2019) has demonstrated that there are associative

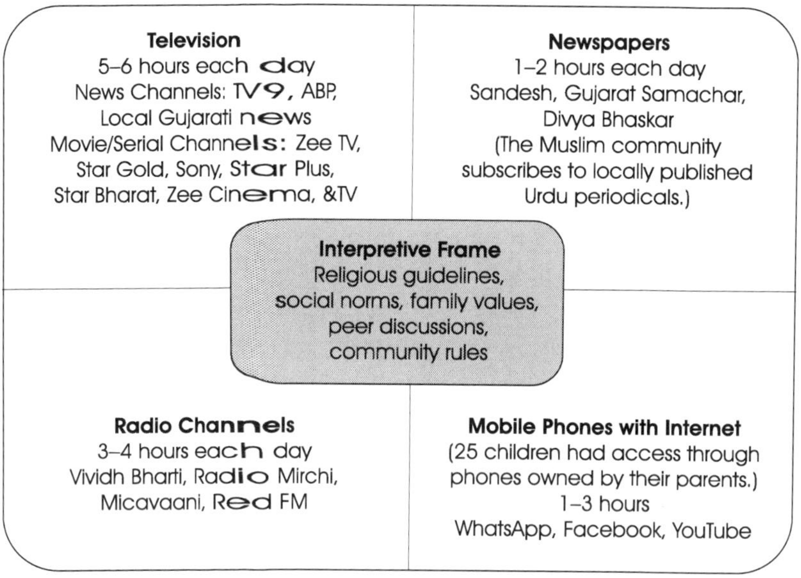

FIGURE 12.2 Media Ecologies of Children

Source: Author.

What is interesting to note here is how this collective media engagement influences the interpretations children draw from the media narratives they consume. Rohan, a 12-year-old Hindu student, explains:

> After dinner, we switch to TV9 [local Gujarati language news channel] for news from the city and state. There are so many things we don't understand, but then I hear what my father and grandfather are discussing. It helps me make sense of the news… One day we were watching news where shops of some Muslim butchers were inspected by some local villagers. I didn't understand it first, but then my father said, 'These people [Muslims] need to be kept under fear or they will start selling beef; they have no respect for our religion. Hindus must come together.' Initially, I thought that police should do the inspection, but then I realised that the Hindus must support this cause and contribute. We must also work if we are to bring a change.

As is evident, the interpretive frame used by children is informed by their family values, religious guidelines, peer discussions and politics in their communities. They use these interpretive frames to make sense of their role as a religious subject in their societies. Rohan, for instance, draws from the conversations his father and grandfather have related to the issue of 'cow vigilantes' (Banaji 2018) and interprets what it means to be a Hindu. According to him, unauthorised surveillance of Muslims is an act of devotion towards his religious community. He consumes media narratives where these actions are portrayed as ethical and justified. Also, the family reads this media narrative for the children to ensure that they learn to perceive various civic issues from the lens of their religious community. Media narratives, therefore, play a crucial role in influencing children to marshal their body capacities to reify their allegiance towards their religious community and enact their subjectivity. When I asked Rohan if such discussions help him re-imagine his relationship with Muslim children from his village, he said, 'Madam, we are different. Hindus want to live in peace, but Muslims are violent. All butchers are Muslims…it means they are violent. Most of the Gujaratis, on the other hand, are vegetarians. We can't allow them to be violent with us. I avoid playing with Muslim children. We avoid them.'

What is evident from this example is that children engage with macro discourses of religious discrimination circulated through local media texts and reinforced through the interpretive frames available in their communicative ecologies. These engagements and macro discourses help define 'us versus the other' and children codify a set of conduct to regulate their behaviour in relation to the religious other. In order to speak to their religious identities, children learn to discriminate against the other and use various disciplinary techniques to systematically erase the other identities and roles in the lived realities of the self (Brubaker et al. 2004). This systemic distancing between the self and the other creates an exclusionary discursive field where the other can be accessed only through the available media representations (Bhatia and Pathak-Shelat 2019). As a result, the influence of media representations, examined through the dominant interpretive frame, becomes one of the primary material sites used to build experiential boundaries within which the religious other is encountered. Media, thus, functions as a channel for circulating the dominant rationality of religious discrimination, thus permeating into routine interpersonal interactions of members from different religious communities as they enact their subjectivity in and through their everyday experiences with the religious other. As a result, many students like Rohan engage in acts of micro-aggression constituted of several actions of self-regulation such as mocking, abusing, avoiding, ostracising and, most importantly, blaming the other.

In the following sections, I present important highlights from this ethnographic study to explain how media discourses which children engage with inform their religious identity. The national and local discourse circulated through media encourages children to enact their religious subjectivity in three ways: (a) discrimination towards the other, (b) intra-community coalition building and (c) disciplining the deviants.

Fear and Paranoia: The Imagined Other

Discussing a newspaper article from *Gujarat Samachar* (2016) titled 'Muslims Will Hold a Meeting in Chikhli to Stop Cow Slaughter', Yashasvi, a 10-year-old Hindu student, said, 'My father says that this is just a show. They [Muslims] want to show the world that they care about Hindus, but they do not. They steal our cows and kill them. They are violent.' The newspaper article she was discussing describes how Muslim communities were organising meetings in Chikhli to create awareness regarding the ban on cow slaughter. This event was also covered on TV9, a local Gujarati news channel, broadcast in these villages. As I sat having food with Yashasvi's family, her father and grandmother were heard discussing two conspiracy theories they had heard on WhatsApp:

> Father: They [Muslims] are afraid that we [Hindus] will show them their place...this is why they are pretending as if they care. My papa [his father] used to say we must be cautious of three kinds of people: the Rabari [lower caste], the police, and the

> mullas [Muslims]. Mullas are the worst…before we know, they will be so huge in numbers that they will wipe off our Hindu religion.
>
> Grandmother: They are doing it already, luring Hindu girls and converting them to their religion.

Soon after dinner, I interviewed Yashasvi to understand how these media stories and discussions around them inform her understanding of what it means to be a Hindu. She explained:

> We live with the Muslims in our villages and so it is important to know of these differences. A Hindu is different from a Muslim; we cannot be friends. This doesn't mean I don't like some of my Muslim classmates in school, but they are trying to suppress us… We should be proud of our religion.

As is evident, we have two crucial insights emerging from this conversation. First, media narratives, especially local Gujarati news houses, and the related family discussions produce the truth that one's religious identity can be defined only in relation to the other. Second, these macro discourses reinforcing the ideology of discrimination often socialise children to analyse and articulate various experiences in their villages as facets of their religious identities. When they define their identity as opposed to the religious other, they reify a Manichean symmetrisation of subjective identities as positive and negative.

For instance, within Muslim families, Hindus are often perceived as 'followers of *shaitan* [the devil]' and considered to be lesser humans. During various conversations I had with children and families in their living rooms, parents and elders often used words such as *mushrik*, *kaafir* and *haraam*[3] in their drawing room conversations. Let us look at one such conversation in the house of Sahida, a 10-year-old Muslim student. I was invited to dine with the family and discuss Sahida's academic performance in school. As the father was browsing through news channels, he paused at VTV Gujarati where the news anchor was reporting a rape case. The father watched the news for long and then said, 'This is haraam! Wearing clothes so short! Have you read this month's issue of *Iman*[4]?

It explains how the kaafirs [non-believers/Hindus] have gone astray and so they are being punished. Girls mean modesty.' Later, I asked Sahida's mother what he meant to validate my interpretation. She explained:

> Oh that! He is a conservative...even I am, but I do not look down upon non-believers. This does not mean we should not take care of our girls. You will not hear about many such cases in our community because we follow all the guidelines of the one true God. We must cover up and be modest. What will happen if you leave a ten rupee note on the road? Someone will take it, right?

Like Sahida, many other Muslim children are socialised to believe that non-believers are deviants and deserve to be punished. These children, thus, take upon themselves to exclude and silence the religious other in order to enact their religious subjectivity. They experience their religious identity largely when they regulate their conduct as the 'true follower of God' by disciplining the others through various forms of punishment such as ostracising them, blaming them for their sufferings, being apathetic to their emotions and refusing to engage with 'lesser humans' or the followers of shaitan. It is, however, crucial to identify that there is an inherent sense of fear and anger towards the other.

When I asked Pappi, an 11-year-old Hindu girl, why she refused to sit next to any of her Muslim friends in school, she said:

> Ma'am, they don't like us. Also, do you not read the newspaper? All the terrorist activities are planned by Muslims. All over the world! Yesterday, on the local news, the reporter said that Muslims in India want to join the ISIS. 100 Muslim youth have joined the ISIS already. What if they kidnap or force me to join them? I don't want to be friends with them.

I investigated the language used by the anchor and it emerged that the anchor did not mention that these youth were 'suspected' to have joined the ISIS. Also, when I unpacked the language used, it was evident that the choice of words, the tone and background score used were all inflammatory. She repeatedly used words and phrases such as: terrorist organisation, Muslims in India, anti-nationals, threat to national security and violent. Pappi, however, argued that the report was true because her father had received a similar message on WhatsApp, warning Hindus from forging close relations with Muslims.

Pappi, therefore, identifies as a Hindu who should fear the Muslim because the imagined other is repeatedly represented as violent, crude, anti-national and *kattar* [hardcore]. On the other hand, Muslim children are socialised to believe that Hindus want to eradicate the Muslim community. Let us look at the following media narrative and how it was interpreted by children from the Muslim community.

The news article titled 'Did Amit Shah Organise a Meeting in Sarangpur to Discuss the "Ram Mandir" Issue in Order to Win the UP Elections?' (*Sandesh* 2016) was circulated and discussed extensively among a few Muslim children in this study. For the families of these Muslim children, this issue and the way it is represented in the media speaks to their religious identities and how they are situated within the wider socio-political context in the country. For instance, Humza, a 12-year-old Muslim boy, argued:

> I was not born when this happened, but my family still discusses this. The media always support the demand of Hindus to build a temple in the place of the mosque. Can you see [referring to the article], how the media is supporting this cause? Doesn't it look intentional? The media never criticise the politicians who say they will construct this temple.

Humza's sister joined this discussion in the courtyard of their house. She has completed her graduation in political science and was more eloquent in articulating her opinions. She explained:

> When they demolish our religious place and construct a temple there, we feel threatened. I know it happened in Ayodhya, but the media and the people here [Gujarat] who are in majority support this. The local media glorifies it. We don't like the local Gujarati channels and newspapers. Also, in the religious sections of the Gujarati newspaper they never have a column on Islamic religious teachings; no, they publish it sometimes, but that is very rare.

> Today, they destroy a mosque; tomorrow they will demolish us and our religion.

Several scholars such as Ahmed (2010), Bhatia (2018), Bhatia and Pathak-Shelat (2017), Jain (2010) and Sonwalkar (2006) support this argument through their studies and claim that many Gujarati media organisations produce narratives with a pronounced pro-Hindutva sentiment. In these polarised representations, Muslims are either demonised or silenced and pushed to the margins.

The local media define ways in which the religious other is perceived, providing interpretive frameworks that resonate across social space (Bhatia and Pathak-Shelat 2017; Rajagopal 2001). Through structures of repetitive explanations, evaluations and assumptions, they juxtapose unrelated ideas to create a dominant narrative. This reinforces stereotypes about the other, creating fear and a sense of aversion towards things, people and practices that challenge the dominant rationality. Children who engage with these media narratives define their religious identity as an ontological space whose boundaries are constituted of guidelines on how to exclude the religious deviant from the experiential realm of the self.

In-Group Solidarity or Echo Chambers

When children in these villages are constantly exposed to a single narrative of religious discrimination through media, they experience a sense of alienation and fear in relation to the religious other. According to Busher (2015), children who are raised in situations of religious and political polarisation tend to develop stronger ties within their religious community and use this in-group solidarity as a 'fleece blanket' against the realities of the polarised world. They learn to use media and communication technologies to increase a sense of belongingness among the members of their religious communities. Building in-group solidarity is often based in the fear of the imagined other and, as a result, the entire discourse of community-building is regulated by the notions of Manichean identities of self/other, good/bad and victim/perpetrator (Pratt 2015).

Let us take the example of Shusruth to understand how young individuals rely on and use media to develop a sense of belonging to their religious community. Shusruth, an 11-year-old male Hindu student, enjoys access to social media applications, especially Facebook and WhatsApp, through his father's mobile phone. He often peruses messages posted in his family group on WhatsApp. He is sometimes allowed to carry his father's mobile phone to school and use it during the lunch hours. In the school, he has a group of Hindu friends, and all the members belong to the Thakur community, an upper-caste community in Gujarat. During a lunch break, his group of friends was watching a news video[5] posted by Zee News of a Muslim family being lynched in Gurugram. The news anchor is heard trying to convince the audience and the panellists that the lynching of the family was a random conflict and not necessarily a hate crime. After watching the video, Gautam, one of the students in the group, said:

> This is what the Muslims do. They want to be the victims and cry. So we should make them victims. My grandmother said the other day [in relation to this incident] that Muslims have been getting so many benefits because they cry that they are the victims. Victims are the Hindus in Pakistan. Do you know how they are treated?

Two things were evident from this conversation: First, news media trivialised this issue of violence and abuse to such an extent that young individuals were desensitised to the pain and suffering of the victim. Media may either refuse to label the violence as a hate crime perpetuated by one community against the other or create confusion in the minds of the audience by questioning the authenticity of the victims' statements. In doing this, media trivialises the insecurity and fear of minorities. Once the audience are desensitised towards the other, building in-group solidarity translates into plans and actions devised to annihilate the other. The religious other is the enemy who gives the group a sense of purpose to stick together. Also, the parents of these young individuals encourage them to identify the other as a 'threat to the well-being of their community. Second, these news media often broadcast disturbing scenes of violence in order to sensationalise an issue or event. They seldom treat the content on communal violence with a responsible rhetoric which is balanced and creates space for interfaith dialogue and exchange to emerge. As a result, children who experience communal discord in their everyday realities and inhabit situations of political polarisation enjoy participating in this hypermedia reality of newsrooms and discussions wherein the blatancy of visual cues and vivid images invoke in them a strong emotional and psychological response to protect their community (Cherian 2016; Tomomi 2013).

Hearing what Gautam had to say about the case of lynching, Shusruth said, 'We can't blame others. If we must protect our community, it starts with us. Like with us [literally]. We must show them that they are the minority. *Jaisa desh waisa bhesh.*'[6] Many children like Shusruth are socialised through their engagements with media and interactions in their families/communities to assume the responsibility of safeguarding their religious communities.

Here, the intentionality to protect one's religious community manifests as acts used to intimidate, exclude and marginalise the religious other. For instance, Hussain, a 12-year-old Muslim student, explains how his Muslim friends use WhatsApp and Facebook to create online groups and circulate pro-Islamic messages and texts. He showed me some messages he shared with his Muslim friends on a WhatsApp group. He explained:

> Ma'am, my grandfather showed me this meme in which Hindus were teasing Muslims with the statement 'We will build the Mandir for sure', and said that the Hindus will unite against us on the temple issue. So, I sent this forward to my WhatsApp group of Muslim brothers [referring to his friends]. If Hindus are together and against us, we must also stick together. Sometimes when there is a fight between a Hindu and a Muslim in the school, we just get a message on our group, and we run to support the Muslim student. We do not even ask them the reason for their fight; that is not important. We just reach the *chowk* [crossroads] with our group.

I requested them to allow me to peruse the messages in their WhatsApp group intimating them about one such fight between young students. He was very reluctant and told me that the language they have used is not appropriate and should not be read by a girl. What was evident through my analysis, however, is that young students regularly use a language of disrespect for the religious other. In this instance, for example, students had posted the following comments on the group:

1. '*Bey chowk agad sadgyu...chalo, bhago badha, aaje toh action cinema!*' (Hey, something's burning [referring to the fight]... let us run to the crossroads; we will have some action today!)
2. '*Pelo Thakur, randi no chokro...enej sharu karyu hase!*' (That Thakur [upper-caste Hindu boy], that s** of a b****...he must have started it!)
3. '*Bauj kapaayu che...aaje kapisu.*' (We have gotten ours cut many times [referring to both the process of oppression and circumcision]...now it is time to cut others.)

Many other students like Hussain are using social media platforms to articulate and express some radical ideas which are considered unacceptable in offline spaces inhabited by multiple and diverse voices. It is important to acknowledge that the materiality of these online networking sites allows students to circulate radical and discriminatory content, often creating closed communication enclaves to reinforce their agenda (Weimann 2010). Young community members, therefore, use discursive violence as a modality around which the identity of the religious other is articulated.

When children operate in such limited religious silos and ideological chambers, they categorise the other as a deviant who must be punished and disciplined. Regulating the conduct of the deviant through disciplinary techniques is the third most important dimension in the study of the socialisation of children as religious subjects. In the next section, I explain how children learn to adopt and practice some disciplinary techniques to punish the religious other. In this analysis, I re-emphasise that media act as a performative site in and through which the children implement disciplinary mechanisms.

Disciplining the Other

Media discourse embodies techniques of representation and reinforces the normalised code of conduct in religious communities. It limits the possibilities of imagining the other by creating linear and 'straightjacketed' narratives delineating the role, positionality, conduct and identity of religious subjects[7] (Brubaker et al. 2004). The dominant media discourse engenders a powerful field of meanings in which interpretations on how to perceive and engage with the other are naturalised (Karim 2003). From an epistemological perspective, children borrow from media language and disciplinary techniques used to identify, label and limit the religious other. According to scholars such as Karim (2003) and Zakaria (2006), media discourse equips children with competencies required to analyse interfaith relations in the political context of Gujarat in ways which do not speak to the structures of power.

To understand this, let us take the example of Babita, a 12-year-old Hindu girl, who regularly reads *Gujarat Samachar*. During her interview discussing how she enacts her subjectivity as a Hindu, she argued that it is her responsibility to support her Hindu community as they fight the Muslims. She explained:

> You don't read the newspapers? Muslims are the invaders. They looted us and destroyed us. If we do not come across as strong, they will do it again. See, I will show you…wait. [She pulled out an old supplement and referred to an article titled 'Alaudin Khilji Has Attacked and Demolished Temples in Gujarat in 1299', published in *Gujarat Samachar* on 11 November 2017.] Look at this, the article clearly explains how Muslims were barbaric and Hindu women had to commit Johar. Haven't you watched *Padmavat*? Back then, we did not fight, but now we will.

As is evident, local media discourse is encouraging Hindus to 'act now' and to claim what Muslims had appropriated from them. Though the macro discourse seems removed from the everyday realities of the children, these interpretations often dovetail into their routines and manifest in the form of acts of micro-aggression. Babita argued,

'We are cordial with them…some of them work for us. We, however, don't socialise with them. Their residential areas are different, and we don't enter those neighbourhoods. I have no Muslim friends. I am a good Hindu and I listen to my parents.'

Teachers in the school have received many complaints against Babita who bullies Muslim girls for not applying *bindi*[8] and for their Urdu accent. In some situations where she was the leader of a dance group, she refused to allow her Muslim classmates to participate. Other Hindu girls in her group supported her decision. Meena, a 12-year-old Hindu girl, said, 'If Ruksana [Muslim classmate] is allowed to be a part of the group, we will have to invite her to our house for dance practice after school. It is not allowed. She can't come to our house.'

It is, however, crucial to note here that many Muslim students harbour the same hatred for their Hindu classmates and often use religious slurs to degrade and insult them. Children from the Muslim community are also raised in a discriminatory ideology, and it compels them to denigrate the religious other. In one such instance, during a conversation with Ehsaan, an 11-year-old Muslim student, the interviewee brought up the topic of 'love-jihad' and he showed me news on Sandesh TV where a Muslim boy is accused of committing love-jihad because the family of the Hindu girl claimed that he lured her with a promise of marriage.[9] He said:

> Have you seen this news? They say Muslim boys will lure Hindu girls. If we ever think of talking with a Hindu girl, my community will disown me. Hindus are stupid. They think our religion is so weak that we must force them to join us. No, they are mistaken. They are the sinners. They do not follow *Allah-talah* [the one God]. It is their fault…but they cannot insult us like that. So, we have decided to ostracise them. If any Hindu child becomes too friendly with a Muslim student in the school, we scare him away. Once, we pulled down the pants of a grade seven Hindu boy because he used to come to our neighbourhood to play with us. We have bats and balls; we are rich. Hindus are poor.

In many local media narratives, love-jihad is defined as an attack of the Muslim community on Hindus and often reported using inflammatory language. In most of the Hindu families, girls at a very young age are taught to 'stay away from Muslim boys'. Bhavana, the mother of a 10-year-old Hindu student, explained: 'In schools, we ask our girls to tie *rakhi*[10] to their Muslim classmates and make them their brothers. Once the boys are their brothers nothing will happen between them.' In several such examples, children are guided and encouraged to discriminate against their classmates, to push the other to the margins of their everyday experiences, and to sometimes enact their religiosity by violating the other.

When children engage with these narratives in their homes, they operate from within the ideological chambers functional in their families and religious communities. The provocative language, content treatment and, in many cases, a pro-Hindutva slant encourage children to commit acts of micro-aggression: bullying, abusing, excluding, silencing and violating. Through these acts of micro-aggression, the deviant other is punished and disciplined. Discrimination against the deviant body is enacted through everyday doings, interlaced with the work of bodily conduct in popular narratives, and in tune with their categorisation of the 'other'.

As children are socialised to enact their religious subjectivity through practices of discriminating, in-group solidarity-building, and disciplining the deviant, an ontological space is created where the existence of the other is silenced. These exclusionary practices are effective because the dominant power structures generate realms of experience where any interfaith engagement is identified as an abnormality and regulated through disciplinary mechanisms. The children, therefore, engage with the religious other based more on media discourse and the dominant interpretive frame, and less on interpersonal experiences.

This can be changed if children are provided with opportunities to collaborate with individuals from different religious communities, negotiate with their own biases and re-imagine the religious other based on new episteme emerging from these experiences, allowing them to extend their civic identities beyond the boundaries of their religious subjectivities. In the following section, I highlight some critical media education initiatives and exercises designed to create interfaith dialogues through classroom-based collaborative work.

Living with Differences: Critical Media Education for Interfaith Dialogues

During my ethnographic immersion in the villages of Gujarat, I also worked as a media educator in the only municipal primary school catering to the educational aspirations and needs of students from all the three villages. Based on my analysis of the role of media in disciplining children as religious subjects, I developed several critical media education exercises to equip children with critical competencies to participate in interfaith teams, initiate dialogues designed to encourage them to collaborate on projects and identify ways to critically examine their biases towards the religious other.

Critical media education is defined as a set of pedagogical strategies used to create for the students an experience of 'critical distance' (Poyntz 2015) from the object of inquiry, here, their religious identities. Media educators must encourage students to participate in exercises designed to create a rupture around the edges of their religious identities; produce a kind of emptiness or a liminal space wherein they are compelled to suspend their primary identities and biases temporarily while engaging with the other. This involves equipping them with critical competencies required to engage with differences constructively by questioning and challenging the boundaries of their interpretive frames and/or meaning-making systems.

Some of these critical media education exercises developed to help children question their uncritical religious identities have been published in previous works (Bhatia 2016, 2018; Bhatia and Pathak-Shelat 2017). Based on my experiences of working as a media educator with primary school children to design media education exercises with the intention of creating safe classroom spaces where students can participate in interfaith teams and dialogues, I suggest a few pedagogical strategies which educators working in similar contexts can adopt and modify.

Critical Competencies

Educators must begin by equipping children with critical competencies required to analyse how media influences their engagement with the religious other. Though such an analysis begins by examining the role of media in the society at large, it is extremely important for children to identify how media informs their meaning-making systems and normalises particular forms of conduct, thus encouraging them to practise their religious identities in specific, antagonistic ways. Media educators must help children trace the influence of media on their everyday interactions with the religious other.

Create and Circulate

Critical media education exercises must have a strong praxis enabling students to create content and/or alternative narratives to challenge biased media representation populating their media ecologies. When students are identified as creators, authors and thinkers, they learn to appreciate the influence of media representations on communities and understand their stake in challenging/reinforcing the biases and/or negative perceptions.

Collaborative Practices

In societies where children are encouraged to enact their religious (social) identities in and through discriminating against the other, it becomes extremely important to encourage children from different communities to work together—occupy same spaces, collectively engage in meaning-making activities, work as members in interfaith teams and participate in critical conversations with the other. Educators can use media technologies as a practice and a space around which children can be encouraged to collaborate with the religious other and work in interfaith teams. Interfaith collaborations over media technologies also involve creating inclusive narratives representing issues concerning different communities to ensure that multiple voices are heard and represented.

Re-imagine and Re-define

Most media education scholars focus on the question of meaning in media cultures: how it is constituted, negotiated and mediated. Based on my work, however, I would also like to emphasise that altering practices of conduct can also change how children associate with and refer to the religious other, thus creating possibilities of change in interfaith relations. One such strategy involves media educators enabling children to re-imagine how public spaces such as roads, residential areas, classrooms, and university campuses can be represented as safe zones for interfaith dialogues and discussions. For instance, in many cities, residential societies are segregated on religious lines such that people from a particular community live in and occupy only areas occupied by their religious community. Religious ghettos or enclaves of minorities in major cities of India are examples of how public spaces are defined and regulated by religious identities; informal religious guidelines are normalised as rules and, as a result, different religious communities refuse to cohabit. Media technologies can be used critically to re-imagine the meanings emerging from and inherent in these spaces to identify ways in which they can be designed as safe zones for interfaith dialogues and presence. Instead of simply critiquing the meaning, critical media education can also be used to insert these spaces with new affective relationality through techniques such as counter-culture mapping, spatial re-arrangements to promote inclusivity and co-habitation, and critical presence—presence of bodies in spaces which otherwise exclude them deliberatively.

Acknowledging Vulnerability

When media educators work with children and students who inhabit societies divided on religious lines, involving them in exercises designed to question power hierarchies in their communities may expose them to threats and abuse. It is, therefore, very crucial to immerse in their communities and develop a relation of trust with its members. Also, media educators must encourage and enable children to enact their agency in relation to participation, contribution and engagement with media education exercises. It is equally important for media educators to articulate their role in this process to ensure that they acknowledge and negotiate with their own biases and/or limitations while creating tensions in the lived realities of children and their families.

Conclusion

Media is integrated into the lives of children and enables them to make sense of and articulate their religious identities. Children learn to navigate through the media narratives smoothly as they borrow meanings which reinforce their sense of religious subjectivity. Dominant discourse defines and limits the conditions under which children experience the religious other. Based on the findings, I argue that many local media narratives in Gujarat create a discursive field wherein Hindus and Muslims are situated within a realm of experienced animosity and hatred. As a result, religious identities manifest in forms of conduct and techniques of discipline designed to exclude religious differences from the realm of lived realities.

Many scholars such as Banaji (2018) and Hoechsmann and Poyntz (2011) argue that children can be equipped with critical skills required to problematise the normalised apathy among different communities. Children can be encouraged to critically engage with media discourse and their religious identities by broadening 'the spectrum of their experiences and relational world' (Davidson 2011: 31). For this, students must be given opportunities to inhabit interfaith sites and engage in interfaith dialogues where they learn to distance themselves from their uncritical subjective identities and re-imagine the process of negotiating with the religious other. This project of unlearning religious biases requires that researchers, scholars and educators conceive projects in critical media literacy and encourage children to acknowledge the boundaries of interpretive frames from within which they are operating in and interacting with the world. According to Foucault, the critical ethos of such a project must be conceived as '…an attitude, […] a philosophical life in which the critique of what we are is at one and the same time the […] analysis of the limits that are imposed on us and an experiment with the possibility of going beyond them'(1997: 50).

Notes

1. It is important to note that the religious socialisation of children is a process which operates in and through various heterogeneous locales of power, especially through social institutions such as local systems of governance, schools, media and community interactions. The focus of this chapter, however, is to highlight how media discourses are implicated in the socialisation of children as religious subjects. In doing so, I have not completely distilled the influence of other social structures and experiences. In our discussion on media as a site wherein children are socialised, I also bring to light how these engagements coalesce with children's lived realities to emphasise the interplay between the various locales of subject formation such as schools, families, peer-groups, local governance and religious communities.

2. I have not revealed the names of the villages and my respondents in order to protect my respondents and the residents from any harm.

3. The words *mushrik* and *kaafir* cannot really be translated. However, for the benefit of the larger audience, these are like abusive words in the Urdu language meant to describe those who do not believe in the 'one God', and can be loosely translated as 'infidels'. *Haraam* means something that is forbidden according to Islamic law.

4. *Iman* is a locally published Urdu periodical which is very famous in these villages. It is written by two *maulvis* (clerics) who manage the central mosque and the *madrasa* (seminary).

5. The video is available online at https://www.youtube.com/watch?v=PQuuvAF4vhY (accessed on 22 October 2022).

6. It is very difficult to translate this quote as it will lose its essence in translation. For ease of understanding I assume the authority to argue that the quote means that people should behave in accordance with the culture of the land. When I verified my interpretation with Shusruth, he explained, 'In India, Hindus are in the majority and so it is a Hindu nation. If the Muslims want to live here, they must learn to live according to the Hindu culture.'

7. This does not mean there are no alternative representations available in the mediascape. These alternative representations, however, are too few to challenge the standardised techniques used by individuals to enact their religious subjectivity.

8. A bindi is a decorative mark worn in the middle of the forehead by Hindu women in India. As it is a religious symbol of the Hindus, practising Muslims are not allowed to wear it on their bodies.

9. The news report is available online at https://youtu.be/a-NfFEII3-M (accessed on 15 November 2018).

10. *Rakhi* is the thread signifying the bond between siblings, tied by the sister on the brother's wrist.

References

Ahmed, Saufuddin. 2010. 'The Role of the Media during Communal Riots in India: A Study of the 1984 Sikh Riots and the 2002 Gujarat Riots'. *Media Asia* 37(2): 103–11.

Amin, Ash. 2010. *Land of Strangers*. Cambridge: Polity Press.

Antal, Carrie. 2008. 'Reflections on Religious Nationalism, Conflict and Schooling in Developing Democracies: India and Israel in Comparative Perspective'. *Compare: A Journal of Comparative and International Education* 38(1): 87–102.

Banaji, Shakuntala. 2018. 'Vigilante Publics: Orientalism, Modernity and Hindutva Fascism in India'. *Javnost* 25(4): 333–50.

Bhatia, Kiran. 2016. 'Understanding the Role of Media Education in Promoting Religious Literacy: A Critical Pedagogy for Primary School Students in Rural India'. *Media Education Research Journal* 7(2): 11–28.

———. 2018. 'Mediating Religious Literacy among Primary School Children in Gujarat: Classroom as a Liminal Space'. *Journal of Media Literacy Education* 10(3): 152–70.

Bhatia, Kiran, and Manisha Pathak-Shelat. 2017. 'Media Literacy as a Pathway to Religious Literacy in Pluralistic Democracies: Designing a Critical Media Education Pedagogy for Primary School Children in India'. *Interaction: Studies in Communication and Culture* 8(2): 189–209.

———. 2019. *Challenging Discriminatory Practices of Religious Socialization among Adolescents: Critical Media Literacy and Pedagogies in Practice*. Switzerland: Palgrave Macmillan.

Brubaker, Rogers, Mara Loveman and Peter Stamatov. 2004. 'Ethnicity as Cognition'. *Theory and Society* 33: 31–64.

Busher, Joel. 2015. 'What Part Do Social Networks Play in Radicalisation?' Available at https://www.radicalisationresearch.org/debate/busher-social-networks/ (accessed on 31 August 2018).

Carrette, Jeremy. 2000. *Foucault and Religion: Spiritual Corporality and Political Spirituality*. New York: Routledge.

Cherian, George. 2016. *Hate Spin: The Manufacture of Religious Offense and Its Threat to Democracy*. London: MIT Press.

Davidson, Arnold. 2011. 'In Praise of Counter-conduct'. *History of Human Sciences* 24(4): 25–41.

de Certeau, Michel. 1984. *The Practices of Everyday Life*. Los Angeles: University of California Press.

Drotner, Kristen, and Sonia Livingstone (eds). 2008. *The International Handbook of Children, Media and Culture*. London: Sage.

Foucault, Michel. 1972. *The Archaeology of Knowledge*, tr. Alan M. Sheridan Smith. New York, NY: Pantheon Books.

———. 1997. *Discipline and Punish: The Birth of the Prison*, tr. A. Sheridan. New York: Random House.

Gujarat Samachar. 2016. 'Muslims Will Hold a Meeting in Chikhli to Stop Cow Slaughter'. 17 July, Ahmedabad.

———. 2017. 'Alaudin Khilji Has Attacked and Demolished Temples in Gujarat in 1299'. 11 November, Ahmedabad.

Hall, Stuart. 1994. 'Cultural Identity and Diaspora'. In *Colonial Discourse and Post-Colonial Theory: A Reader*, eds P. William and L. Chrisman, 392–403. New York: Columbia University Press.

Hoechsmann, Michael, and Stuart Poyntz. 2011. *Media Literacies: A Critical Introduction*. Oxford, UK: Blackwell Publishing.

Jain, Anuja. 2010. 'Beaming It Live: 24-Hour Television News, the Spectator and the Spectacle of the 2002 Gujarat Carnage'. *South Asian Popular Culture* 8(2): 163–79.

Karim, Karim. 2003. *Islamic Peril: Media and Global Violence*. Montreal: Black Rose Books.

Lallement, Maxime. 2014. 'Foucault's Biopolitics: A Critique of Ontology'. *Journal of the British Society for Phenomenology* 43(1): 76–91.

Lemish, Dafna. 2015. *Children and Media: A Global Perspective*. Oxford: Wiley Blackwell.

Lemke, Thomas. 2001. 'The Birth of Biopolitics: Michel Foucault's Lecture at the Collège de France on Neo-liberal Government'. *Economy and Society* 30: 190–207.

Poyntz, Stuart. 2015. 'Conceptual Futures: Thinking and the Role of Key Concept Models in Media Literacy Education'. *Media Education Research Journal* 6(1): 63–79.

Pratt, Douglas. 2015. 'Reactive Co-radicalization: Religious Extremism as Mutual Discontent'. *Journal for the Academic Study of Religion* 28(1): 1–10.

Rajagopal, Arvind. 2001. *Politics after Television: Hindu Nationalism and the Reshaping of the Public in India.* Cambridge: Cambridge University Press.

Sandesh. 2016. 'Did Amit Shah Organise a Meeting in Sarangpur to Discuss the "Ram Mandir" Issue in Order to Win the UP Elections?'. 9 June, Ahmedabad.

Sonwalkar, Prasun. 2006. 'Shooting the Messenger? Political Violence, Gujarat 2002 and the Indian News Media'. In *Conflict, Terrorism and Media in Asia*, ed. B. Cole, 82–97. New York, NY: Routledge.

Sud, Nikita. 2012. *Liberalization, Hindu Nationalism and the State: A Biography of Gujarat.* New Delhi: Oxford University Press.

Tomomi, Yamaguchi. 2013. 'Xenophobia in Action: Ultranationalism, Hate Speech, and the Internet in Japan'. *Radical History Review* 2013(117): 98–118.

Weimann, Gabriel. 2010. 'Terror on Facebook, Twitter, and YouTube'. *Brown Journal of World Affairs* 16(2): 45–54.

Yagnik, Achyut, and Suchitra Sheth. 2005. *The Shaping of Modern Gujarat: Plurality, Hindutva and Beyond.* New Delhi: Penguin India.

Zakaria, Rafiq. 2006. 'Covering Indian Muslims'. In *The Indian Media: Illusion, Delusion and Reality*, ed. A. Mathur, 58–65. New Delhi: Rupa.

NOTES ON THE CONTRIBUTORS

VASUKI BELAVADI is Professor, Department of Communication, University of Hyderabad. He specialises in video production and has good grounding in radio programming and production. His research interests include pedagogy of video production and community media. He is also the deputy director of the E-Learning Centre at the University of Hyderabad.

KIRAN VINOD BHATIA is Assistant Professor (Activist Media), Tulane University, USA, and Program Director at a Sudanese non-profit. Her research examines the role of digital media technologies, state and corporations in enabling and sustaining the marginalisation of minority groups in global South countries. She also studies the interlinkages between digital technologies, protest cultures and social movements.

ADITYA DESHBANDHU is Lecturer of Communications (Digital Media Sociology) in the Department of Communication, Drama, and Film at the University of Exeter. His research interests include new media studies, digital cultures, the various conceptions of the digital divide and the emerging field of video game studies. He is a columnist and writes on video games and the gaming industry.

SUMANA KASTURI is a writer and researcher, and works in the field of international higher education. Her research interests include children's media, feminist media studies and digital cultures of the everyday. She has a master's degree in media studies from The Pennsylvania State University, and a master's degree and PhD in communication from the University of Hyderabad.

ARCHANA KUMARI is Assistant Professor, Department of Mass Communication and New Media at Central University of Jammu. Before joining academia, she was a journalist and media professional. She is currently involved with initiatives that fight fake news. Her research interests are media economics, media literacy, development communication, new media and digital journalism, media research and advertising.

SAMINA MISHRA is a documentary filmmaker, writer and teacher based in New Delhi, with a special interest in media for and about children. Her work uses the lens of childhood, identity and education to reflect the experiences of growing up in India. Her recent work is a research project on children and citizenship.

KAMALA MUKUNDA works at a teacher-run school, Centre For Learning, outside Bangalore. She received a PhD in educational and developmental psychology from Syracuse University and has published two books for educators and parents. She has worked with government educational agencies to share both psychological insights and her experience as a teacher for two decades.

ANITA SAREEN PARIHAR is a media practitioner and senior visiting faculty for television, film and new media studies. Her interests include television production and direction, script writing, media literacy and gender. She has scripted and directed 20 educational television programmes at Educational Multimedia Research Centre (EMMRC), Savitribai Phule Pune University, for telecast.

MANISHA PATHAK-SHELAT has taught and worked as a media consultant and researcher in India, Thailand and the US. Her publications address young people's media cultures, new media, civic engagement, transcultural citizenship, media literacy and gender. She is also the editor of the *Journal of Creative Communications* published by MICA.

USHA RAMAN is Professor, Department of Communication, University of Hyderabad. Her research and teaching interests include cultural studies of science, health communication, children's media, feminist media studies, journalism pedagogy, and the social and cultural impact of digital media. She edits a monthly magazine for school teachers and is serving as co-vice president on the executive board of the International Association for Media and Communication Research (IAMCR) from 2020 to 2024.

NIMMI RANGASWAMY is Professor at the Kohli Centre on Intelligent Systems, Indian Institute of Information Technology (IIIT), Hyderabad. She brings an anthropological lens in understanding the impacts of AI research and praxis. She works in the human technology interactions research area combining theoretical analysis and ethnographic field research to understand technology use in developing countries.

DEVINA SARWATAY is Senior Research Fellow (UGC-NET) and PhD student, Department of Communication, University of Hyderabad, and Graduate Student Member, Media Education Lab, USA. Her research interests are children and media, social media, digital cultures, and digital and media literacy. She also served as the editorial assistant for this volume.

MEHAK SIDDIQUI is a writer who works at the intersections of education and technology. She holds a master's degree in communication from the University of Hyderabad. She received an Erasmus Mundus Scholarship 2022–24 to pursue the international master's in children's literature, media and culture, jointly offered by the University of Glasgow and other European institutes.

DEEPA SREENIVAS teaches at the Centre for Women's Studies, University of Hyderabad. Her research interests include visual culture, childhood studies and feminist pedagogy. Her research articles have appeared in various journals. She is also the series editor for a collection of illustrated books for children, drawing on the experiences and stories from marginalised communities.

INDEX